Skywatch West

The Complete Weather Guide

Revised Edition

Richard A. Keen

Library of Congress Cataloging-in-Publication Data
Keen, Richard A.
  Skywatch west / Richard A. Keen.—2nd ed.
    p. cm.
Rev. ed. of: Skywatch. 1987.
Includes bibliographical references and index.
  ISBN 1-55591-297-4
  1. West (U.S.)—Climate. I. Keen, Richard A. Skywatch. II. Title.
QC984.W38K44 2004
551.6978—dc22

                                                2003020282

Project Editor: Daniel Forrest-Bank
Design: Patty Maher
Front cover photographs: top—storm cloud over dirt road
copyright © Corbis Images; left—rainbow copyright © Image Club Graphics Inc.;
middle—tornado courtesy of NOAA; right—lightning copyright © Corbis Images
Back cover photograph of tornado: copyright © Corbis Images
Interior images copyright © Corbis Images, except where otherwise noted.

Printed in China
0 9 8 7 6 5 4 3 2 1

Fulcrum Publishing
16100 Table Mountain Parkway, Suite 300
Golden, Colorado 80403
(800) 992-2908 • (303) 277-1623
www.fulcrum-books.com

To Mom and Dad—
Thanks for reading the rain gauge all these years.

CONTENTS

FOREWORD

Weather is something most of us are affected by every day. We are out and about in it all the time, often without giving it much thought. That is, until a sudden rainstorm ruins our afternoon picnic or a big snowstorm delays, or even cancels, our vacation flight to someplace warm and sunny. But we shouldn't blame the weather forecasters! They can only do their best to let us know just what kind of weather is on its way. In the West, like no where else in the world, there is much that affects the weather. A big example is the mountains ... that beautiful Continental Divide. But that's why I think forecasting the weather is so much fun, yet equally challenging. It can be different almost every day (sometimes hour to hour!), and seeing the forces that help us conjure those forecasts is fascinating. They can be gentle and pleasant, or forceful and destructive, and just about everything in between.

I have been forecasting the weather for nearly 30 years here in the West with lots of sophisticated and expensive equipment, and as you know, I can still get fooled. There's the rub. Weather is not an exact science. "A" plus "B" does not always equal "C." The book you are holding in your hands will explain much of that mystery. Some of the terms weathercasters seem to use so casually will be explained here. You'll be amazed at what can help cause the weather and just how it does. You'll see how weather hinders, but how it also helps. And it is help we often need. You'll learn what *graupel* is. Ever cried over "spilled ice"? Probably not, but you'll learn what it is in this book. Did you know there are four kinds of lightning? Can lightning hit you while skiing? Could that tornado really have lifted Dorothy's house in *The Wizard of Oz?* Read the chapter on tornadoes. You'll read about hurricanes with benign names causing destruction in the millions of dollars and how they really can affect landlocked areas of the West. The strongest winds. The heaviest snows. The most flooding rains. The hottest. The coldest. The oddest! And the where, when, why, and how of them all.

Whether you're a casual weather observer or someone who depends upon the weather for a living, this book will be an excellent reference for all your weather questions. It may even help you forecast the weather. Just don't get too good at it! Young and old alike can enjoy, benefit, and understand our ever-changing and totally unpredictable weather like never before with *Skywatch West*. I will surely make it a standard text in the Stormcenter at News 4. It should prove invaluable.

Get ready for an adventure in weather and a thrilling and fascinating journey all the way. I wish you good reading ... and good weather!

—Ed Greene
Meteorologist, News 4
Denver Colorado

PREFACE TO THE REVISED EDITION

Much has happened since the original *Skywatch: The Western Weather Guide* reached its first readers in the Fall of 1987. The air that we all breathed back then has since circled the planet a hundred or so times, and has created a lot of fantastic weather on its way. Many weather records have been broken (especially for heat, cold, drought, and snowfall), and this new edition of *Skywatch West* notes these new records. When the original *Skywatch* went to press, a powerful El Niño that had upset the West's weather was still warm news; since then, five more Niños have come and gone, including one in 1998 that some say was even stronger than the 1983 event. In 1991, clouds of gas shot high into the atmosphere by a volcano in the Phillipines called Pinatubo, perceptibly chilled the climate of the West. And just in the past couple of years, a summer of forest fires turned the sun a deep crimson and the moon salmon pink and rained charred pine needles on my house, while a spring storm left many residents of Colorado, including me, snowbound for a week.

Equally important as the continuing saga of the weather is the slow but steady improvement in our understanding of the weather. Perhaps the most dramatic improvements have come in the science of forecasting small and short-lived, but very dangerous, weather events. In the 1980s and early 1990s, I participated in several experiments aimed at using Doppler radar and other technologies to predict and detect tornadoes, hailstorms, and microbursts. The experiments succeeded, and Doppler radar is now part of the Weather Service's regular retinue of resources that have made storm warnings more timely and accurate and which have doubtlessly saved hundreds of lives. And while it may not be saving as many lives, improvements in satellite imaging has certainly made for some spectacular pictures of the weather as seen from space.

While forecasting of storms and daily weather changes has improved, the causes of the slower changes of climate remain as elusive as ever. Although much has been learned about how the oceans—particularly the Pacific—can influence the West's weather, the 1998 El Niño caught as many forecasters by surprise as did the last big one in 1983. And those who try to forecast the climate are still arguing with those who try to measure it, all about a few tenths of a degree.

As for me, I have learned a lot about severe weather from "chasing" tornadoes and hail storms during those weather experiments, and have learned a lot about climate by simply following it for another 15 years and by obsessively poring through reams (and megabytes) of climate records. As a result, I've changed and added some things in this second edition. In 1996, I was invited to be a meteorology instructor with the Juneau (Alaska) Ice Field Research Program, a summer field program aimed at teaching a select group of college students about glaciers. I've returned to that magnificent location (broad expanses of ice and snow punctuated by tooth-like pinnacles, much as I imagine Colorado to have looked during the Ice Age) every summer since, and have become rather familiar with the hearty climate of that part of Alaska and neighboring British Columbia. My experiences in the North Country inspired me to extend the domain of *Skywatch* to include Alaska and western Canada, which are, after all, parts of the same Rocky Mountain and Coastal Range terrain as the western "lower 48."

One thing hasn't changed since the first edition, however. From Alaska to Alberta to Arizona, the wind still sweeps the mountains, plains, coasts, canyons, and glaciers of the West, producing some of the most dramatic weather in the world. In words and pictures, *Skywatch West* chronicles this encounter between the wind and the land. Leaf though its pages and enjoy the sometimes wild, sometimes delightful weather of the West!

ACKNOWLEDGMENTS

I must confess from the start that writing *Skywatch West* wasn't really my idea! For years I have been giving lectures to the Colorado Mountain Club about the strange and spectacular weather that hikers and mountaineers might encounter, and the idea for this book actually came from the audience one evening—in particular, from Betsy Armstrong, a former editor at Fulcrum Publishing, who thought that the weather of the West would make a lively subject for a book, and whose contagious enthusiasm got the project rolling. Along the way, the folks at Fulcrum, especially Hunter Holloway and Dr. Archie Kahan, gave many useful comments and suggestions that greatly improved the text of the first edition. Likewise, Patty Maher and Dan Forrest-Bank contributed their talents to this second edition. Thanks are also due to dozens of fellow weather buffs—old friends and new acquaintances alike—who provided all sorts of assistance. Among these, Dave Blanchard, Jon Eischeid, Ron Holle, Paul Neiman, Dennis Rodgers, and others of the National Oceanic and Atmospheric Administration were especially helpful, as was Nolan Doesken of the Colorado Climate Center.

Other organizations that contributed to this book in one way or another are the National Center for Atmospheric Research, National Weather Service, the National Aeronautics and Space Administration, U.S. Forest Service, U.S. Geological Survey, Federal Emergency Management Agency, the Meteorological Service of Canada, the Universities of Alaska, Alberta, Chicago, Colorado and Hawaii, Colorado State University, Western Oregon University, the Western Regional Climate Center, the U.S. Army, the Juneau Ice Field Research Program, the Public Broadcasting System, *Weatherwise* magazine, the Lightning Data Center, FMA Research, and the Boeing Company. In addition, the weather buffs whose names are credited beneath each of the photos are all true artists!

I'd like to add a special acknowledgment of the late David Ludlum, founder of *Weatherwise* magazine and author of many books about weather history. His writings have been a great source of weather facts, figures, and anecdotes, always written in an informative and engaging style. When I skim through *Skywatch West,* I realize how much influence his works have had on my efforts.

On the home front, where I wrote *Skywatch West,* Sarah, Daniel, Michael, Amanda, and Samantha provided help in a variety of forms ranging from smiles and giggles to assistance with weather observations. Strangely, a couple of critters made the process of writing more pleasant—Qatiyana, the pint-size dog, by letting me know when I need to take a break and accompany her on a walk through the woods (several of the photos in *Skywatch West* were taken on these walks), and Mouse, the pint-size cat, who graces me with her quiet company when I'm deep in thought.

A very special appreciation goes to my wife, Helen, for her encouragement, good humor, good company, and so much more.

A wild lady named Hazel also deserves mention. When this great storm visited my hometown in Pennsylvania one October evening in 1954, she brought misery to millions. To at least one wide-eyed seven-year-old boy, however, she brought a sense of wonder and lasting fascination. In a way, that dark and stormy night half a century ago is where this book really began.

—Richard A. Keen
May 1987 and January 2004

INTRODUCTION

To many, the West conjures up images of rugged scenery and even more rugged souls who spent their lives trying to tame it. Names like John Wesley Powell, Geronimo, Wyatt Earp, and John Wayne have become legends around the world. Millions of people cross oceans and continents to visit places like Pikes Peak, Death Valley, the Grand Canyon, and Glacier Bay. With the eruptions of Lassen Peak in California and Washington's Mount Saint Helens, and of numerous Alaska volcanoes (such as the titanic blast of Katmai in 1912), we have even seen the capricious landscape explode in our faces! It is fitting that the weather of the West is every bit as awesome and fickle as the land it sweeps.

Those who live in the twelve states, three provinces, and two territories that make up the region we call the West, are already familiar with the power of their weather. Westerners have seen winds strong enough to send parked airplanes into unwanted flight and airborne planes crashing to the ground. They have seen tempests destroy bridges and flatten trees by the millions, coastal storms wash neighborhoods into the sea, mountain snowstorms strand trains and bury houses, and desert whirlwinds send terrified jackrabbits sailing skyward!

The West can get hot—only the Sahara Desert in Africa has recorded higher temperatures than Death Valley, and in Alaska the heat has exceeded anything seen in many equatorial countries! Alaska and Canada's Yukon territory can get

"Frankly, I don't like the looks of the weather." Norris, *The Vancouver* (B.C.) *Sun*

xiii

The Earth—Our oasis in space—with the moon in the distant background. Hurricane Linda swirls off the coast of Mexico. This image was produced by NASA's Goddard Space Flight Center from cloud, land, and ocean data gathered by several NOAA and NASA satellites. NASA

colder than any place on Earth, excluding the ice sheets of Greenland and Antarctica (and a few villages in Siberia), which is probably no surprise, but 1,500 miles closer to the equator, similarly cold weather has visited Montana and Utah. Between the extremes, the temperature has been known to fall 100 degrees overnight and to rise almost as much during the day. Yet, for the most part, the climate of the West is pleasant. Sunshine is abundant throughout much of the region, and those few cloudy areas are compensated by moderate temperatures.

Remarkable changes occur in western weather from one day to the next, from summer to winter and from year to year. Changeable weather is common in the middle latitudes, and the old quip, "If you don't like the weather, wait a minute," is invoked in many languages in many places. In the West, though, one can also add, "If you still don't like the weather, go a few miles." An hour's drive will take many westerners from forest to desert or from summer heat to a snowfield.

This variety hasn't gone unnoticed. Many segments of the economy—from agriculture to recreation—thrive on it. Tropical fruits are grown with water drawn from nearby snow-clad mountains and, in return, the mountains receive hordes of skiers from warm cities in the lowlands. Yet, these same activities can also suffer from the varied weather—frostbitten oranges and snowless ski runs are among the many reminders of the whims of western weather.

What makes the West's weather the benevolent prankster that it is? It's a simple question with many answers, and those answers are what this book is all about. Descriptions of the fascinating variety of western weather—through words, pictures, and numbers—make great reading. But this book intends to go beyond that, I hope, and leave the reader with an understanding or, better yet, a *feeling* for how the West's peculiar weather works. This is where the real satisfaction lies. It's like looking under the hood of a car and knowing why the distributor is there, or realizing how a human heart does its job.

Some reasons for the West's unique climate are obvious. It's a region of mountains and valleys with the world's largest ocean next door. But for a real explanation, we must go far beyond local topography. Shifting currents in the equatorial oceans and the frozen wastes of the North and South Poles are every bit as important to western weather as are the Rockies and the Sierras.

The importance of all these factors, however, is dwarfed by the role played by ancient volcanoes that have since eroded into sand. The story of these 4-billion-year-old eruptions unfolds in the first chapter.

It may seem strange that the third photograph in chapter 1 is a landscape from the planet Venus, but a real lesson can be learned from our sister planet. Over the eons since those primordial volcanic eruptions, Earth slowly became the garden that it is today—while Venus turned into a searing visage of hell. If nothing else, a look at the different fates of the two planets should help us appreciate how truly fortunate the Earth and its inhabitants are. Think about it the next time you see lightning cracking the skies over the Grand Canyon or "flying saucer" clouds hovering above Mount Rainier. It's a sight you'll see nowhere else on Earth or—barring some parallel solar system out of a *Star Trek* episode—in the entire universe!

Admittedly, western weather is far too complex to be stuffed into a single book. Like many things in life, the best way to learn about weather is to observe it in detail. The book's last chapter, "Watching the Weather," offers tips on tracking the daily passage of foul and fair weather. I hope that your learning experience has just begun when you put this book down.

Between the creation of the atmosphere and the construction of your personal weather station, *Skywatch West* progresses in an orderly and logical manner. Each chapter is meant to be read independently of the other chapters. So if you have a hankering to read about hurricanes, you can do so without having to flip through the entire book.

Finally, a word about metric versus English units of measurement. I've always felt that the main purpose of a measurement system is to communicate information. Since most readers of this book are probably more familiar with the English (or American, as it's known in some remote valleys) system of measurement, English units it is. Snow and rain fall in inches, hailstones are weighed in pounds, wind blows in miles per hour and all temperatures are in degrees Fahrenheit. True, it's an old system of measurement and its arithmetic gets a bit tricky (quick: how many inches in a mile?), but as long as we both know how deep a foot of snow is, it works quite well.

WHY IS THERE WEATHER?

CHAPTER 1

Why is there air?
There is air to fill the basketball with!

—Bill Cosby

Air is wonderful stuff. We breathe it, fly airplanes in it, burn things with it, and, yes, fill basketballs with it. Most importantly (at least to meteorologists!), it gives us weather. Without air, there would be no weather; with it, weather is inevitable. And that's a good thing—even though sometimes it may seem that rain and snow exist only to make our lives a bit more miserable, without the weather, the Earth would be uninhabitable, and our lives wouldn't be possible at all.

It takes more than just air, though, for Earth to have the kind of weather we've become so used to. Five basic factors combine to create the alternation of sun and storm and of warm and cold that we call weather. The first and most obvious factor is that Earth has an atmosphere. Second, Earth is sunlit. Third, is the Earth's rotation. The fourth factor—and one unique to our planet—is Earth's vast supply of liquid water. Finally, there is geography—the variety of surfaces, from oceans to continents to ice sheets, that cover Earth. In recent years, we have been treated to close looks at other planets in our solar system, where the factors that control what might be called "weather" are incredibly different from ours. A survey of the conditions leading to Earth's weather will help us understand why our weather is the way it is, and comparisons with other planets will let us appreciate its uniqueness.

THE ATMOSPHERE

Earth has approximately 6 million billion tons of air. Numbers this large make even the national debt seem small. But there are always ways to make small

HOW TO MAKE WEATHER

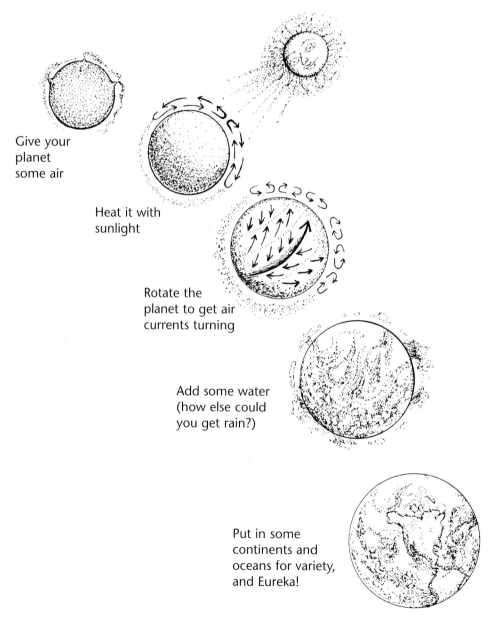

Give your
planet
some air

Heat it with
sunlight

Rotate the
planet to get air
currents turning

Add some water
(how else could
you get rain?)

Put in some
continents and
oceans for variety,
and Eureka!

ILLUSTRATION BY BEVERLY POWELL

numbers look big and big numbers look small. To make the bulk of the atmosphere seem small, consider this: all those millions of billions of tons of air amount to a mere millionth of the weight of the entire planet Earth. Another way to look at the equation is to imagine a winter cold enough that the air itself freezes and falls to the ground as a layer of solid nitrogen and oxygen. This layer would be about 20 feet thick. That's a lot of frozen air to shovel your car out of.

Where did the atmosphere come from? Four and a half billion years ago, when the planets formed out of dust and gas surrounding the newborn sun, leftover gases collected around the infant planets. These gases were mostly composed of hydrogen and helium, the two most abundant elements in the universe. But hydrogen and helium are also the lightest of the elements, and Earth's gravity—strong as it may seem to us—was too feeble to keep them around for long. Farther from the sun, the gases were cooler and therefore more able to stick around the young planets. To this day, the distant planets Jupiter, Saturn, Uranus, and Neptune still have the massive atmospheres of hydrogen and helium. Earth, however, like Mars, Venus, and Mercury, soon found itself without an atmosphere.

What Earth lost to space, it soon (geologically speaking) created from within. Heat in Earth's core sent columns of molten rock to the surface, erupting as volcanoes. Substances trapped in the rocks, such as water,* carbon dioxide, methane, sulfur, and nitrogen, spewed into the vacuum (or space

Weather—Combine the five ingredients in the proper proportions, and the result is the weather of Earth. NASA

*Studies of comets—especially Halley's Comet—have revealed that comets are composed largely of water ice, leading some researchers to speculate that the atmosphere may have received its water from space, rather than from within, in the form of falling comets. For the time being, I am sticking with the traditional volcanic theory. However, an interesting point arises: the science of meteorology is named after a Greek word, meteoros, meaning "high in the air." Ever since, meteorologists have had to explain that they do not study what we now call meteors (from the same Greek word), those burning bits of space dust often referred to as "shooting stars." Astronomers have long known that this space dust is the remnants of disintegrating comets. So if water vapor, that all-important ingredient of what meteorologists do study, actually does have a common origin with meteors, then the distinction between the terms loses some of its significance.

Venus—This view of the surface of Venus, imaged by radar on NASA's Magellan spacecraft, is a scene straight out of Dante's *Inferno*. In size, Venus is Earth's twin sister, and its early days were probably much like Earth's. Along the way, however, Venus evolved into a parched hell with a thick 850-degree atmosphere. Life as we know it is completely impossible on Venus. NASA

Earth's Atmosphere—The layers of the atmosphere become strikingly apparent in this sunset image from the space shuttle *Endeavour*. Thunderheads and cirrus clouds lace the lowest layer, the troposphere; above lies the pale blue sky of the stratosphere, which blends into the deep blue of the mesosphere. NASA

where the primordial atmosphere was before it was lost) surrounding Earth. Unlike hydrogen and helium, these heavier gases remained close to the Earth's surface. Thus, our atmosphere was born.

By today's standards, this early atmosphere was a vile affair, consisting largely of carbon dioxide, steam, clouds of sulfurous gases, and no breathable oxygen. A little chemistry and, later, biology took care of the oxygen shortage. Most of the water fell as rain to form the oceans. For the first billion years or so, carbon dioxide mixed with water vapor to make rainfalls of carbonic acid. This acidic rain leached calcium from the surface rocks. The ensuing chemical reactions formed calcium carbonate, which was carried into the oceans, where it sank to the bottom, forming the thick limestone layers now scattered around the globe.

It is interesting to compare Earth's history with that of Venus, 26 million miles closer to the sun. Although Venus is similar to Earth in size and (probably) composition of volcanic gases, its atmosphere is a hot, dense soup made up of mostly carbon dioxide. Intense sunlight on Venus prevented the planet from cooling quite enough for water vapor to condense into liquid. Without liquid water, no rains of carbonic acid could fall onto the rocks below. Venus's carbon dioxide remains in its atmosphere, while Earth's is locked in underground limestone, and all because of the relatively slight difference in distance from the sun. One may speculate on how narrowly Earth escaped Venus' hellish fate, or how narrowly Venus missed becoming the paradise that is Earth.

Half the diameter of Earth and one-tenth its bulk, the little planet Mars never had enough volcanoes to create much of an atmosphere. Like that of Venus, Mars's air is mostly carbon dioxide, but it is incredibly thin—only 1 percent as dense as the Earth's, and a mere ten-thousandth the density of Venus's. Nonetheless, thanks to trace amounts of water vapor and a rotation rate nearly identical to Earth's, Mars has more Earth–like weather than any other place we know of in the universe. Automated weather stations sent to the red planet have detected fronts, cyclones, clouds, snow, and even tornadoes. But Mars is still a desert planet, and, so far as we know, lifeless.

Meanwhile, back on Earth, at the tender age of one billion years, plant life began releasing oxygen (through photosynthesis) into the atmosphere. Eventually, about half a billion years ago, there was enough oxygen to allow a layer of ozone (a molecule of three oxygen atoms) to form. Ozone constitutes only the tiniest fraction of the atmosphere—less than one molecule in a million. However, this minuscule amount is extremely important because it absorbs the sun's ultraviolet radiation, helping to protect us from sunburn and

Mars—More familiar to earthlings, perhaps, is this view of a Martian landscape, taken by NASA's *Spirit* rover that landed in December 2003. The scene could be Death Valley or the Sahara Desert, but it's not—it's Mars. The weather on Mars might seem familiar, too, with clouds, frost, snow, fronts, and dust devils. However, Mars' thin atmosphere is less than once percent as dense as Earth's, and even in the Martian tropics, nighttime temperatures regularly reach 125 degrees below zero. With no liquid water, Mars is an eternal desert that is, so far as we know, lifeless. NASA

skin cancer. (This beneficial shield of ozone, 10 to 20 miles high, shouldn't be confused with local concentrations of ozone that form around today's cities.) Protected from ultraviolet rays, early plant life increased dramatically. The greening of Earth led to a rapid increase in the amount of atmospheric oxygen, leading in turn to oxygen-breathing animals, such as dinosaurs and, eventually, human beings. The modern-day status of the atmosphere is comprised of 76 percent nitrogen, 23 percent oxygen, and 1 percent other gases.

SUNLIGHT

All this air would simply sit still without some source of energy to move it around. That source of energy is the sun. It may seem obvious to us that the sun is the main source of heat for the atmosphere, but there are planets where that isn't the case. On Jupiter, the largest of the planets and five times Earth's distance from the sun, sunbeams are so feeble and the planet's center so hot that the atmosphere is actually heated more from below than above. On Earth, though, most of our heat comes from the sun.

Not all places on Earth get the same amount of heat. In the tropics, when the noontime sun passes directly overhead, the ground gets the full effect of solar heating: a 1-foot-wide beam of sunlight heats up a square foot of ground. At higher latitudes outside the tropics, the noontime sun doesn't pass overhead, and its light strikes the ground at some oblique angle. Forty-five degrees from the equator, the foot-wide sunbeam has to heat one and a half square feet of ground, and at 60 degrees latitude the sunbeam is spread over two square feet. At the poles, 90 degrees from the equator, the sunbeam hits the ground at such a low angle that it is spread over many square yards. Accordingly, the equator is heated more by the sun than are the poles.

The West from Space— Astronauts aboard the space shuttle *Columbia* caught this sweeping vista covering five states (Colorado, Wyoming, Utah, Montana, and Idaho). The isolated white dot in the lower right is Pikes Peak; several ranges of the Colorado Rockies dominate the center of the picture; and the Uinta and Wind River ranges are in the distance. The pale blue patch in the upper left is the Great Salt Lake, next to the Bonneville Salt Flats. NASA

As the sun heats Earth in its non-uniform manner, the planet warms up. If this heating went on forever, the planet would eventually melt. Since Earth as a whole is not heating up, there must be some way for the planet to get rid of the solar heat as fast as it receives it. Earth does this by sending energy out to space in the form of infrared radiation. *Infra-red* is a mixture of Latin and English meaning "below red," and refers to light waves whose frequency is less than that of red light. Although we cannot see infrared radiation, there are times when we can feel it—such as the warmth we feel coming from a hot stove or from a radiator (hence the name!).

On the average, Earth must lose as much heat through radiation as it receives from the sun. As with sunlight, this loss of heat is not uniform around the globe. A hot object radiates heat faster than does a cold one; at a temperature of 80 degrees, for instance, the tropics radiate heat twice as fast as does the zero-degree Fahrenheit Arctic. Not only do the tropics receive more heat than do the poles, they also lose it faster. Gains and losses, however, do not balance out locally, though they do balance for the globe as a whole. In the tropics, there is a net gain of heat, as the incoming sunlight is greater than the loss through radiation. Conversely, the arctic regions see a net loss of heat. It is this difference in the net heating between the equator and the poles that drives Earth's weather.

The West from the Air— In this slightly less sweeping view of the Earth from a commerical airliner, glaciers radiate from the Ha-Iltzuk Ice Field (surrounding Silverthrone Mountain) in British Columbia. RICHARD A. KEEN

Were the net heating of the tropics and the net cooling of the arctic regions to continue unhindered, Earth would end up with three equally obnoxious climate regions—an unbearably hot equatorial zone bounded on either side by two frightfully cold polar areas. The atmosphere, however, keeps this from happening. Remember that hot air is lighter than cold air, so as the air over the equator heats up, it rises. Conversely, the cooling of air over the Arctic causes it to sink. The rising equatorial air moves toward the equator. In this manner, the uneven heating of Earth sets up atmospheric currents that modify what would otherwise be extreme temperature differences between the equator and the poles. To this day, meteorologists call this current of air the "Hadley circulation," after the Englishman who thought of the idea in 1735.

A simple household analogy to this global current of air can be seen in a pot of boiling water on a stove. The stove supplies heat to the bottom of the pot, and the water loses heat by releasing steam at the top. Rising water at the pot's center carries the heat upward, and the returning, cooler (but still hot!) water sinks down near the edge of the pot.

This pattern of uneven heating and circulating currents of air changes during the course of a year due to the effect of the seasons. During the summer, the sun passes overhead at 23 degrees north latitude, while the overhead passage of the winter sun is at 23 degrees south. The latitude of the greatest heating of the ground is correspondingly farther north during the summer months. In turn, the resulting atmospheric currents shift to the north. Meanwhile, the North Pole, which sees no sunlight at all from October through March, is bathed in 24-hour sunshine during summer. This decreases the difference in net heating between the tropics and the Arctic, thereby weakening the heat-driven currents. Thus, seasonal variations in the solar heating of Earth's surface lead to shifts in weather patterns, with the patterns being, in general, farther north and weaker during summer.

As the Earth Turns

Now we have a simple heat-driven current that carries cold air to the equator and warm air aloft to the poles. This means that here in the West, the winds (at ground level) must always blow from the north, right? Of course, they don't, because the wind flow is complicated by the well-known fact that the Earth turns. The 7,918-mile-diameter Earth rotates once every 24 hours, spinning the people, houses, hills, trees, animals, and air on the equator around and around in an eastward direction at a zippy 1,038 m.p.h.

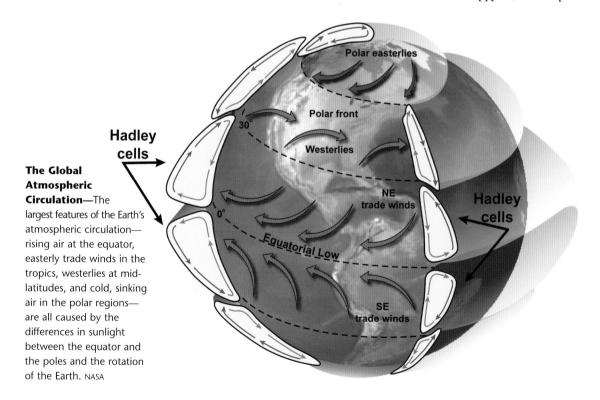

The Global Atmospheric Circulation—The largest features of the Earth's atmospheric circulation—rising air at the equator, easterly trade winds in the tropics, westerlies at mid-latitudes, and cold, sinking air in the polar regions—are all caused by the differences in sunlight between the equator and the poles and the rotation of the Earth. NASA

Hadley cells

Hadley cells

Polar easterlies

Polar front

30°

Westerlies

NE trade winds

0°

Equatorial Low

SE trade winds

Meanwhile, on the poles, where there are much fewer houses and occasional people, things are carried along at a sluggish zero m.p.h. As the rising equatorial air moves toward the poles, its eastward motion of 1,038 m.p.h becomes increasingly greater than the eastward motion of the ground below. Unless something slows it down, the air will be moving 60 m.p.h faster than the ground at 20 degrees latitude, and 140 m.p.h faster at 30 degrees latitude. This rapid eastward flow of air is known as the subtropical jet stream or the "subtropical jet." It is one of the strongest and most consistent winds of the world.

By the time air reaches the subtropical jet, its eastward motion is far greater than the poleward motion, and our simple heat-driven circulation no longer is so simple. While this pattern can be seen in the tropics, up to about 30 degrees latitude on either side of the equator, it ends at the subtropical jets in each hemisphere. Farther from the equator, winds still blow east, but with nowhere near the regularity of the subtropical jet. This belt of winds is known as the "prevailing westerlies," from the meteorologist's (and mariner's) habit of referring to winds by the direction they blow *from*.

Meanwhile, up around the poles the simple circulation pattern tries to re-establish itself as radiatively cooled air piles up and heads south (in the Northern Hemisphere), but this, too, is broken up by Earth's rotation. In between, in that region known to meteorologists as the mid-latitudes, the poleward transport of warm air and the equator-ward flow of cold air is accomplished by a real mish-mash of swirling eddies of many sizes and shapes, all embedded in the general west-to-east flow of the prevailing westerlies. We know these eddies as cyclones and fronts, and they are the subject of the next chapter.

The 7,918-mile-diameter Earth rotates once every 24 hours, spinning the people, houses, hills, trees, animals, and air on the equator around and around in an eastward direction at a zippy 1,038 m.p.h.

WATER

Think of it—a world without clouds, where nary a drop of rain or a flake of snow ever fell from the sky. No cooling fog, no dewy summer dawn, no frost on the window. Pretty dull? That is what weather would be like if there were no water vapor in the air. Remember the composition of the atmosphere, with its 99-percent nitrogen and oxygen and 1-percent other? Only a fraction of that remaining 1 percent is water vapor. And yet, slight as it is, that small concentration of water in the air is responsible for much of what we call weather. In fact, nearly all of the visible phenomena that make the weather so interesting are comprised of water in one form or another.

The importance of water in the atmosphere goes far beyond its role in making weather visually appealing. Water's place in the history of the Earth is assured, having kept our planet from becoming a Venus-like carbon dioxide pressure cooker. Even now, this most mundane of liquids is an essential ingredient of our weather. In its vapor state, water contains vast amounts of energy, which, when released, can literally unleash a storm. The energy in water vapor is called "latent heat." *Latent* means "present, but not visible or felt," and while latent heat cannot be felt as what we normally sense as heat (called "sensible heat"), it is very much present in moist air. Latent heat gets into water when it evaporates from the sea surface or wet ground. You know the cooling sensation of water evaporating from your skin—a cooling caused by water taking away from others of their kind, allowing the molecules to remain a vapor. When the vapor does condense back into liquid water, the latent heat is released into the atmosphere as sensible heat, where it causes rising currents of air.

Earth's oceans weigh 1.5 billion billion tons, or 300 times more than the atmosphere.

Earlier, we talked about the heating of Earth by sunlight. Since 71 percent of Earth's surface is covered by water, most sunlight falls onto oceans. Earth's oceans weigh 1.5 billion billion tons, or 300 times more than the atmosphere. Most sunlight that strikes the oceans goes into heating that huge bulk of water, and very little goes into directly heating the atmosphere above. Rather, the atmosphere receives solar energy in the form of latent heat, as tropical breezes evaporate water from the ocean surface. The amazing thing about latent heat is that it can be carried thousands of miles from its source before being let loose. Thus, energy absorbed from the sun by water vapor over the tropical Pacific Ocean may eventually fuel a storm over Montana. The mobility of latent heat allows the heat-driven motions of the atmosphere to concentrate over certain parts of the world, leading to some of the particular weather patterns that circle the Earth.

GEOGRAPHY

Even if Earth were as smooth as a billiard ball, with no oceans, continents, or mountain ranges, it would still have many of the familiar features of our weather such as storms, fronts, jet streams, and the like. But there would be none of the local variations that are so characteristic of western weather. San Francisco, Colorado Springs, and Saint Louis, being at nearly the same latitude, could expect the same climate. This, of course, is not the case, and the reason is geography.

We have seen how the heating of Earth's surface by sunlight is the ultimate energy source that drives the weather. The way the sun heats the atmosphere is, however, profoundly affected by the nature of the underlying surface, be it lowland, highland, or ocean. Furthermore, heat can be moved thousands of miles by ocean currents before entering the atmosphere as latent heat, and yet thousands more miles by ocean currents before entering the atmosphere as sensible heat. Mountains, by their sheer obstructive mass, can divert or destroy storms and shift jet streams.

The effects of geography on weather are as varied and detailed as geography itself. Western weather is influenced by one of the greatest geographical features on Earth—the continents and oceans of the tropics. Strangely, while most solar energy received by the tropics is absorbed by the oceans, the bulk of this energy ends up being released over land. Water vapor evaporated from the three tropical oceans—Indian, Pacific, and Atlantic—is carried by trade winds to the three landmasses of the tropics—Africa, South America, and the islands of Indonesia. Over these landmasses, latent heat is released in huge clusters of thunderstorms, resulting in rising currents of air that lead to powerful but localized Hadley circulation patterns.

The effects of geography on weather are as varied and detailed as geography itself.

The Hadley circulations over the three landmasses are stronger than over the oceans and consequently generate subtropical jet streams that are faster and farther north. These speedy subtropical jets—with winds averaging 150 m.p.h—usually cross the Middle East, Japan, and the southeastern United States. Elsewhere, such as over western North America, the subtropical jet stream is weaker and closer to the equator (and therefore well south of the western states). The winds of the subtropical jet stream often supply energy to mid-latitude storms, so we can begin to see how thunderstorms over Indonesia and South America can shape the weather of the West.

FRONTS, JETS, AND CYCLONES

The power of the world always works in circles,
and everything tries to be round. ... The sky
is round ... and so are the stars. The wind,
in its greatest power, whirls ...

—Black Elk, *Words of Power*

In chapter 1, we learned how the great winds of the world—the subtropical jet stream and the prevailing westerlies—are powered by sunlight falling on a rotating planet Earth. Important as these air currents are, they are not what we normally perceive as "weather." We think of weather as something smaller and more changeable, and indeed, less global and more "down home." Here in the mid-latitudes, including the West, it is the day-to-day passage of fronts and cyclones, of high and low pressure, that really makes up the weather. While these weather systems are not on as grand a scale as their globe-circling counterparts, they are caused by the same forces and are as essential a part of the atmosphere.

To geographers, the mid-latitudes are the zones (one in each hemisphere) between 23 and 66 degrees latitude that separate the tropics from the Arctic and the Antarctic. Meteorologists define the mid-latitudes as the region dominated by the prevailing westerlies. Their location on the globe changes from day to day and season to season, but, roughly, the mid-latitudes extend from 30 to 60 degrees latitude. More important, the mid-latitudes are where fronts and cyclones perform the vital task of carrying surplus heat northward from the tropics and returning cold air to the south. In the process, the opposing air masses clash and eventually mix, giving us our ever-changing weather.

THE MAKINGS OF A STORM

What happens when warm air meets cold air? First, there is a boundary between the two types of air, which is called a *front*. This term was taken straight out of military books by Norwegian meteorologists who came up with the concept shortly after World War I. Indeed, to this day, fronts are shown on weather maps in a fashion identical to battle lines on military maps. Usually more than one front separates the tropical and arctic air masses. One front may divide tropical air from cooler air to the north, with another front between that cooler air and downright nippy air north of that, and yet another front between the nippy air and the bitterly cold arctic air near the North Pole. To understand these meteorological battles, we first will consider a single front.

Fronts are three-dimensional. There's cold air to the north, warm air to the south and a boundary between the opposing air masses that often runs east to west. Air masses also have depth, so fronts extend upward into the atmosphere. The upper section of the front usually looks quite different from the part near the ground. Meteorologists like to slice the atmosphere into five or six layers, each at a different height, to get a more complete idea of its

Anatomy of a Storm— This schematic cyclone shows the major features of a low-pressure system. West of the low, cold air plunges south along a cold front, lifting the warm air ahead of the front to make clouds and rain. Meanwhile, the warm air pushes eastward over entrenched cold air, rising and making stratus-type clouds and light precipitation in the process. Ascending air near the center of the low creates more clouds there. Above it all, the jet stream—caused by the temperture contrast between the polar and tropical air masses— imparts some of its energy to the storm as it pushes the entire system to the east. Meanwhile, near the center of the low, the cold front has caught up to the warm front, creating an "occluded" front that has cold air on both sides. The development of the occluded front means the temperature contrast that powers the storm is beginning to disappear, so this storm is past its prime and is now weakening. ILLUSTRATION BY MICHAEL T. D. KEEN

Low

Cold Air

Jet Stream

Warm Front

Cold Front

Warm Air

Copyright Michael Keen 2003

workings. Let it suffice here to slice it into two layers—an upper level around 20,000 to 30,000 feet, and a lower level near the ground.

Pressure—that number read off a barometer—is simply the weight of the overlying air. That's why the pressure goes down when you (and the barometer's reading) go up. There's less air overhead at higher elevations. Furthermore, at the same pressure (and, roughly speaking, the same elevation), cold air is denser than warm air, meaning that the

same amount of air is packed into a smaller volume. For example, if you go up 1,000 feet, you'll rise past more air if it's cold. Thus, in cold air the pressure drops faster with increasing altitude. Conversely, in warm air the pressure drops more slowly. The end result is that high above a front of 30,000 feet, the pressure will be lower on the cold side of the front and higher on the warm side. Sometimes this is complicated by pressure differences across the front at ground level. If the surface pressure is higher on the cold side of the front, the pressure at 30,000 feet will be correspondingly higher on the cold side. Most of the time, though, this effect isn't great enough to change the final result: that cold air has lower pressure at high altitudes.

Air tends to move from high pressure to low pressure. Open the valve on an inflated tire, where the pressure is higher inside than outside, and you'll see what I mean. At 30,000 feet, air tries to blow from the warm side to the cold side of the front. Remember though that the Earth is still turning. The warm air at, say, 40 degrees north and moving eastward with the Earth rotating at 796 m.p.h. heads north to 50 degrees latitude, where the ground below is moving at only 668 m.p.h. The air ends up moving east at 128 m.p.h. Strong westerly winds (blowing from the West) are usually found along fronts at the upper levels of the atmosphere and are called jet streams, or just jets.

Unlike the subtropical jet, these frontal jets come and go as their fronts develop, move, and dissipate. Frontal jets can sometimes form near enough to the subtropical jet to pick up some of the subtropical jet's wind speed. Because the subtropical jet is usually fairly weak and well to the south of the western states, the frontal jet streams over the West tend to be weaker (but not always!) than they are over the East and elsewhere.

Dusty Cold Front— Everybody is familiar with cold fronts as those blue lines that adorn weather maps. Once in a while, cold fronts can also be seen in real life. Here, a cold front sweeping southward across the plains of Colorado is made visible by dust lifted from dry fields. The front is framed by the towers of the National Center for Atmospheric Research in Boulder, Colorado.

LYNETTE RUMMEL

With cold air to the north and warm air to the south, a front initially extends in an east–west direction with a westerly jet blowing along its upper edge. This situation doesn't last long, as eventually the cold air starts moving southward, and the warm air northward. This must happen for the arctic and tropical air masses to mix. At this point, the east–west front begins to twist. The southward bulge ahead of the advancing cold air is called a "cold front," and, not surprisingly, the northward bulge leading the warm air is a "warm front." These are the beginnings of a storm.

Let's get back to the rotating planet Earth. We've seen, in several instances, northbound winds turned to the east by the rotation of the Earth. Conversely, southbound winds are deflected west. In either event, the airflow is swerving to its right. No matter which way the air is moving, it always tends to curve right in the Northern Hemisphere (we see the opposite effect in the Southern Hemisphere, south of the equator). This is called the "Coriolis effect," after Gaspard Coriolis, the French engineer who proved it mathematically in 1843.

There are some important sidelights to the Coriolis effect. Initially, a low-pressure center sucks in air from all sides, leading to inward currents converging on the center. By bending each of these currents to its right, the Coriolis effect sends the air flowing *around* the low-pressure center in a counterclockwise direction (in the Northern Hemisphere). As always, the opposite holds true for high pressure. The counterclockwise winds blowing around a low-pressure center are also worked on by the Coriolis effect, which tries to make the winds start moving *away* from the low-pressure center. Meanwhile, the low pressure tries to suck the air back in. The end result is a sort of balance, with the air going around and around in a counterclockwise direction, but never heading into or away from the low-pressure center. In reality, this balance never exactly occurs, and some air leaks into or away from the "low," as meteorologists are fond of calling low-pressure areas. The near balance, however, keeps the low from either collapsing in on itself or flying apart and allows the storm to continue spinning as long as it does (for a week or so).

Types of Fronts—The weather and cloud types associated with the three major types of fronts— cold, warm, and stationary—are displayed in this National Weather Service diagram.

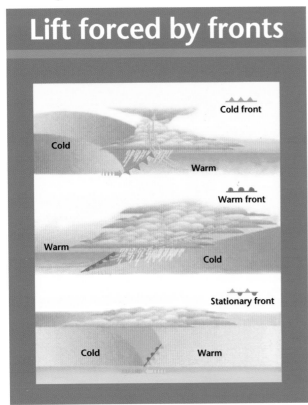

Lift forced by fronts

Cold front

Cold

Warm

Warm front

Warm

Cold

Stationary front

Cold

Warm

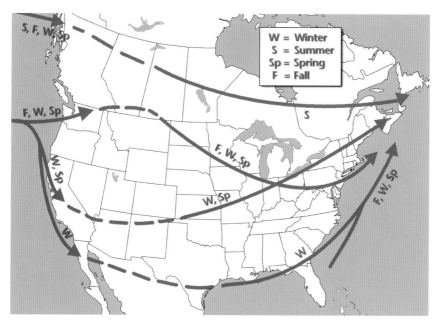

Major Storm Tracks of North America—Solid lines show the main storm tracks; Dashed lines show the frequent paths of storm that break up over the Rockies and regenerate over the plains or along the Gulf of Mexico. The seasons when each of the tracks are most active are marked. RICHARD A. KEEN

We return now to the bulging fronts. Let's take the case of a cold bulge occurring west of a warm bulge. The cold air heads south and tries to turn west, while the northbound warm air tries to head east. The two flows are trying to move away from each other. With air moving away in two directions, a partial vacuum develops in the middle. In other words, a low forms. The low pressure then counteracts the diverging warm and cold air flows and starts to pull them back toward the center. This creates a low center, with cold air pouring down the western side and warm air streaming up the eastern side— otherwise known as a "cyclone."

West of the cold bulge may be another warm bulge. Between the bulges, the turning effects are the opposite of those leading to a cyclone, and the result is known as an "anticyclone." This is a region of high pressure, so it is called a "high." In the Northern Hemisphere, winds blow clockwise around a high. The eastern edge of the high, where winds arc from the north, is colder than the western side.

Meanwhile, back at 30,000 feet, the jet is twisting with the bulging fronts. The jet dips south with the cold front and bows north with the warm front. The line depicting the jet on a weather map may take on the sinuous appearance of a snake. The northward bends of the jet overlying the warm air are called "ridges." The southward bending "troughs" arc above the cold air, so pressure in the trough is lower than in the ridge. Near the surface, the cyclone remains in the middle of the whole mess, with the ridge to its east and the trough to its west. So a peculiar thing happens—the center of low-pressure aloft is not above the surface cyclone, but to the west of it.

As the storm continues to develop, the cold air plunges even farther south. The trough often becomes so sharp that it breaks off from the rest of the jet stream, forming an "upper-level low." Sometimes the "upper-low" (an interesting combination of terms!) separates from the low-level storm, and the two go on their separate ways. This actually happens frequently in the West, where mountains have a way of destroying the low-level cyclone. When storms split like this, they often wither and die. Sometimes, however, the upper-low may wander along and overtake another front, where it finds new life as another cyclone.

WEATHER PATTERNS OF THE WEST

Autumn Cold Front—As it plunges southward, the heavier cold air behind the front flows like molasses spilled on a table—only faster. The leading edge of the cold air—the cold front—takes on the same curved shape as the front edge of the spreading molasses. Moisture in the cold air mass makes this front visible as a fog bank advancing into the Colorado Rockies. RICHARD A. KEEN

Although jets may bend and bow, their winds still blow, for the most part, to the east. Everything associated with a jet, including cyclones, fronts, and even the ridges and troughs, is carried eastward with the jet's winds. We may therefore think of jet streams as "storm tracks," the paths taken by cyclones as they live out their lives. This is one reason jet streams are such important features on weather maps—their average positions give a good idea where the main storm tracks are found.

Except for the Pacific Coast and the first one or two mountain ranges inland, such as the Sierra Nevada, Cascade, and Coast ranges, the West is the driest part of North America. Of course, there are reasons for this. Lack of an available supply of moisture isn't the answer, because the Pacific Ocean lies

right next door to the entire West Coast. Moist air doesn't do any good without some mechanism to wring water out of the air and drop it to the ground. Storms, which provide the most effective way to squeeze out this moisture, tend to skirt the western states. That is why the West is dry. Although it sometimes seems otherwise, much of the West usually is ignored by the world's major storm tracks.

Let's consider what causes storms. Sharply contrasting air masses are a must for healthy cyclones, and having a strong subtropical jet nearby doesn't hurt. In winter, these conditions are met to a T over the eastern coasts of North America and Asia, where chilly air over the continents clashes with balmy air above the warm offshore currents. The West never sees the eastern North American storms, which track off in the opposite direction. Meanwhile, East Asian storms have to cross the Pacific before reaching western shores. Many of these storms end up stalling and dying in the Gulf of Alaska, feeding into the semi-permanent vortex known as the "Aleutian Low." Since it takes about a week to cross the Pacific, the storms that do make it to the West Coast usually have lost much of their punch and only the remains of the upper low make it to California.

Occasionally, some storms are still going strong when they reach the West Coast, particularly if they get a boost from the temperature contrasts along the south coast of Alaska. And sometimes the Aleutian Low spins off new storms that pound the coast with fresh vigor. Even a powerful storm striking the West Coast meets its match when it tries to cross the highlands of the West. The vast region between the Sierras and the Rockies is, on the average, the most-elevated terrain in North America, with nearly a million square miles of land lying 1–2 miles above the sea.

Crossing a 2-mile-high and 1,000-mile-wide mass of mountains is a real hurdle in the life of a cyclone. Think of the storm as a rotating swirl of air extending from sea level to 6 miles up. To cross the barrier, 6 vertical miles of storm must squeeze into just 4 miles. The cyclone responds to this squeeze by spreading horizontally, which, in turn, slows the cyclone's rotation, just as a twirling figure skater spins slower when the arms are extended outward. This squashing all but destroys many storms and leaves others in a severely weakened state. We can see why many storms skirt along the Mexican and Canadian borders of the western states, where the mountains aren't quite as imposing. Many less-ambitious cyclones are content to remain just offshore, spinning out their lives without ever seeing land.

If a storm squashes and weakens when it encounters high terrain, what does it do when it moves back over lower ground? As is so often the

Although it sometimes seems otherwise, much of the West usually is ignored by the world's major storm tracks.

Few major storm tracks cross the West in summer. … Sunny, dry weather is the rule; rarely do fronts and weak cyclones invade the West.

case in meteorology, the exact opposite happens. The storm stretches vertically, tightens inward horizontally, and spins faster once again. Although the mountains weed out weaker storms, those storms that make it across stand a good chance of redeveloping when they reach the High Plains east of the Rockies. This is especially true if there is a strong frontal boundary crossing the Plains, a common situation in the winter. The front gives a new source of energy to the storm system, and a new and powerful cyclone may sweep into the Midwestern states. These ensuing storms have been named "Colorado" and "Alberta" lows, after the favored places for the regeneration process.

In winter, Pacific storms crash into the West Coast, especially in the Pacific Northwest, and break up as they try to cross the mountains. Their upper-level remnants track along the northern and southern borders of the United States and give birth to new storms when they once again reach lower ground and fresh fronts of warm and cold air. This double storm track is a peculiar feature of the West and leads to what is known as a "split jet." The powerful jet that frequently streaks across the North Pacific divides in two as it traverses the West, rejoining into one jet over the Midwest. Occasionally, the subtropical jet joins the action, breeding upper lows south of Hawaii that sweep into the Southwest and southern Rockies.

During summer, the South American thunderstorms that kick off the Hadley circulation and the subtropical jet move into Mexico and Central America, while Indonesian thunderstorms migrate north to Southeast Asia. This pushes the Pacific and northern United States storm tracks farther north into Canada, and the southern storm track—the one that runs along the Mexican border in winter—disappears completely. Few major storm tracks cross the West in summer, and the area remains under an upper-level ridge. Sunny, dry weather is the rule; rarely do fronts and weak cyclones invade the West.

The cloudless skies of summer help perpetuate the upper-level ridge that caps the West at this time. Intense heating of the 1- or 2-mile-high ground by the nearly overhead sun warms the air at these altitudes. Warmer air leads to higher pressure aloft, and so the upper ridge, once it sets up in the early summer (usually in early June), becomes a persistent feature for the next three months.

Late in the season, the mass of tropical thunderstorms over Mexico may extend into the Southwest. This is the "summer monsoon," a brief rainy season that brings fleeting, but occasionally drenching, rains to the deserts. The ridge itself starts breaking down in late August or early September, when the sun has dropped too low in the sky to provide enough heating to reinforce the ridge.

Storm tracks of the in-between seasons, autumn and spring, have features of both the summer and winter patterns. In general, the storm tracks are slightly farther north than in winter. The Canadian border track is well into Canada, while the Mexican border track cuts across the southwestern states. The storms that take these paths are usually not as strong or as frequent as in winter. In spring, though, the regenerating storms along the east slopes of the Rockies can become quite intense. The boundary between lingering arctic air over the northern plains and moist air surging north from the Gulf of Mexico can breed powerful cyclones that bring heavy snows and rains to the eastern Rockies and High Plains, and tornadoes to the Midwest.

STORMY WEATHER

The passage of cyclones and anticyclones brings the West its never-ending variety of weather. Like snowflakes, no two storms are identical. And as cyclones progress through their life cycles, the type of weather they bring also changes. However, most cyclones have some common features that are worth describing. The most important and simple guide to understanding the weather of high- and low-pressure areas is to remember that rising air brings clouds, rain, and snow, while sinking air brings clear skies. Three principles

White Sands Gypsum Storm—A crowd awaiting the landing of the space shuttle *Columbia* in 1982 watches apprehensively as high winds whip clouds of gypsum dust thousands of feet into the sky. The poor visibility on the landing strip forced a one-day delay in the landing.
RICHARD A. KEEN

MEMORABLE WESTERN CYCLONES

November 1861–January 1862—A nonstop series of Pacific cyclones struck the entire West Coast, causing severe flooding from San Diego to Olympia, Washington. The central valleys of California turned into a "sea," and, up in Olympia, a resident wrote that "everybody's roof leaked."

January 1921—The "great Olympic blowdown" swept the coasts of Washington and Oregon with gusts as high as 150 m.p.h. Gales destroyed eight times as much Douglas fir lumber as did the eruption of Mount Saint Helens in 1980.

October 1934—Hurricane-force winds raked western Washington, unroofing buildings and sinking boats in Puget Sound. One casualty was the liner *President Madison,* which ripped loose from her moorings, hit several other ships, and sank.

November 1940—Not a huge storm, but enough to send the Tacoma Narrows Bridge in Washington into the drink. Flaws in the bridge's design caused it to vibrate and twist when winds were just right. Already bearing the name "Galloping Gertie," the bridge was unable to survive this storm. One dog reportedly died in the collapse.

October 1962—The "Columbus Day storm" in western Washington and Oregon was, in part, the remnants of Pacific Typhoon Freda. It was possibly the most powerful storm ever to pound the West, with winds reaching 170 m.p.h. in Oregon's Tillamook Forest and 116 m.p.h on a bridge in downtown Portland.

January 1969—Ten days of storms brought floods, mudslides, and falling trees to much of California. More than 40 people drowned or were buried in mudslides.

December 21, 1977—Powerful winds, due to the pressure difference between a huge high system centered in Utah and an approaching Pacific low, raised millions of tons of soil from California farmlands, converting fertile fields into sand lots. Highways were blocked by dirt drifts, and some cars were literally buried in dust. Gusts reached an estimated 192 m.p.h. in Arvin, near Bakersfield.

MEMORABLE WESTERN CYCLONES, CONTINUED

March 29, 1982—Gusts of nearly 60 m.p.h. lifted huge clouds of gypsum dust above the landing strip at White Sands, New Mexico. The near zero visibility forced the space shuttle *Columbia* to delay its landing until the next day. (See photograph on page 21.)

November 1982–April 1983—One of the strongest and most extended series of cyclones pounded the California coast. Storms brought wind, rain, surf, and even tornadoes to southern and central California, damaging or destroying more than 3,000 homes and businesses. One storm dumped 25 inches of rain on the Santa Cruz mountains and 102 inches of snow near Lake Tahoe. Many of the storms continued into the Rockies with heavy snows—a Christmas blizzard shut down Denver with 2 to 4 feet of snow, and an April storm dumped 65 inches near Fort Collins, Colorado. The siege of storms was caused by the strongest El Niño in decades, and was voted the "Top Weather Event of the Century" by National Weather Service forecasters in California.

February 1986—Twelve days of torrential rains, totaling as much as 49.6 inches, drenched northern California. Dam and levee breaks flooded cities in the Sacramento Valley, including Yuba City and Linda, causing nearly half a billion dollars of property damage.

November 29, 1991—A low over southern California whipped up 60 m.p.h. winds, which, in turn, whipped up dense clouds of dust along Interstate 5. Visibility was particularly poor along a 2-mile stretch near Fresno, where 164 vehicles piled up in 6 minutes, killing 17 motorists. It was the worst multiple vehicle accident in U.S. history.

December 11–12, 1995—An "explosively" developing cyclone (these storms are nicknamed "bombs" by forecasters) off the California coast moved ashore in Washington, bringing all-time low pressure records to Seattle and Astoria, Oregon. It also created gusts reaching 119 m.p.h. on the Oregon coast and 134 m.p.h. at Kregor Peak, near San Francisco.

October 17, 1996—Another "bomb" blasted Vancouver Island, B.C., with 100 m.p.h. winds on the coast and waves as high as 100 feet on the open ocean. Falling trees knocked out power, and numerous boats were ripped from their moorings and set adrift.

of physics make this so: atmospheric pressure decreases with increasing altitude; air expands and cools when it rises into the realm of lower pressure; and cool air is less able to hold water vapor, so it condenses back into droplets of liquid water (or crystals of solid water) and forms clouds. With enough moisture in the air, the droplets and crystals coalesce into raindrops and snowflakes.

The twisting fronts around a cyclone determine where the air currents rise and where they fall. Since most lows move east, the northward moving warm front is ahead of the low center—the "warm before the storm"—and the southbound cold front follows the passage of the low. Being lighter, warm air tends to overrun the cold air. This usually brings thickening and lowering clouds followed by steady precipitation in the form of rain or snow. As it plunges south and east, the heavier, cold air cuts under the lighter, warm air. The undercutting cold front shoves the warm air upward, often in a fairly narrow line, setting off brief but heavier precipitation in showers, squalls, and thunderstorms.

Many cyclones reach the West Coast near the end of their lives. These old storms usually don't have well-defined fronts and can be best described as spinning whirls with little up-and-down air motion. The weather is as lackluster as the cyclones themselves, often appearing as drizzle along the coast and light snow in the mountains. Quite a few of these old storms drift slowly southward along the coast, finally retiring off the shores of Mexico. Others move inland, occasionally finding new life as regenerating storms.

The world-record heaviest snowfall, 7 feet in just over a day, was dumped on Colorado in April 1921 during one of these springtime reversals of the prevailing westerlies.

There is nothing like a good mountain range to complicate this picture of the sequence of weather brought by a passing cyclone. Simply put, when winds reach a mountain range, they blow up and over the ridge and down the other side. Since rising air brings precipitation, the *upwind* side of a mountain range gets an extra dose of rain or snow. With prevailing westerlies most of the year, the western slopes of the Cascades, Sierras, and Rockies get quite a boost to their annual precipitation from upslope winds. Sometimes in these areas, rain or snow continues for a day or more after the skies have cleared elsewhere.

The rain and snow that soaks the western slopes removes moisture from the air blowing over the mountain, which means that the air descending the eastern slopes will be drier air and will drop much less precipitation. Prevailing downslope winds give many of these regions a desertlike climate; all of Nevada and parts of eastern Washington, Oregon, and California, along with some valleys in British Columbia are clear examples of this so-called "rain shadow" effect.

The eastern slopes of the Rockies, from New Mexico to the Yukon, are also subject to rain shadowing much of the year. Springtime in the Rockies, however, is a different story. Regenerating cyclones over the High Plains

Aerial of North Pacific Storm—A vigorous cyclone ruffles the waters of the North Pacific Ocean in this image from NASA's Terra satellite. The storm shows a well-developed spiral flow into its center. A ship passing through this storm would likely encounter gale-force winds and squalls. NASA

draw humid air from the Gulf of Mexico and swirl it around the north side of the low center, directly into the Rockies. Riding winds from the east, this Gulf moisture can be unloaded in copious quantities onto the foothills. The world-record heaviest snowfall, 7 feet in just over a day, was dumped on Colorado in April 1921 during one of these springtime reversals of the prevailing westerlies.

The south-facing mountains of northern Arizona, New Mexico, and southwestern Colorado see upslope precipitation when the winds are from the south, often ahead of an approaching cyclone. With the convoluted terrain of the West, it is easy to realize why the weather can vary so greatly from one county to the next.

The cyclone passes, and its potpourri of precipitation has come and gone. It is now the anticyclone's turn to take charge of the weather. This high brings clearing and cooling, but, as the high moves east, southerly winds usher in warming. High-level clouds appear on the horizon, foretelling the approach of the next cyclone.

At many places in the mid-latitudes, cyclones pass at three- or four-day intervals. This rule of thumb works well in the eastern states. But the West

These sluggish weather patterns can bring days of lingering inclement weather followed, fortunately, by an equally long spell of fine weather.

has its "split jet" and double storm track. Frequently, alternating cyclones take each route: one goes north, the next goes south. On each storm track, cyclones pass once a week rather than every three days. What this means for westerners is that storms often arrive at weekly intervals. Sometimes the jet doesn't split or only splits after it has reached well inland. These weather patterns can subject parts of the West Coast to a near continuous battering by Pacific storms, with the skies scarcely clearing after one storm before clouds from the next cyclone start rolling in. There are also the occasional "blocking" weather patterns, so named by the action of large, slow-moving highs or lows (or a combination of both) that block the regular west-to-east flow. These sluggish weather patterns can bring days of lingering inclement weather followed, fortunately, by an equally long spell of fine weather.

One reason western weather never gets boring is that weather patterns can change several times during the course of a season. Months may pass without a good, healthy storm, but then the pattern breaks. Suddenly, cyclones queue up across the Pacific from California to Japan, each impatiently waiting its turn to march ashore. Then, unexpectedly, they're gone. Watch the weather maps and satellite photos in your newspapers and television broadcasts and you'll see this happen. It's fascinating!

WATER FOR THE WEST

All the streams run to the sea,
but the sea is not full;
to the place where the streams flow,
there they flow again.

—King Solomon, *Ecclesiastes* 1:7

One of the West's most remarkable climatic features is its fantastic variability from place to place. In many parts of the West, an easy hour's drive takes you from verdant forest to sagebrush desert. To a large extent, these stark contrasts of vegetation are due to differences in the amount of moisture that drops from the sky. This moisture falls in many forms, some liquid and some frozen. Rain, sleet, hail, snow—all those inclemencies mail carriers must go through—are all lumped together under the common name "precipitation."

Precipitation is the depth of rain, melted snow, hail, and other frozen stuff that would be standing on the ground after a storm if none ran off, soaked into the ground, or evaporated. The measurement of precipitation reflects this concept. Frenchman Denys Papin put out a bucket to measure the rain in 1669. Ever since, no matter how sophisticated they may look, most measuring devices for precipitation are still essentially buckets. Some use heating elements or automobile antifreeze to melt snowfall and some have digital readouts. But all are still cans that show the water depth at the end of a storm. Add these measurements over the course of a year and you get the annual precipitation for your locale. Do this for several years and you can get the average annual precipitation. This number—average annual precipitation—is one of the single numbers that best describe the climate.

The wettest weather station in the West is Henderson Lake on Vancouver Island, British Columbia, which averages 262.10 inches of precipitation per

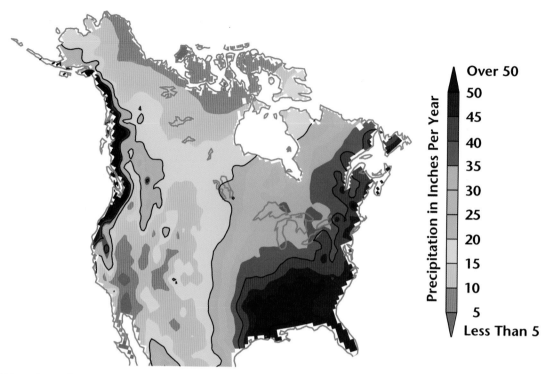

Mean Annual Precipitation for North America—

Precipitation includes rain and melted snow, and average amounts range from less than 5 inches in the Southwest to 50 inches and more in the dark blue areas along the Pacific Coast and in the Southeast United States.

NOAA/CIRES CLIMATE DIAGNOSTICS CENTER

Precipitation in Inches Per Year

- Over 50
- 50
- 45
- 40
- 35
- 30
- 25
- 20
- 15
- 10
- 5
- Less Than 5

year. Little Port Walter, in the Alaska panhandle, enjoys 223.71 inches of rain and melted snow in an average year, and farther south, the wettest place in the western "mainland" United States is Wynoochee Oxbow, Washington, on the Olympic Peninsula, with an average annual rainfall of 144.43 inches. These locations all have rain and snow gauges, but between the gauges, there are doubtlessly places where more unmeasured precipitation falls. One such spot may be near the 10,000 foot level in the mountains between Glacier Bay, Alaska, and the Pacific Ocean, where climatologist George Taylor of Oregon State University estimates the annual total of rain and melted snow to be a whopping 450 inches per year. If real, this estimate, which is based on elevation, topography, and data from nearby weather stations, would make this part of Alaska (not far from Mount Fairweather) the wettest place in the world!

Henderson Lake receives 116 times as much as the West's driest spot, Death Valley, California, with only 2.3 inches a year. The extreme variability of the West contrasts with the evenness of annual rainfall across the eastern states. For the 26 states east of the Mississippi River, the extremes are 80 inches in the hills of South Carolina and 28 inches in western Wisconsin. Amazingly, this range of average annual precipitation can be found between sites 12 miles apart within Clallam County, Washington, and 16 miles apart in Shasta County, California.

As best as it can be figured, the averaged annual precipitation for the 12 western states is about 17 inches. The rest of the "lower 48" states average more than twice as much—about 36 inches. While the West may be the driest part of the country, the amount of water that falls is nonetheless enormous. Seventeen inches a year comes out to half a million gallons per acre. Over the 1,193,826 square miles of western states, the annual soaking amounts to 319 cubic miles of water, or 1.5 million million tons of the stuff. That's 10 times the volume of Washington's Puget Sound—and this doesn't include western Canada or Alaska! The amounts are awesome. Where does it all come from?

Water vapor is always part of the atmosphere overlying the western states. The amount of this vapor varies considerably from season to season and even from day to day, but on the average the total volume of moisture over the West is about 10 cubic miles of liquid equivalent. This is enough to cover the region with a half inch of liquid water. However, again on the average, a half inch of precipitation falls on the West every 10 days. This means there must be a continuous replenishment of atmospheric moisture over the West.

There is no single source for the West's water. Sources change from state to state and from season to season. We know that moisture evaporates off the surfaces of the world's oceans because, ultimately, that is where it all returns—as noted by King Solomon in the opening quote. In fact, oceans are the West's primary water source. The cycle of evaporation from oceans, transport by winds to land areas, precipitation, runoff into rivers, and return to the oceans is known as the "hydrologic cycle."

In reality, the hydrologic cycle is complicated. Water can be stored for long amounts of time in lakes, soil, underground water supplies, and even in snowpack and glaciers before being released back to the oceans. Even atmospheric transport of moisture can be circuitous—water can precipitate and evaporate several times before reaching its "final" destination.

Rain (or Snow) Seasons Across the West—In some parts of the West, winter is the wettest season of the year, while other regions receive their moisture during the summer. This map shows which of the four seasons receive the most precipitation for different areas. RICHARD A. KEEN

WINTER MOISTURE

The Main Streams of Moisture—In a schematic way, the arrows depict the flow of water vapor from the North Pacific Ocean, the Gulf of California and nearby areas of the Pacific, and the Gulf of Mexico, along with the seasons each moisture stream is important. The width of the arrows gives a rough idea of the relative importance of each of the moisture sources. RICHARD A. KEEN

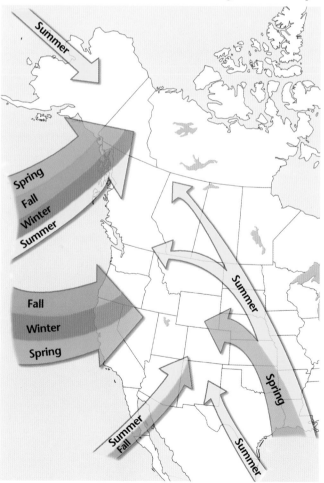

Maps of precipitation distribution across the West, and of the seasons in which most of it falls, provide strong clues as to its source. In general, the coastal states and provinces (California to coastal Alaska) are wetter than the interior states and provinces. In these coastal areas, the western slopes of the mountains are wetter than the eastern slopes. Most of the annual precipitation in these regions falls during the winter, when the prevailing westerlies are most pronounced. It is therefore a simple deduction that the West Coast and the western slopes of the interior mountain ranges receive most of their moisture from the Pacific Ocean.

It is no big surprise that the Pacific supplies much of the West's moisture, considering its size and placement. However, many of the places that rely on Pacific moisture are the same places that are dry during summer. The ocean is still there, of course, but the means of getting Pacific moisture onshore and then squeezing it out of the air is not. The storms that lash the coast during the winter are gone, and only occasionally do weak storms brush the Pacific Northwest. Summer is dry on the West Coast (at least, south of Canada— farther north, along the Alaskan coast, it rains regularly all year-round). Mark Twain succinctly summarized the nature of West Coast rain in his description of San Francisco's weather in his book *Roughing It*:

> *When you want to go visiting or attend church, or the theatre, you never look up at the clouds to see whether it is likely to rain or not—you look at the almanac. If it is winter, it will rain—and if it is summer, it won't rain, and you cannot help it.*

SUMMER MOISTURE

Summer is the wettest season over much of the interior Southwest and along the High Plains east of the Rockies. Each of these regions has its primary moisture source. The southwest region—Arizona, southern Utah, western New Mexico and southwestern Colorado—gets its moisture from the warm waters of the Mexican Pacific Coast and the Gulf of California. These tepid waters can be considered separately from the main mass of the Pacific Ocean, which supplies winter moisture to the coast, because each feeds moisture to a different region at a different time of year through the action of a different kind of storm. Winter moisture is brought by cyclonic storms, while most summer rains fall in thunderstorms. The summertime flow of tropical air into the desert Southwest is called the "Southwest monsoon," after its larger and stronger Asian counterpart.

Like its Asian cousin, the Southwest monsoon can vary from year to year and even during the course of an individual season. It is often intermittent with rainy spells lasting several days or weeks, interspersed with similarly long dry spells. Some years the monsoon barely reaches into southern Arizona, while other years its thunderstorms can be followed into Idaho and Oregon.

The other region with predominant summer rains, the High Plains, stretches 1,300 miles from border to border in the United States and another 300 miles into Canada. This area includes western Texas, the eastern sections of New Mexico, Colorado, Wyoming, Montana, and Alberta, the Black Hills of South Dakota, and southern Saskatchewan. The imposing barrier of the Continental Divide separates this region from the tropical moisture of the Southwest monsoon. In its place, water vapor streams in from the Gulf of Mexico to feed the summer storms of the High Plains. At this time of year the Gulf of Mexico simmers at 85° F, allowing large amounts of water to evaporate into the overlying air. The Gulf is such a prodigious source of moisture that it supplies much of the rain that falls over the entire United States east of Rockies. During the summer, some of it finds its way into the Rocky Mountains

Annual Precipitation for 11 Western States, 1895–2001—More than 100 years of annual precipitation, averaged over the 11 western states, show a great deal of year-to-year variability. The wettest year, 1983, saw twice as much water fall from the sky as did the driest year, 1929. NATIONAL CLIMATIC DATA CENTER DATA

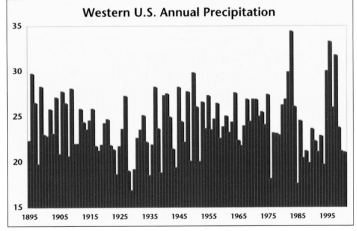
Western U.S. Annual Precipitation

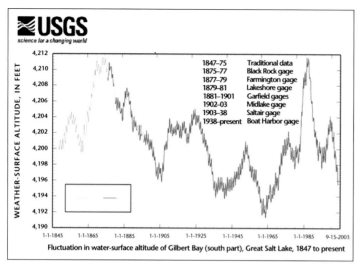

1847–75	Traditional data
1875–77	Black Rock gage
1877–79	Farmington gage
1879–81	Lakeshore gage
1881–1901	Garfield gages
1902–03	Midlake gage
1903–38	Saltair gage
1938–present	Boat Harbor gage

Fluctuation in water-surface altitude of Gilbert Bay (south part), Great Salt Lake, 1847 to present

Level of the Great Salt Lake—Perhaps no single record tells more about the recent climate of the West than the changing level of the Great Salt Lake. Located directly in the middle of the West and draining four of its states, the lake acts as a huge natural rain gauge for measuring western precipitation. Decreasing lake levels in the 1870s, 1890s, 1930s, and 1950s show hints of a 20-year drought cycle, while wet weather in the 1860s sent the lake rising to 4,211.8 feet above sea level in 1873. In April 1987, heavy precipitation, including some caused by the 1982–83 El Niño, raised the lake level to 4,211.85 feet—an inch above the 1873 record.

U.S. GEOLOGICAL SURVEY

themselves. On occasion, Gulf moisture occasionally drifts way north across eastern British Columbia, the Yukon, and even (rarely) into the interior of Alaska—all places where the annual cycle of rainfall peaks in the summer months.

The river of humid air flowing north from the Gulf of Mexico normally stays several hundred miles east of the Rockies. The summertime boundary between the usually hot and dry air of the West and the humid mass of Gulf air often lies near the 100th meridian, a line that runs from central Texas to the middle of North Dakota. Frequently, this boundary forms a sharply defined front called the "dry line." The dry line separates wet and dry rather than warm and cold air masses, but it is every bit as important to the daily weather of the summer months. Severe thunderstorms, and sometimes tornadoes, like to form along the dry line; however, most of the time these storms form too far east to be considered "western" weather.

Like other fronts, the dry line does not stand still. Its westward excursions allow Gulf air to flow right into the foothills of the Rockies. This happens often enough to bring 5 to 10 inches of summer rain all along the High Plains.

The moist streams from the two Gulfs, the Gulf of California and the Gulf of Mexico, sometimes meet over the Rockies of northern New Mexico. The result is the most pronounced summer rainfall maximum in the West, with some spots receiving half their annual precipitation in July and August alone. Most of this rain falls in thundershowers, which occur more often here than anywhere else in the country.

SPRING MOISTURE

Never mind what the song says; springtime in the Rockies is the *wettest* time of year. Along the Rockies and their eastern foothills from Denver northward, the three spring months—March, April, and May—see more rain and snow fall from the sky than any other season. In these areas, summer is the second wettest season, and the source of the moisture is the same—the Gulf of Mexico. The dry line is there too, especially in late spring. However, the means for bringing moisture to the mountains is a lot more vigorous in the spring than it is in the summer.

The eastern plains of Colorado are a favored location for the regeneration of cyclones that make it across the mountains. The counterclockwise rotation of these storms swirls the humid Gulf air north and then westward around the storm's center, flinging moisture against the slopes of the Rockies. Although this may happen only a few times a year, the resulting precipitation (usually in the form of snow) can be extremely heavy.

AUTUMN MOISTURE

Autumn is the wettest season in a small area of northeastern Utah and north-western Colorado, and even in these regions it is just barely moister than the other seasons. Located on the northern fringes of the Southwestern monsoon, this area's autumn maximum is earned in those occasional years when the monsoon continues into September. August, September, and October have been known to bring hurricane remnants into the southwestern states and, although rare, their rains can be torrential. Over the long run, hurricanes provide a significant portion of the late summer and fall precipitation for much of the Southwest.

The other part of the West whose precipitation peaks in autumn is the Pacific Coast of Alaska from Kodiak to Ketchikan. The source of the moisture is obvious—the Pacific Ocean—and in the autumn, the still-mild waters are able to feed more moisture into the storms that gather around the Aleutian Low.

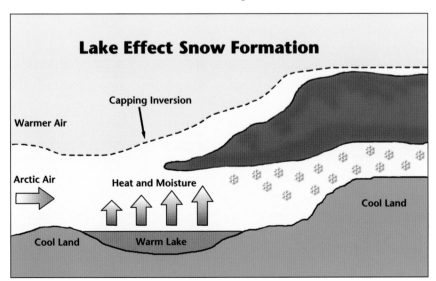

Lake Effect Snow—Cold air passing over relatively warm water (such as the Great Salt Lake, Puget Sound, or large reservoirs) can pick up enough moisture to create localized snow storms on the downwind shore.
NATIONAL WEATHER SERVICE

LOCAL MOISTURE SOURCES

There are three main oceanic sources of water for the West—the Pacific Ocean, the Gulf of California, and the Gulf of Mexico. Of course, the path of a water molecule from the ocean to your backyard may not be a direct one. Much of the moisture blown in from the ocean and dumped on the West collects on the ground and in lakes, where it evaporates and becomes an important moisture supply for later storms. It is quite possible that some of the water in a local rainstorm has been "recycled" several times since it evaporated from the ocean surface.

The soil is one place where water can be stored for recycling. Heavy storms are often followed by lighter showers, which are fed, in part, by moisture evaporated from the soaked ground. Storage of moisture in the soil is one way that wet spells and, conversely, droughts perpetuate themselves. In summer droughts, rain showers are less likely to develop as long as the ground remains dry. Dry ground is more readily heated by the summer sun, since less solar energy goes into evaporating moisture from the soil. The more efficient heating of dry ground and of the air above it helps maintain the upper-level ridge, which, in turn, helps suppress the development of showers.

Mountain snowpack, like wet soil, can also be a local source of moisture for the atmosphere. The major difference is that the moisture is lying on top of the ground. Evaporation from melting snowpack is one source of water vapor for showers forming over mountain areas in late spring and early summer.

Perhaps the West's most unique local moisture source is its largest body of surface water, the Great Salt Lake in Utah. Lakes of this size deliver large amounts of water vapor into the atmosphere, particularly when the lake is warmer than the air blowing across it. This occurs in late autumn and early winter, when the first outbreaks of arctic air reach a lake still retaining the warmth of summer. On the coldest days, moisture can be seen entering the atmosphere as twirling streamers of mist above the lake surface. Take a cup of hot coffee outside on a winter day and you'll see this in miniature. Usually, this moisture doesn't rise very high into the atmosphere; but when the lake is warm enough and the air cold enough, low clouds and "lake effect" snow can develop over the downwind side of the lake.

"Lake Effect" Clouds— Zero-degree air crossing Fort Peck Lake in Montana made these lake effect stratus clouds. The power houses at Fort Peck Dam disappear into the very low cloud deck. ANDREW POHL, NATIONAL WEATHER SERVICE

In October 1984, one lake effect storm dumped up to 40 inches of snow on different parts of the Salt Lake City area. Between the lake and the crest of the Wasatch Mountains, some 50 million tons of snow dropped from the sky— enough to make a mile-high snowman! Similar storms have resulted from the passage of polar air across Washington's Puget Sound, and no doubt every inlet, bay, and fjord along the coast north of Puget Sound has generated its own little snowstorm.

How small can a lake be and still make a snowstorm? In December 2002, zero-degree air whisking across Fort Peck Lake (a 70-mile long reservoir approximately 5 miles wide) created a lake effect storm that dropped 2 inches of fluffy snow near Glasgow, Montana. Smaller lakes, those a mile or less across, usually freeze over when the air gets really cold. But when a lake is used to cool the burners in factories and power plants, its water stays warm all winter long. Occasionally, when the atmospheric conditions are just right, miniature snowstorms coat the ground downwind from factory-heated lakes and even large cooling towers. One of these "backyard blizzards" whitened a 2-mile-wide section of Boulder, Colorado, near the local power plant one January morning in 1981. There was only a skiff of snow, enough to fill the cracks in the sidewalks, but piled all in one place it may have weighed 5 or 10 tons. That's not a whole lot of snow, but these little storms do illustrate the hydrologic cycle on a scale that we can grasp.

The Great Salt Lake may be enormous compared to a heated pond, but it is still puny compared to the vast expanse of the Pacific Ocean. Likewise, its real importance as a moisture source is relatively unimportant. The big lake effect snow in 1984 supplied only .003 percent of the West's total precipitation that year. We are left realizing the real sources of water for the West are the surrounding oceans, and that some of this moisture entered the atmosphere half a world away.

SNOW AND RAIN

CHAPTER 4

*Hamlet: Do you see yonder cloud that's almost in
    the shape of a camel?
Polonius: By the mass, and 'tis like a camel indeed.
Hamlet: Methinks it is like a weasel.
Polonius: It is backed like a weasel.
Hamlet: Or like a whale?
Polonius: Very like a whale.*

—William Shakespeare, *Hamlet*

In the previous three chapters we have seen how the sun makes the wind blow and how the wind brings enormous amounts of water from the world's oceans into the West. That leaves us on an average day with 5 or 10 cubic miles of water sitting over the western states. This water, however, is in the air and, instead of being a refreshing liquid that animals and plants can enjoy, it's all vapor. That brings us to the question of how to get all this water out of the sky and onto (and into) the ground.

CONDENSATION

Water vapor is a gas and, therefore, will never fall. To return to earth it needs to turn into liquid water or solid ice through a process called "condensation." Did you ever notice how your laundry on the line dries faster when it's warm outside? Warm air has less trouble evaporating water because it can contain more water vapor than cold air can. If air containing water vapor gets chilled, it eventually reaches a point where it can no longer hold its supply of vapor. The excess vapor condenses into tiny drops of liquid water. If the air is cold enough, the vapor may form ice crystals through a process called "sublimation."

Spring Snow—Spring storms in higher elevations of the West often occur when the temperature is near freezing. Here, the rain–snow line is located a few yards up the trail in Chautauqua Park, Boulder, Colorado. RICHARD A. KEEN

Later we'll see how vapor condenses into liquid water at temperatures well below the freezing point, although the drops may later freeze.

One way to describe the amount of vapor in the air is to measure the temperature at which condensation occurs. This temperature is called the "dew point," and the higher the dew point, the more moisture the air contains. Roughly, the amount of vapor in, say, a cubic foot of air doubles for every 20-degree increase of the dew point. An 80-degree dew point means four times the moisture as 40 degrees.

There's an old army saying that "the only things that fall from the sky are rain and paratroopers." Of course, meteorologically speaking, this just isn't true. It's not just rain and snow, either. Water can condense into an astounding variety of shapes and sizes before it falls from the sky. The form of precipitation that reaches the ground tells you a lot about what's happening miles overhead.

CLOUDS

Most of the time, there must be clouds before there's precipitation. Amazingly, if the atmosphere were completely "pure" and contained only gaseous molecules like oxygen and water vapor, we would never see a cloud. Even though air may cool below its dew point, water vapor still needs something to condense *on*. Water can't just condense in thin air. Fortunately, the air isn't pure; it is chockful of minuscule particles of dust, pollen, sea salt, smoke, and even tiny drops of turpentine blown from trees. The amount of these "condensation nuclei" varies greatly from place to place, but usually there are between a thousand and a million of them in every cubic *inch* of air. Of course, there are more above cities than over countrysides and more over land than over sea. Nonetheless, water vapor molecules rarely have to go very far to find a place to condense.

There are two main ways to cool air down to the dew point. The first is to lift the air; as it goes higher, the pressure around it falls off, and the air expands and cools. At a given altitude the temperature falls to the dew point, and condensation occurs. This altitude is the "condensation level"; above this level sits a cloud. Often, this lifting of air takes place in cyclones, as described earlier. Sometimes, particularly in summer, solar heating of the ground can send warm air "bubbles" up to the condensation level. Another way to lift air is for it to blow uphill along a mountainside.

The second way to chill air is to set it out at night and let its heat radiate into space. At first, most of the radiation leaves the ground, not the air, and the air gets cold by contacting the cold ground. When stones and blades of grass cool below the dew point, dew or frost condenses; when the air gets to the dew point, a cloud-fog forms near the ground. Blanketed by a layer of fog, the ground no longer radiates its heat directly to space. Now the radiational cooling occurs at the top of the fog bank, and the fog thickens and deepens. This is how valley fog forms. A variation on this theme is to run air over a cold surface, be it ground or ocean. Fog off the California coast develops this way.

The drops of water that condense to make clouds are incredibly small, averaging much less than a thousandth of an inch in diameter. It would take 10,000 water droplets to cover the head of a pin. Drops this small would take a week to fall to the ground, except that they never make it. Once outside the cloud, they evaporate in minutes. These lazily floating droplets are the answer to that nagging question of childhood: how do clouds stay up? But don't be fooled. There are a lot of these droplets in a cloud, and even the smallest puffy cloud on a summer afternoon can easily outweigh an automobile.

Dew—Heavy fog left drops of dew on these heather plants growing on a rock outcrop in the Juneau Ice Field, Alaska.
RICHARD A. KEEN

North American Snow Cover, February 2002—
The amount of snow coating the continent in this image based on data acquired by NASA's Terra and Aqua satellites is fairly typical for mid-winter. Most of Canada and Alaska has snow on the ground, while most of the continental United States is snow-free. Exceptions are the snow-covered mountains of the western United States and a huge swath of snow from the southern plains to the Great Lakes. That swath was laid down by a major storm on February 1st; most of the snow was gone within a week. NASA

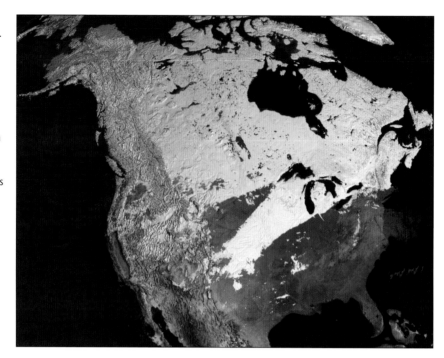

RAIN

We know that rain falls and clouds don't, so raindrops must be a lot heavier than cloud droplets. It takes about a million cloud droplets to make one average raindrop. Initially, a cloud droplet grows by condensing more water vapor onto its tiny spherical surface. Eventually, it gets large enough to start falling through the cloud. On its downward journey, the growing drop bumps into and absorbs some of the many droplets still hanging in the cloud. This growth process is called "coalescence." When the drop gets as large as a sixteenth of an inch across, it's a genuine raindrop and down it goes.

Coalescence works well in thick clouds with a good supply of very moist air, so the droplets have plenty of opportunities to bump into each other. This process happens a lot in the tropics. Coalescence doesn't work very well, however, in the cooler and drier climate of the West. If clouds are thinner and there's not as much water vapor around, drops don't grow to full size. These immature drops fall as drizzle, a common form of precipitation from the thin clouds and fog along the coast. If the air doesn't have the moisture to form even a drizzle, the cloud releases no precipitation.

SNOW

While coalescence may seem like a perfectly reasonable way to make rain, the truth is that in the West, and everywhere else outside the tropics, most rain is really melted snow (or hail, in the summer). This is partly because in mid-latitudes any cloud big enough to precipitate is probably tall enough to have its top portion well below freezing. Another factor is the way snowflakes grow faster than raindrops.

Raindrops may begin their lives as snowflakes, but there's yet another twist: snowflakes start out as water droplets! When water vapor condenses out of the atmosphere, it nearly always does so as droplets of *liquid* water. When the air is colder than –40° F, vapor may condense into minute ice crystals, but this is relatively rare. When the air temperature is between 32° F and –40° F, condensation results in peculiar creations: droplets of "supercooled" water whose temperature is below freezing.

You have probably heard stories about ponds in the north woods that have cooled below 32 degrees but haven't frozen over. An unfortunate duck alights in the water, and the pond immediately freezes around the poor critter's feet. There's reason to believe that ducks never suffer this ignominy, but the duck's tale does illustrate a point: supercooled water freezes immediately when disturbed. In the air, disturbances come as little particles called "freezing nuclei." Just as condensation nuclei start the condensation of vapor into droplets, freezing nuclei start the freezing of droplets into crystals.

Most freezing nuclei are the same kind of dust and smoke particles that work so well as condensation nuclei, although it may be that nuclei with different shapes and sizes do better at freezing. Even meteor dust—the ashes of "shooting stars"—might do the job. Then there are the artificial nuclei, such as silver iodide

Snow Flakes.
RICHARD A. KEEN

crystals, that cloud-seeders (people who seed clouds) intentionally put into the air to trigger the freezing and (hopefully) increase precipitation. Duck feet do not work well.

Once a droplet freezes into a little crystal, it turns into a wolf among sheep. Ice particles act as both condensation and freezing nuclei, grabbing moisture out of the air more efficiently than water droplets could. Growing ice crystals even steal moisture from nearby droplets and become snowflakes within 10 or 20 minutes.

Cloud Temperature	Ground Temperature						Type of Crystals
below –20°	below 0°						hexagonal columns
–20° to 0°	0° to 15°						hexagonal plates
0° to 20°	15° to 30°						dendrites
20° to 32°	30° to 40°						needles

Types of snow crystals—The size and shape of snow crystals depend largely on the temperature (along with moisture content) of the air they form in. These standard types of flakes were categorized by Japanese meteorologist Ukichiro Nakaya in the 1930s. UKICHIRO NAKAYA

Snowflakes are famous for their variety of six-pointed shapes, and it's probably true that no two are alike. Each snowflake is made up of thousands of billions of billions (or sextillions) of water molecules that can be arranged in quadrillions of septillions of centillions of ways. The number of flakes that fall annually on earth is in the sextillions—far, far fewer than the number of possible different flakes. So it's likely that in the entire lifetime of our planet, there will never be a snowflake that's identical to any other past, present, or future flake.

All these centillions of possible snowflakes can be lumped into several categories. The category a snowflake will fall into is pretty much decided by the temperature at which the flake forms. Flakes that grow from the skimpy water supply at –20° F or colder form six-sided (hexagonal) "columns" that look like pieces of a six-sided pencil. Around 0° F to –10° F, the crystals take the shape of flat, six-sided wafers called "hexagonal plates." With the more plentiful supply of water vapor at 0° F to 20° F, crystals can grow into the large but delicate six-pointed stars that typify our idea of snowflakes. These crystals are called "dendrites," from the old Greek word meaning "branched like a tree." The warmest crystals, those that grow between 20° F and 32° F, are splinter-shaped bits of ice known as "needles."

In moderate snowstorms, individual crystals can reach the ground without hitting and sticking to other crystals. With a magnifying glass you can see an incredible variety of crystal shapes. They show up well on dark surfaces such as wooden railings or winter coats. When snowfall increases, however, crystals stick together. These aggregates can get quite large at times, sometimes growing to several inches across.

For skiers, the best snow is the light powder, which means the aggregate flakes contain lots of air and little water. The biggest crystals—dendrites—make the fluffiest flakes. The biggest dendrites form when air temperature is about 5° F. Since most snowflakes in a snowstorm are formed several thousand feet up, ground-level temperature where these flakes fall is 20° F or 25° F. What this means is that the fluffiest, lightest snow falls when the temperature at ground level is in the low 20s. On the average, 13 inches of this snow melts down to an inch of water.

When the ground-level temperature is closer to freezing, snow comes down as bunches of needle crystals, looking somewhat like a handful of pine needles. These densely packed crystals make a heavier layer of snow on the ground; 10 inches of snow makes only about an inch of water. Interestingly, when the ground-level temperature is below 10 degrees, the snowfall also gets denser. The little hexagonal plates and columns don't stick to each other very easily, and the layer they make on the ground doesn't hold very much air. However, it never gets too cold to snow—Yellowstone National Park has had snow with temperatures of –20° F or colder. Extremely cold air doesn't contain much moisture, but what there is can be made into ice crystals. There just isn't very much of the stuff.

Rimed Fence—A night of fog at subfreezing temperatures can leave thick deposits of rime on trees, grass, fences, and anything else that juts above the ground.
RICHARD A. KEEN

Rime Close-Up—This close-up of rimed pine needles shows their true nature. The rime spikes, less than a quarter of an inch long, are each composed of hundreds of frozen water droplets.
RICHARD A. KEEN

DIAMOND DUST

When it's really cold—at zero or below—cloud droplets don't last too long before they freeze. This means extremely cold clouds are made largely of ice crystals, most of which are hexagonal columns and plates. When fog forms at extremely low temperatures, it too freezes quickly into crystals. This "ice fog" is common

Capulin Mountain—
After a night in the clouds, these trees atop Capulin Mountain, New Mexico, sport a thick coating of rime. RICHARD A. KEEN

during Alaskan winters. Often the air is full of fairly large plate crystals falling slowly from a clear sky—there are so few water droplets that any fog or cloud is invisible. The twinkling and glistening of these crystals in sunlight has earned the spectacle the name "diamond dust." The meteorological name is more direct—"ice crystals." At night the crystals sparkle in flashlight and headlight beams, as thousands of flat plates reflect the light right back at you.

Diamond dust crystals fall with their flat sides parallel to the ground. This cloud of minuscule mirrors, each facing straight down, leads to one of the weirdest nighttime lighting effects that weather can produce. All along the horizon, above every distant street lamp and approaching headlight, are long, straight, and narrow rays pointing straight up like searchlight beams—light reflecting off millions of crystals between you and the light source. The shifting beams above moving cars can even look like the northern lights!

SNOW GRAINS

Sometimes, when a cloud is warm enough (but still below freezing), supercooled droplets can coalesce to the size of drizzle before freezing. If the cloud deck is fairly thin, perhaps less than a thousand feet from top to bottom, the frozen droplets leave the bottom of the cloud before they grow much more. The white, sand-sized bits of snow that fall to the ground are called "snow grains." Few roads have been closed by falls of snow grains, which rarely amount to much more than a dusting.

GRAUPEL

Yet another form snow can take is "snow pellets," also known as "soft hail" and, more commonly, by the German name, graupel. These roundish or cone-shaped, pea-sized snowballs usually come down in quick showers and bounce once or twice. Heavy graupel showers sometimes occur with thunder and lightning. The snow pellets grow as turbulent air currents inside the cloud carry them through swarms of water droplets, which freeze onto their crystal structure. Since they pick up whole droplets, snow pellets are heavier, grainier, and lack the delicate features of snowflakes.

GLAZE ICE

On a sultry summer afternoon, it doesn't seem believable that the rain shower steaming from the sidewalks started out as a snowstorm. But the higher you go, the colder it is, and eventually the temperature falls below freezing. This "freezing level" changes from day to day, but even in the heat of summer—indeed, even in the tropics—it never gets higher than 19,000 feet above sea level. Summer thunderheads often tower to twice that height, so the top halves of their clouds actually harbor raging snowstorms. At a rate of 3 to 5 degrees every 1,000 feet, the snowflakes warm as they fall. When they drop below the freezing level, they melt into raindrops. Most of the time, the raindrops stay melted and soak into the ground or run off into streams. However, a nasty thing happens if there is a layer of cold air near the ground: the rain freezes on everything in sight. Trees, wires, grass, and even roads can be coated with a sheet of glossy ice called "glaze" or, appropriately, "freezing rain."

The beauty of these "ice storms" can't be denied; even the most mundane of objects, from trees to television antennas, assume the elegance of fine crystal. Unfortunately, the reality is that glaze often reduces the value of whatever it touches. Heavy accumulations bring down wires and branches, and driving and walking can become treacherous. Glaze ice is usually a fraction of an inch thick, but two-inch-deep coatings have been seen on wires and trees. At that rate, a 100-foot length of wire would be burdened with 600 pounds of ice, and the branches of a typical spruce would be loaded with several tons.

Freezing rain often occurs when a lingering arctic air mass gets overrun by warm air ahead of an approaching storm, creating an inversion. The temperature near the ground may be 10 degrees below the freezing point, but several hundred or thousand feet aloft there lies a warm layer of above

Ice Storm—Freezing drizzle leaves a beautiful coating of clear ice on a pine bough. Thicker coatings of ice can become quite destructive.
RICHARD A. KEEN

freezing air. Above that, it cools off in the usual manner. Arctic air that settles into the interior valleys of the Pacific Northwest is not easily dislodged by coastal storms, which themselves bring no shortage of melted snowflakes. Some of these locations get glazed an average of 10 or more days a year.

Ice storms are rare in the Southwest, where it just doesn't get cold enough, and in most mountain locations, where suitable temperature inversions don't happen. Rime ice, a close relative of glaze, is more common in the western mountains. Supercooled fog, rather than rain, freezes directly onto whatever gets in its way, leaving a white coating of ice. Usually, rime forms quarter-inch-long spikes that grow especially well on pine needles. In heavy rime storms, the thick coating looks like the stuff that used to fill freezers before the days of frost-free refrigerators.

SLEET

If the low layer of cold air is deep enough, raindrops may freeze solid on their way down. At other times, raindrops are blown back up to the colder levels of a storm, where they freeze and fall back to earth. In either case, these clear pellets of frozen rain are known as "sleet," which bounce when they hit the ground. Although usually less than a sixteenth of an inch in diameter, sleet pellets are round and slippery, and it doesn't take much of the stuff to foul up traffic. Sleet is most common along the Pacific Northwest Coast and in the Bitterroot

Clear and White Hailstones—Hailstones tell a lot about themselves from the way they appear. The transparent stones on the left spent much of their time in the warmer, lower parts of the storm cloud, where they collected liquid water which later froze into clear ice. The white centers of the stones are rime ice gathered near the top of the cloud. Some stones have several layers of clear and white ice, telling of two or more up-and-down trips through the storm. The mothball-like stones on the right are almost entirely rime ice collected in the colder parts of their storm cloud. RICHARD A. KEEN

Spilled Ice—Excess ice from Alaska's Saint Elias Mountains oozes down to the sea in the giant Malaspina Glacier. The 60-mile wide glacier covers 1,500 square miles and is 1,000 feet thick. Repeated surges of the glacier picked up rock debris to make the fancy striped patterns. Photo from the space shuttle *Columbia*.
NASA

Mountains of Montana and Idaho, where it can occur eight or more times a year.

Sleet pellets, being small and solid, fall faster than snowflakes. They are more likely to reach the ground without melting when the temperature is above freezing. That is why places that rarely see snowflakes do get to see sleet once in a while.

HAIL

The last member of our precipitation potpourri is one of the nastiest. Hail causes millions of dollars worth of damage to crops every year, and storms have driven unlucky farmers out of business in less than 10 minutes. People have been killed by hail, although, fortunately, these cases are rare. Cattle have less opportunity to find shelter when hail strikes, and their casualties over the years have been much higher. Damaged roofs, broken windshields and dented automobiles all bear testimony to the destructiveness of hail.

Hail is yet another form of refrozen raindrops. It begins just like sleet, with rain blown back up into colder parts of the cloud. With hail, though, the upward winds are much stronger. A frozen drop may spend enough time high in the cloud to gather a frosty layer of ice crystals; when it falls back down it picks up water droplets. The growing pellet may then be blown back up a second time. When the coating of water droplets freezes, the pellet picks up another layer of frost. This up-and-down cycle can happen 10 or more times before the hailstone becomes too heavy for the winds to keep it up.

Ground Blizzard in the Rockies—Winds of 20 m.p.h. can cause drifting of snow, but it takes gusts of 30 m.p.h. or more to lift the blowing snow to eye level or higher—a phenomenon commonly called a "ground blizzard" in English, or "piqsiqtuq" in Inuit. RICHARD A. KEEN

Next time it hails, cut one of the stones in half with a warm knife. You'll see concentric rings of white and clear ice—alternating layers of accumulated frost and frozen droplets. The number of layers tells you how many loops the stone made through the storm cloud.

Hailstones can range in diameter from an eighth of an inch up to 4 inches or more. It takes a mighty powerful updraft to send the biggest stones back up for more ice. The heftiest thunderstorms are in the Midwest and the Great Plains. A stone weighing nearly 2 pounds and measuring half a foot across landed in Dubuque, Iowa, in 1882. The impact of a large stone can be lethal, with baseball-sized hailstones hitting the ground at 90 miles an hour, the speed of a major league fastball. Notice what baseball catchers wear to protect themselves from such forceful flying objects! In the West, cities and farms just east of the Rockies from Alberta to New Mexico are most likely to endure huge hail, and the cities of Edmonton, Calgary, Cheyenne, Denver, and Pueblo have been especially hard hit. Fortunately, large hail is a rare occurrence west of the Continental Divide.

Sastrugi—A Russian name for snow sculpted by sun and wind, sastrugi graces a tundra meadow on James Peak, Colorado. The Inuit name for this is "qimugjuk." RICHARD A. KEEN

ICE FROM THE SKY

It's amazing how much trouble something as ordinary as ice can create when it comes out of the sky. For example ...

June 29, 1805—A trail party of the Lewis and Clark expedition was pounded by a hailstorm near Great Falls, Montana, and several members were injured. According to Joseph Whitehouse, "In the afternoon their arose a storm of hard wind and rain and amazeing large hail at our Camp we measured & weighed Some of them, and Capt. Lewis made a bowl of Ice punch of one of them they were 7 Inches in Surcumference and weighed 3 ounc[e]s."

October 1846—Early snows in the Sierras trapped the wagon trains carrying the Donner party to California. Only half of the 81 pioneers survived and were rescued four months later.

January 11–13, 1888—The "Blizzard of '88" killed 200 people and thousands of cattle across the Plains from Montana and Wyoming to Minnesota. A more famous "Blizzard of '88" struck New England two months later.

March 1, 1910—At Stevens Pass, Washington, an avalanche swept two trains into a ravine, killing 96 people. It was the deadliest avalanche in U.S. history.

February 21–23, 1919—Supercooled fog around Cheyenne, Wyoming, froze directly onto trees and wires, causing $150,000 in damage.

April 14–15, 1921—A 32-hour storm left 95 inches of snow at Silver Lake, Colorado, in the mountains northwest of Denver. The one-day total of 76 inches set a national record. A sloppy mixture of rain and snow broke trees and power lines in Denver.

January 1–10, 1949—A series of heavy snowstorms struck the West; some wet snow even fell over San Diego. The worst storm was the blizzard of the century in Wyoming and northeastern Colorado. Three days of gales, snow, and near-zero temperatures plagued Cheyenne and stranded thousands of cattle out on ranches. The army came to the rescue of the starving livestock with Operation Haylift.

January 13–14, 1950—On Friday the 13th, a near-blizzard left 21 inches of wind-driven snow in Seattle. Overall, 1949–1950 was Seattle's coldest winter ever.

December 29, 1955—Sixty-two inches of snow in one day set a state record at Thompson Pass, Alaska, on the road north of Valdez.

January 1–3, 1961—Freezing fog in northern Idaho coated wires with rime ice 8 inches across.

ICE FROM THE SKY, CONTINUED

June 29, 1963—A Canadian one-day snow record, 44 inches, fell at the Livingstone, Alberta, fire lookout station. (Yes, that's correct—it was at the end of June!) The record stood for 11 years.

December 12–20, 1967—Two back-to-back, slow-moving storms sauntered across the Southwest, blanketing the Four Corners states with massive snowfalls. Seven feet fell on Flagstaff, Arizona, collapsing roofs and farm buildings. A repeat of Operation Haylift saved the lives of many people and cattle on the Navajo reservation in northeastern Arizona. San Diego saw a light fall of graupel, and even Yuma, Arizona, had a few flakes.

December 30, 1968–January 3, 1969—Moist Pacific air streaming over a record cold air mass dripped five days of freezing rain across much of Oregon. Falling on top of earlier snows, the ice blocked roads and downed power lines, closing businesses and stopping traffic around Portland for several days.

June 24, 1972—Four inches of snow at Paradise Ranger Station, 5,427 feet up Washington's Mount Rainier, topped off the snowiest winter ever recorded in the United States at the time. Total snowfall since September 1971 measured 1,122 inches, or nearly 94 feet.

January 17, 1974—Forty-six inches of snow at Lakelse Lake, British Columbia, eclipsed the June 1963, 24-hour snowfall record for Canada.

Winter 1976–1977—Here's an example of what a lack of snow can do. An extremely dry winter left many of the West's ski slopes bare, and skiers found other things to do. In Colorado, a 40-percent drop in visiting skiers cost the state several hundred million dollars. Four years later, another "snow drought" had similar results.

July 30, 1979—Softball-sized hail descended on Fort Collins, Colorado, killing a three-month-old baby—the first American hail fatality since 1930.

December 24–25, 1982—The "Christmas blizzard" shut down Denver with 2 to 4 feet of wind-driven snow. The city paid $4 million to clear the snow from its streets and airport.

June 13, 1984—Hailstones, some as large as grapefruit, pummeled Denver for 3 hours, punching holes in roofs and reshaping automobiles. Total damage was nearly half a billion dollars.

July 10, 1990—Over its 6-hour life span, a large, rotating thunderstorm dumped hail along a 200-mile long swath from Laramie, Wyoming, to Colorado Springs, Colorado. Along the way, baseball-sized hailstones pounded Denver, exacting $650 million in damage (the author's car is included in this total). It was the most devastating hailstorm in U.S. history until a costlier storm struck Dallas, Texas, in 1995.

ICE FROM THE SKY, CONTINUED

September 7, 1991—It was Canada's turn to have its most damaging hailstorm, as a 30-minute fall of golf ball–sized stones cost Calgary $360 million.

February 17–18, 1994—A heavy snow storm dumped 53 inches on Lodgepole, California. One week later, another fast-moving storm unleashed 65 inches of snow in 24 hours at Crystal Mountain, Washington, the heaviest one-day snow ever recorded in that state.

June 8, 1997—Hail, driven by 58 m.p.h. winds, piled 3 inches deep in Fairbanks, Alaska, unusually far north for severe thunderstorm weather.

July 16, 1996—The second major hailstorm in five years pounded Calgary, Alberta. Hail piled several feet deep, enough for children to make "hailmen" and to go tobagganing. Eight days later yet another storm dropped baseball-sized hail on the same city. Over the previous six summers (1991–1996), Calgary had endured a dozen storms with damaging (walnut-sized or larger) hail.

December 28, 1996—Canada's mildest city, Victoria, British Columbia, was buried under 31 inches of snow. Up to 40 inches fell elsewhere in southern British Columbia, crushing roofs and making this the costliest storm in the province's history.

October 23–24, 1997—In eastern Colorado, it was known as the "October Blizzard," with upslope easterly winds dumping as much as 30 inches around Denver and Boulder, and 53 inches in the nearby foothills. In western Colorado it was the "Great Blowdown," as downslope winds (still from the east) flattened millions of trees north of Steamboat Springs. Five years later, huge fires raged through the fallen and rotting trees.

February 11, 1999—Canada's largest and most recent 24-hour snowfall record, 57 inches, fell at Tahtsa Lake, British Columbia. The record snowfall was caused by a moist, mild southerly flow overrunning a shallow layer of cold, arctic air. Just south of the border, this and other storms left a winter total of 1,140 inches at Mount Baker Ski Area, Washington, a record for North America.

March 16–17, 2002—Alaska's largest city, Anchorage, received 28.7 inches of snow in a surprise snow blitz that nearly doubled the previous record. The remarkably localized storm concentrated on the area near the airport, while the normally snowier foothills east of the city received only 5 to 10 inches.

March 17–19, 2003—A "perfect storm" (meteorologically speaking) dumped up to 87 inches of heavy, wet snow along the eastern slopes of the Rockies in Colorado and Wyoming. At the author's home west of Denver, the snow contained 9 inches of moisture—as much as what fell during the preceding summer, fall, and winter combined.

THE 100 INUIT WORDS FOR SNOW

It has been said that the Inuit (the Eskimo people who inhabit the arctic coastal regions of Alaska, Canada, and Greenland) have 100 words for snow—or 200, or 500, depending who's doing the saying. Some claim that this is an urban legend, and that there are only 14 (or some other smallish number) of words. Others point out that it depends on what the definition of "word" is—after all, in English we have snow, snowing, snowed, snowfall, snowflake, and so on—all words derived from the same root, snow. We also have assorted euphemisms for snow that don't include "snow," such as blizzard, Seattle cement, slush, powder, base (as at a ski area), flurries, the white stuff, diamond dust, winter storm, and so on. The World Meteorological Organization has decided that of the 100 standard kinds of weather (used for coding weather reports on weather maps), 25 include snow in one form or another—such as steady light snow, heavy snow showers, snow pellets, mixed rain and snow, drifting snow, and more. And that's not to mention the scientific names for the different kinds of snow crystals—columns, plates, dendrites, needles, graupel, and so on. So perhaps the marvel should be that the Inuit probably don't have as many words for snow as we have in English!

To check for myself how many Inuktitut (the Inuit language) words there are for snow, I looked at the Inuktitut Living Dictionary (on the Nunavut Department of Culture website, www.asuilaak.com). In summary, I found more than 40 words for snow, snowfall, or different forms of snow on the ground, and even more for various uses of snow. But the numbers aren't as interesting as the words. Here's a sampling.

A Sampling of Inuit Words for Snow

Aniuvak—snow that has fallen on the side of a hill, and which could cause an avalanche
Apigianngaut—first snowfall in autumn
Apijuq—soft snow that is so deep that it is hard for people to walk
Apimajuq—snow covering objects to the extent that you can't see them; depth is usually several inches

THE 100 INUIT WORDS FOR SNOW, CONTINUED

Apisimajuq—snow deep enough to cover the ground, but not deep enough to prevent cars or people from moving about and getting to other settlements

Apusimatiqtuq—snow storm

Aput—snow (the substance, flakes)

Aputi—snow lying on the ground

Aqillupiaq—mixed snow and water that is thawing

Aqillutaq—new snow that has recently fallen

Autturunniq—pressed, melted, and frozen snow where a dog slept

Iglu—snowhouse

Isiriaqtaq—snow that falls yellow or reddened (by dust or smoke)

Manngutuq—snow decreasing in depth because of melting

Masak aput—slushy snow that may freeze if the temperature falls below freezing

Mauja—soft snow made of large flakes

Misaliraq (or matsaq)—slush

Naannguaq—a small well-rounded mound of snow

Natiruvaaktuq—blowing and drifting snow near the ground

Piqsiqtuq—blowing and drifing snow at eye level, making it difficult to see

Pukaangajuq—snow that is sufficiently crystallized to make a snow house

Pukajaak—sugar snow (snow crystals ground apart by sunshine and wind)

Qaniut—the amount of snow accumulated on the ground

Qannipiluktuq—snow flurry

Qanniqtuq—snowflakes falling from the clouds and landing on the ground

Qimugjuk—snow drift (a mound or pile of snow that has been blown by the wind)

Qimutjuk—snow streaks on the ground made by a gale

Qiqirrituq—snow that squeaks underfoot

Qiqsuqaktuq—snow on the ground with crust formed by melting from sunlight or packing by strong winds

Qiqumaaqtuq—snow coated with ice, after a slight thaw

Qukaarnaqtuq—light snowfall of small flakes or crystals of snow

Salittutaq—snow decreasing in depth because of a warm wind

Sikiitu—snowmobile

Sitilluqaq—hard snow that is easy to cut into snow blocks to make igloos

Umippaa—snow that gets stuck between two things, such as the runners of a sled

HOW MUCH SNOW?

Snow lovers and snow haters alike have no trouble finding their favorite climates somewhere in the West. At the snowy end of the scale, Paradise Ranger Station in Mount Rainier National Park, Washington, receives an average of 679 inches per year. Three winters—1955–1956, 1970–1971, and 1971–1972—each dumped more than 1,000 inches of snow at Paradise, but all those records were eclipsed by a 1,140-inch season at Mount Baker Ski Area (Washington) in 1998–1999. Another Cascades volcano, Oregon's Crater Lake, averages 526 inches a year, with 879 inches falling in the winter of 1932–1933. Other places that have seen more than 800 inches of snow in a winter are Thompson Pass, Alaska, with 974 inches during the winter of 1952–1953; Kildala Pass, B.C., 888 inches in 1956–1957; Tamarack, California, 884 inches in 1906–1907; Alta, Utah, 847 inches in 1982–1983; and Wolf Creek Pass, Colorado, 837 inches in 1978–1979.

Key West, Florida, has never seen a flake of snow.

These are all locations where a real live weather observer has actually measured the snow. However, if Alaska's Fairweather Range actually receives the estimated 450 inches of precipitation each year, and most of that falls as snow, those glacier-clad peaks may be buried under 4,000 miles of snow in an average year—six times Mount Rainier's annual dose!

At the other extreme, most of the coastal cities of California have seen just one or two snowstorms in the 2- to 4-inch range, while Phoenix, Arizona, has on two occasions suffered 1-inch snowfalls. Two cities of the West—Yuma and San Diego—have never had a snowfall deep enough to measure. In the past century, flakes have been sighted at Yuma three times, in 1932, 1937, and 1967. However, flurries have struck San Diego only twice, in 1949 and 1967. San Diego is the most snow-free city in the West, although by a very thin hair. Don't forget, however, that Key West, Florida, has never seen a flake of snow.

THUNDERSTORMS

Tall, dark columns of thunderclouds seem to boil up through flatter layers and climb into the upper atmosphere. ... Electric flashes of lightning brilliantly illuminate from within the thunderclouds that generate them. The huge clouds seem to light up instantly and magnificently like enormous bulbs, and a single lightning bolt often seems to trigger a chain reaction of flashes from cloud to cloud so that the lightning appears to be walking its way for hundreds of miles across the darkened earth.

—Joseph P. Allen, *Entering Space*

Whether from the perspective of an astronaut orbiting on board the space shuttle *Columbia,* or of the rest of us stranded here on Earth, few phenomena of nature are more impressive than lightning. Lightning and its inseparable offspring, thunder, are the necessary attendants of thunderstorms, and combined they give the West some of its deadliest and most beautiful weather.

As with almost every other kind of weather, thunderstorms range from extremely rare to commonplace in different parts of the West. In the Rockies of New Mexico and Colorado, thunderstorms strike on 70 or more days a year, while San Francisco averages only two annually. Like snow and heat waves, thunderstorms are seasonal, but even this differs with location—most of the West's thunderstorms rumble during summer; along the coast, winter is the thunderstorm season.

Western thunderstorms are, in general, not as severe as their larger midwestern cousins. That is not to say, though, that severe weather has never visited the West. Tornadoes, hail, gusty winds, and downpours have struck every state of the West, and at times with terrible losses of human life and property.

CLOUDS AND CONVECTION

Clouds need water if for no other reason then just to be seen. Clouds are liquid droplets of water condensed from the vapor contained in rising currents of air. However, thunderstorms need water for more than droplets—it's the latent heat they're really after. When water vapor condenses in rising air currents, its latent heat is released, warming the air surrounding the new cloud droplet. Like a bubble in a pool, this warmer—and lighter—air rises more swiftly, leading to even more rapid condensation. Meanwhile, increasing amounts of fresh air drawn into the base of the cloud keep the condensation going. This process of rising, condensation heating and faster rising currents is called "convection." Without it, there would be no thunderstorms.

Even the meanest thunderstorm needs something to get it going. Nothing happens until air starts rising. For most western thunderstorms, updrafts begin with air heated by the sunlit ground below. Some storms, though, start

Cloud Types—The main cloud types are arranged by height above the ground. Layered clouds are called "stratus" (or strato-), while billowy clouds are labeled "cumulus" (or cumulo-). The names are further modifed by their altitude category, with mid-level clouds (typically 5,000 to 20,000 feet above the ground) receive the prefix "alto-", while the highest clouds are "cirrus" (or cirro-) clouds.

ILLUSTRATION BY MICHAEL T.D. KEEN

with the air currents in different sections of cyclones, especially where the cold front wedges under warmer, moist air and shoves it upward.

There is plenty of water in the air and no shortage of sunlight and fronts to get those currents going. Nonetheless, thunderstorms are relatively infrequent. Even those places that get thundered on 70 days a year *don't* get thundered on the other 295 days. The average storm lasts an hour or so, which means only about 100 hours—or four days—out of the 70 are actually thundering. So even in the thunderstorm capitals of the West, it's actually thundering only an average of 1 percent during the year. Most people spend more of their lives in the shower than they do hearing thunder.

Stratus Clouds—The lowest of clouds, stratus, hugs a mountain near the author's home. Since the cloud actually touches the ground in places, it can also be called fog.
RICHARD A. KEEN

Clearly, atmospheric conditions have to be just right for thunderstorms to develop. The necessary condition is called "instability," the opposite of "stability." To physicists, a stable object (or situation) is one that returns to its original position after being moved (or changed). A bowling ball sitting in a ditch is stable—give it a shove, and it will roll back to where it was. A bowling ball balanced on a roof is unstable—give it a kick and off it goes.

Like a bowling ball, the atmosphere can be stable or unstable. Cold air in a valley—an inversion—is stable, because the air becomes warmer with height. Lift the cold air off the ground, say, 100 feet, and it is surrounded by warmer, lighter air. Let go, and the cold air returns to the valley floor. With stable air, those little rising currents don't get very far.

With unstable air, the temperature drops off fairly rapidly with height—about 25 degrees per mile. If ground-level air is lifted, it expands and cools as the pressure gets lower. Despite this cooling, however, the lifted batch of unstable air remains warmer than the air around it and keeps going up. Instability is even stronger if there's water vapor in the air to release its latent heat. If you give an upward kick to part of an unstable air layer, that part continues to soar upward in a relatively warm stream.

You can't have rising currents of air everywhere, or the lower atmosphere would soon run out of air. That's why thunderstorms are so scattered. The clear spaces between thunderstorms, which are much wider than the storms

Fair Weather Cumulus—Cotton ball cumulus scattered above the eastern plains of Colorado offer little chance of rain, and are commonly called "fair weather" clouds. RICHARD A. KEEN

Cumulus Clouds—"The clouds must look like many sheep before the rains will come," says a Navajo proverb. RICHARD A. KEEN

themselves, are where the air is sinking back to the ground. With air bubbling up here and sinking over there, afternoon thunderstorms are part of an extremely complex pattern of up-and-down currents.

THUNDER IN THE HILLS

Now we know how to cook up a thunderstorm. All we need is some unstable, moist air and something to kick it with. Clearly, this doesn't happen very often along the West Coast, especially along that stretch between the coastal ranges and the sea. In Washington and Oregon, Quillayute and Astoria average seven thunderstorm days a year (for the record, a thunderstorm day is a day on which thunder is observed at a weather station; it doesn't matter if there's one distant peal or twelve hours of constant close lightning). Along the coast of California, Eureka averages four thunderstorm days and Los Angeles has six. The lowest frequencies of thunder, just two days per year, are found around the San Francisco Bay area. Unlike thunderstorms in every other western region, coastal storms prefer the winter months.

The ocean-chilled air along the California coast is the most persistently stable layer in the country. Two thousand feet up, temperatures may be 30 degrees warmer than at sea level. This strong inversion lasts from spring until fall and is very effective at keeping thunderstorm activity down. The coastal inversion is so strong that its cool air pours through the Golden Gate to suppress thunderstorms in the Central Valley. The inversion isn't quite so strong farther north, but is still strong enough to do its job. In winter, the air aloft isn't nearly as hot, and the coastal inversion weakens. At times (twice a year, to be exact), a winter cold front is strong enough to get things convecting, and San Franciscans marvel at the flashes in the sky.

The farther inland you go, the more thunderstorms there are. In the Sierras there may be 20 or 30 thunderstorms in a year; the plateaus and mountains of Arizona and Utah, as well as the High Plains from eastern Montana to New Mexico, may see 50 or more. But nobody hears more thunder than the residents of the Rockies, from New Mexico into Colorado. The thunderstorm capital of the United States lies somewhere in the eastern Rocky Mountains in New Mexico and Colorado, where it storms at least 60 days per year. Based on the high number of thunderstorms at my weather station and noting where most of those storms appear to develop, it's my opinion that 14,256-foot Mount Evans, west of Denver, is *the* thunderstorm capital of western North America. Elsewhere in the United States, the area around Lakeland, Florida, is considered by some to have the most thunderstorm days, about 100 per year, while farther south, numbers approach 200 in Panama.

Notice that the West's most thunder-prone locations are in the mountains and that the highest mountains—the central Rockies—have the most storms of all. Even within mountainous areas, there are more storms in the highlands. At 9,000 feet elevation, I've recorded an average of 84 thunderstorm days per year, while Denver, 28 miles away and 4,000 feet lower, averages only 42. That's a two-fold difference between places within sight of each other!

Towering Cumulus—The characteristic "cauliflower" appearance indicates a rapidly growing cloud.
RICHARD A. KEEN

Why do mountains get so many thunderstorms? If you live near a mountain, you've probably noticed that the first puffy clouds of the day form over the mountains and that the mountain clouds grow faster than their lowland counterparts. Mountains get off to an early start because their air is less stable than in the valleys. Overnight, cold air drains from the highlands to the lowlands, leaving the valleys full of cold, stable air. By the time the sun heats up this stable layer, clouds are already billowing over the hills.

LIFE OF A CUMULONIMBUS

Similar to humans, thunderstorm clouds change their size and shape as they grow, reach their prime, and then get ready to check out. The first clouds to

Rain Shower—This towering cumulus has grown so large and so vigorously that it is producing a light rain shower. RICHARD A. KEEN

form are white, cottony puffs called *cumulus* clouds, a Latin word meaning "pile" or "heap." Who among us has never seen fleeting forms of sheep, camels, and dragons in these heaps of water droplets? As they turn more vapor into droplets, cumulus clouds grow into billowing cauliflowers named "towering cumulus."

Three or four miles up (lower in the winter) lies the freezing level. Above this line, the air is colder than 32° F, and clouds that go higher may freeze. It usually takes a while for an ascending droplet to find a freezing nucleus, so for several thousand feet above the freezing level, the cloud is made of subfreezing, but still liquid, water droplets—supercooled water. The cloud may reach 30,000 feet before its droplets start to freeze.

With a frozen top, the cumulus cloud becomes a different animal. The cloud top loses its solid, cauliflower appearance, and takes on the stringy, fuzzy appearance characteristic of ice clouds. High winds aloft may blow the ice crystals away from the main cloud; the flat, spreading tops of ice are often called "anvil" clouds.

The changing appearance is a sign that something more meaningful is happening in the cloud. In the moist interior of the cloud, ice crystals grow rapidly into snowflakes, which fall and melt into rain. *Nimbus* is the Latin word for rain, and our cloud has matured into a *cumulonimbus,* meaning, loosely, a raining heap!

While cumulus and towering cumulus clouds are growing, air currents all head upward. But as ice crystals form, some of this air starts coming back down, bringing with it snow and rain. As the downdrafts reach the ground, they spread out, bringing us the first gusts of cool air that so often are followed by sudden rains. On the ground, a storm has begun.

If a raindrop loses its downdraft, it may blow back up above the freezing level to become hail. The up- and downdrafts can approach 100 m.p.h. in a mature cumulonimbus cloud. Loaded with hail, these vertical winds give pilots good reason to avoid thunderstorms. Even on the ground, hail may arrive on hurricane-force winds, giving the earthbound equally good reason to seek shelter from the storm.

At some point, the supply of fresh, warm, moist air runs out, and the thunderstorm begins to fade. Inside the cloud, the updrafts weaken, shrink, and finally cease, leaving sinking currents of rain- and snow-filled air. The cloud's edges begin to evaporate, taking on a ragged appearance. Above, the ice-crystal anvil cloud may separate and blow off with the high-level winds, while below, light rain falls out of a disappearing cloud. The entire cycle of growth, maturity, and decay may take 2 or 3 hours, and by the fourth hour there may be no visible remnants of a once mighty storm!

Most western storms are started by solar heating. While the first cumulus generally appears over the mountains by late morning, if the air is especially moist and unstable, clouds may pop up within a couple of hours after sunrise. On dry, stable days, they may never appear. Several studies of the timing of daily thunderstorms have found that, in general, peak thunderstorm activity—when the most storms are going on at the most places—is around 4 P.M. In the high mountains, peak storm activity is earlier, around 1 P.M., while the lowlands see most of their storms lingering until midnight or later. Veteran mountain climbers know these patterns well and know the advantages of starting their climbs early in the morning.

These statistics reveal an important pattern. Thunderstorms develop first over the mountains and, as afternoon wears on, move out to the foothills. The mountains may already be clearing while the foothill storms are just beginning. Some storms move onto the plains and into the valleys during evening, but most die off by 10 P.M. If the lowland air is especially moist and unstable, however, storms may continue until dawn.

Rarely can individual storms be traced from the mountains to the lowlands throughout the course of the daily cycle. What happens is more like a moving "wave of activity," within which storms live their several-hour lives

Canyonland ▲ **Thundershower**—As is typical of many western thundershowers, much of the precipitation (visible as dark streamers falling from the base of the cloud) evaporates before reaching the ground. RICHARD A. KEEN

Mature Cumulonimbus Cloud—This impressive sight is topped by a spreading "anvil" cloud of ice crystals. DAVID O. BLANCHARD ▼

and are replaced by new storms. These waves can travel considerable distance. The wave of thunderstorms that begin over the Colorado Rockies around 2 P.M. can sometimes be traced to eastern Kansas, 400 miles east and 12 hours later. There have even been occasions when the thunderstorms continue well into the next day, by which time they're approaching the Mississippi River. This pattern seems to hold for all parts of the West, from the Rockies to the Sierras, although it's most pronounced where storms occur most frequently.

Mammatus Clouds—
These pouch-like formations hanging from the side of a cumulonimbus are called "Mammatus" clouds, from their remote resemblance to the breasts of some female mammals. The cloud formations are caused by downdrafts of cool, moist air, and are most often seen after the storm has passed. RICHARD A. KEEN

Why does this wave of thunderstorms happen at all? It is, essentially, the thunderstorms way of looking for greener pastures. Being generally cooler and drier, mountain air usually doesn't contain a lot of moisture to feed thunderstorms, and those first mountain storms soon run out of fuel. However, their cold downdrafts spread across the foothills and, acting like small cold fronts, start another generation of storms. These new storms use up their local moisture supply, start off a third generation, and so on. Over and over this cycle continues, as new storms feed on untapped moisture supplies ever farther from the mountains. If the mountain storms clear off early enough, the sun may kick off another round of thunderstorms; sometimes there are several waves during the course of a single day. What hour of the day has the most thunderstorms at your home? Keep records for a year and you'll get a pretty good idea. It's an easy, interesting, and cheap weather project.

While the vast majority of western thunderstorms are started by sunlight, sometimes it is an advancing front—particularly a cold front—that gives the air its upward shove. Thunderstorms pop up here and there along the front, sometimes merging into a line extending tens or even hundreds of miles along the length of the front. The approach of a "squall line" can be an imposing spectacle, with a wall of dark, thundering clouds stretching from horizon to horizon. Squall lines are rare in the West, but along the coast—where solar-powered storms are virtually nonexistent—most of the few thunderstorms that do occur are set off by fronts.

▲ Dissipating Anvils— These evaporating anvils mark the final stage in the lifetime of a thunderstorm. As happens so often with mountain and desert thunderstorms, this final stage is occurring at sunset. RICHARD A. KEEN

◄ Alaskan Altocumulus— A deck of altocumulus clouds fills the sky above a layer of billowy stratocumulus. The stratocumulus clouds drifted in from the Pacific Ocean and surrounded the peaks on Alaska's Juneau Ice Field. RICHARD A. KEEN

Altocumulus Rolls—
Changing winds, or "wind shear," a couple of miles up creates these wavelike patterns in altocumulus clouds. RICHARD A. KEEN

◀ Gathering Storm—
A thickening sheet of translucent altostratus clouds often means rain or snow within a few hours.
RICHARD A. KEEN

Cirrus—The first sign of an approaching storm is often the appearance of feathery cirrus clouds in the southwestern sky. Composed mostly of ice crystals 5 to 8 miles up, cirrus clouds form as warm air rises over a warm front on the eastern side of the storm center. RICHARD A. KEEN
▼

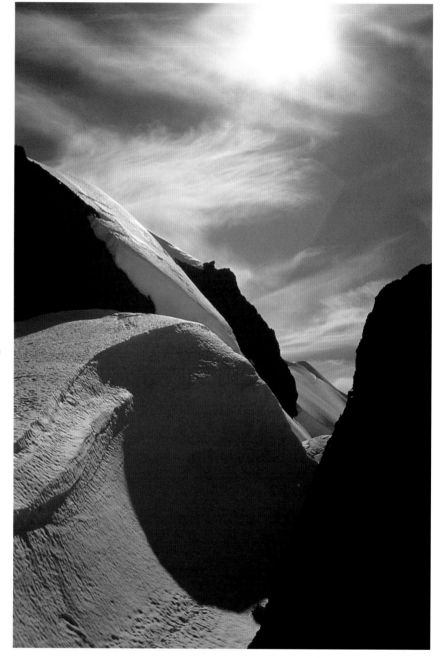

Cirrus over Mount Olympus—Fortunately, there was no storm following these cirrus clouds, and the rest of the ascent of Washington's Mount Olympus was made in delightful weather!

RICHARD A. KEEN

▲ **Cirrus and Altocumulus**—Clouds of a given type rarely occur alone. Here, high cirrus clouds share the evening sky with mid-level altocumulus. RICHARD A. KEEN

◀ **Desert Cirrus**—These cirrus clouds are actually high altitude showers, with snow crystals forming in cotton-like puffs and falling in thin streamers of snow trail behind the puffy clouds, which are being blown toward the left by high winds at these altitudes (30,000 to 40,000 feet).
RICHARD A. KEEN

Cirrostratus—Cirrus clouds that spread into a layer covering most of the sky are called cirrostratus clouds. The hallmark of these high layers of prismatic ice crystals is a halo around the sun or moon, along with sun dogs and other phenomena. RICHARD A. KEEN

Cirrocumulus—Puffy cumulus-type clouds that occur so high (above 20,000 feet, usually) that they are made mostly of ice crystals. RICHARD A. KEEN

Polar stratospheric clouds—Also known as nacreous clouds, these rare clouds form in the normally clear and dry stratosphere. They occur only in mid-winter at high latitudes, require very cold air at their altitude of 15 or 20 miles, and are generally seen over mountainous areas such as Alaska and Scandivania. Because nacreous clouds are so tenuous, they are seen around sunset and sunrise, when the sunlit clouds can be seen against a darker sky. LAMONT POOLE, NASA

Noctilucent Clouds— These clouds resemble cirrus in appearance and, probably, in composition (ice crystals). However, they float an incredible 50 miles above the ground—so high, in fact, that they remain sunlit for one to two hours after sunset and before sunrise, earning them the name "noctilucent," meaning "shines at night." Noctilucent clouds are extremely rare and are sighted only north of 50 degrees latitude and usually in mid-summer (when they may shine all night long!). These noctilucent clouds shimmer above the Juneau Ice Field at midnight in July. RICHARD A. KEEN

LIGHTNING

First let me talk with this philosopher—
what is the cause of thunder?

—Shakespeare, *King Lear*

The Norse had an answer—the mischievous Loki forged bolts and gave them to Thor, who pitched them earthward. When Thor rode his chariot, thunder rumbled across the heavens. However, Vikings saw even fewer thunderstorms than Californians, so perhaps we shouldn't consider them the experts. Their explanation was as good as any, though, until Benjamin Franklin performed his legendary lightning experiment in 1752.

We all recall how Franklin flew his kite into an approaching thunderstorm. Contrary to popular belief, his kite was not struck by lightning; if it had, Franklin's signature would have never appeared on the Declaration of Independence. The developing storm was generating a lot of static electricity, though, and sent fibers on the kite cord standing on end. Suspecting the presence of electricity, Franklin touched a metal key tied to the end of the cord. His suspicions were brilliantly confirmed.

Two centuries after Franklin's experiment, the source of all this electricity is still a mystery. A recent pamphlet on lightning by the National Oceanic and Atmospheric Administration (NOAA), our nation's largest weather research outfit, noted that "no completely acceptable theory explaining the complex processes of thunderstorm electrification has yet been advanced. But it is believed that electrical charge is important to the formation of raindrops and

Life Cycle of a Thunderstorm—During its lifetime, which may last one or several hours, a thunderstorm goes through three stages: the **towering cumulus stage,** with updrafts building the cloud; the **mature stage,** with updrafts feeding moisture into the cloud, to fall as rain in downdrafts; and a **dissipating stage,** in which the supply of fresh moisture is cut off, and the water in the storm is "raining out." DIAGRAM COURTESY NATIONAL CENTER FOR ATMOSPHERIC RESEARCH/ NATIONAL SCIENCE FOUNDATION

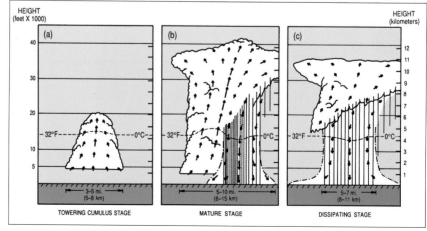

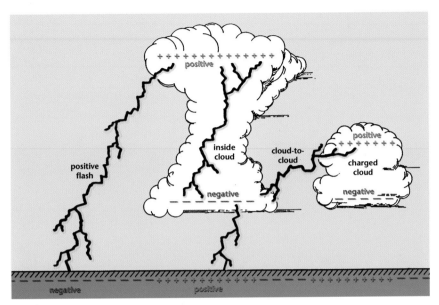

Four Kinds of Lightning—All forms of lightning connect oppositely charged regions inside clouds or on the ground. RICHARD A. KEEN

ice crystals, and that electrification closely follows precipitation."

In other words, electricity appears to be produced by the freezing of super-cooled water droplets. For some reason, when some drops freeze, the ice crystals take on a positive charge, and the remaining droplets become negative. Not only does the ice crystal anvil formation atop a cumulonimbus portend rain, it also means lightning and thunder. That's why cumulonimbus clouds are more popularly known as thunderclouds.

At this point of freezing, the electrical charges in the cloud separate, with the positive charges gathering near the icy cloud top and the negative charges gathering in the lower parts. Under normal conditions, the ground is also negatively charged. Now, however, the concentration of electrons in the lower cloud repels the negative ground charge (like charges repel; opposites attract), leaving a positively charged ground for several miles around the cloud base.

As the charges gather, voltages build up to as high as 100 million volts within the cloud and between cloud and ground. Air is a terrible conductor, meaning that it is fairly effective at holding electrical charges apart. In clouds, air can separate voltages at the rate of 3,000 volts per foot, or 15 million volts per mile. Eventually, enough is enough, and when a thundercloud's 100 million volts show up, something has to give.

Sparks fly when cloud voltage reaches the breaking point, but their flight is not a direct one. One hundred feet at a time, a "leader stroke" makes its way downward from the base of the cloud. Too faint to be seen, the leader ionizes the air along its path, meaning that this air can now conduct electricity. It

Intense Electrical Storm—Two kinds of lightning are seen here—inside cloud, and cloud-to-ground. RICHARD A. KEEN

pauses for a few millionths of a second, then jumps another 100 feet. After a hundredth of a second, the leader stroke arrives within a few hundred feet of the ground. At this point, similar leader strokes stream upward from hilltops, trees, antennas, golfers, and the like to join the downward leader. This meeting completes an electrical circuit between the cloud and the ground.

With cloud and ground connected with a conducting "wire" of air, the electrical charges go into action. A "return stroke" shoots up the leader path at one-sixth the speed of light. Sometimes return strokes follow each of the branching leader channels up from the ground, to join in a single massive stroke several hundred feet up. The intense electrical currents, concentrated in a path a few inches across, heat the air almost instantaneously to tens of thousands of degrees—several times as hot as the surface of the sun! We see this glowing channel of hot air as the familiar and spectacular flash of lightning.

The return stroke doesn't last long; in less than .00005 seconds, it's over. If there's still some electrical charge left in the cloud, another leader stroke may head down the path of ionized air left over from the first stroke. When it

Desert Lightning—Distant lightning strikes a mesa near Arches National Park, Utah. RICHARD A. KEEN

reaches the ground another powerful return stroke heads back up the channel. Every .05 seconds, this cycle repeats itself until the cloud is discharged. There's often enough electricity to make two or three separate strokes. Sometimes there are 10 or more, giving some lightning a flickering appearance. Properly speaking, these repeated strokes are called "flashes" of lightning. The popular term "bolt" is not precisely defined and is considered colloquial by meteorologists.

This sudden heating literally explodes the air all along the length of the flash, and we hear the detonation as thunder. Thunder can usually be heard 8 to 10 miles away from the lightning that produced it, but there are some reports of the sound being heard 20, 30, and even 70 miles away. You can measure the distance of lightning by counting the seconds until you hear the thunder. The boom of thunder travels at the speed of sound, 0.2 miles per second, so by dividing the elapsed time by five you'll get the distance in miles. Next time your ears are rattled by a thunderbolt, just remember that less than 1 percent of lightning's energy goes into making noise.

Lightning that zaps from cloud to ground is called, with the usual scientific honesty, a "cloud-to-ground" flash. Lightning also jumps between differently charged regions within a cloud, such as from the lower regions to the icy top. This "inside-cloud" lightning actually occurs with more frequency than the cloud-to-ground variety. Lightning connecting differently charged parts of *different* clouds is called, as you might expect, "cloud-to-cloud."

These three types of lightning are well known to meteorologists, and each has its own abbreviated code name for transcribing onto weather reports. Recently, another fourth kind of lightning has been documented, and it may be the nastiest kind of all. Recall that cloud-to-ground flashes go from a negatively charged cloud base to the positively charged ground directly underneath. Meanwhile, several miles away from the storm, the ground is *negatively* charged. This sets the stage for cloud-to-ground lightning to jump from the positively charged cloud top to the negative ground. Since these flashes discharge from the positive region of a cloud, they are often called "positive" flashes.

Positive lightning flashes are not just negative flashes going the opposite direction. For one thing, the distances they traverse can be enormous. From a 40,000-foot cloud top to the ground five or more miles from the storm, a single flash may extend 10 or even 20 miles—five times the length of a typical negative flash. Positive flashes are often among the last thrown off by an about-to-die storm. They seem to prefer winter thunderstorms—perhaps because the positively charged icy parts of the cloud are closer to the ground.

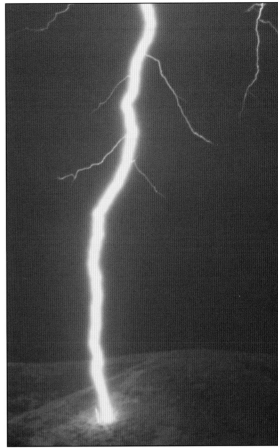

Ground Streamer—This photo leaves no doubt where lightning struck the ground, but it also reveals the lightning's second choice of a target. The short upward streamer probably was attempting to contact the downward progressing "step leader" when a rival streamer from a nearby tree beat it to the punch. KEN LANGFORD

Lightning Strike—
Qatiyana, the wonder dog, inspects a lightning damaged tree near the author's home. The lightning current traveled down the trunk, heating moisture beneath the bark to explosive temperatures. Although the tree lost some of its bark, the dog kept all of hers. RICHARD A. KEEN

There is a treacherous quality to these positive flashes. Coming from a storm miles away, they may appear to strike out of a clear sky. I once saw one of these flashes come from a storm passing several miles to the south. The lightning left the storm, passed across blue sky directly overhead, and connected to a ridge off to the north. There are doubtlessly some unfortunate souls who took the proper precautions during a thunderstorm, only to be struck by a "bolt from the blue" as the storm moved on and the sun was shining.

I know from firsthand experience that the old adage "lightning never strikes twice in the same place" is not so, having once been in a truck that was struck three times in five minutes, and on another occasion having watched a utility pole endure three strikes in 20 seconds. In neither case was there any damage! These six strikes illustrate how much lightning there actually is. The National Lightning Detection Network (operated by Vaisala, Inc.) has picked up more than a million cloud-to-ground strikes per summer over the western states, or about one every square mile. Some mountain areas have been bombarded with five or more per square mile during the few short months of summer. With that much lightning to go around, some is bound to find a target that's been struck before. And if there is any truth to the adage, it's because some targets just aren't there after the first strike.

The power of lightning can be described with some very large numbers. The *instantaneous* peak rate of energy usage may exceed a trillion watts, equivalent to the *average* consumption rate of the entire United States. But lightning strokes are incredibly brief, ranging from millionths to thousandths of a second long, and the total electrical energy expended by an average lightning flash is several hundred kilowatt hours—costing about $50.

It is a bit more meaningful to measure the power of lightning in terms of what it does to its targets. Perhaps the most impressive and lasting monuments to lightning are glassy masses of melted and solidified sand called "fulgurites." Fulgurites often mark the path of electricity as it skims along the ground. They may be several inches across and 20 to 40 feet long, and their total weight can run up to several hundred pounds. Sand melts at 3,100° F;

now consider the energy it takes to heat 200 pounds of sand to that temperature, all in a fraction of a second!

It is no wonder that lightning is one of the West's deadliest weather phenomena. Over the past 25 years, lightning has killed an average of 86 Americans annually, nearly as many as tornadoes and hurricanes combined, and injured 280 more. Colorado and New Mexico led the 12 western states in lightning casualties, while Alaska has never had a lightning fatality.

Many of those people killed and injured by lightning were engaged in outdoor activities such as boating, golfing, and baseball. Hikers above timberline are particularly vulnerable; atop a mountain, a climber may be the most tempting lightning target in the state. Even some indoor activities can be dangerous during a thunderstorm—people talking on the telephone have died in mid-conversation when a nearby strike came "over the wires." Lightning is beautiful and spectacular, but it also deserves a great deal of respect.

"Bolt from the Blue"— Positive lightning flashes across clear sky, from the positively charged top of the thundercloud to the ground several miles from the storm. RICHARD A. KEEN

HOW NOT TO GET STRUCK BY LIGHTNING

Of course, no one wants to get hit by lightning, and over the courses of our lifetimes, most of us won't. You can better your odds of never being struck by paying attention to the following "Proactive Plan" (from Ron Holle, Raul Lopez, Ken Howard, James Vavrek, and Jim Allsopp "Safety in the Presence of Lightning." *Seminars in Neurology* 1995; 15 (4): 375–380.) It is the best summary of practical advice about lightning I have ever read.

PROACTIVE PLAN

The following is an example of how you should use this information about thunderstorm life cycles, the flash-to-bang method, and storm monitoring when taking a two-day hike with several people in an unfamiliar mountainous region in July. Information presented in this sequence will apply to boating, camping, and other activities that last several days, and portions of the sequence will apply for an activity that lasts less than one day.

DAYS BEFORE ACTIVITY

- Become aware of the types of storms, and their time of day, that form in the area during the season of the activity. Listen to weather broadcasts by the media and NOAA Weather Radio for general outlooks in advance of the hike.
- Decide on rules about whether to postpone the hike, the time of day to start, how to decided when to stop the hike, and where to take shelter if storms develop.

DAY OF ACTIVITY

- At all stages of the hike, be aware of where shelter is and how long it will take to reach it if lightning becomes a threat.
- During difficult stages of climbing or crossing rivers, for example, designate a spotter who watches for lightning. Develop a method to inform the larger group of the lightning threat. In the case of team sports, a designated spotter watches the sky

Red Sprite—After years of reports from pilots, astronauts, mariners, and others of seeing weird red flashes and other lights above thunderstorms, researchers began seriously looking for these lights in the 1990s. This image of a "red sprite," caught by an airborne low light level video camera in 1994, shows the spectacular colors of these flashes. However, sprites are quite faint, and to the unaided eye look like small red patches of aurora that last but an instant. DANIEL L. OSBORNE, GEOPHYSICAL INSTITUTE, UNIVERSITY OF ALASKA

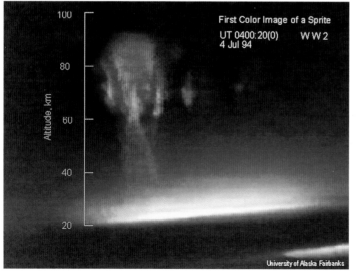

First Color Image of a Sprite
UT 0400:20(0)   W W 2
4 Jul 94

University of Alaska Fairbanks

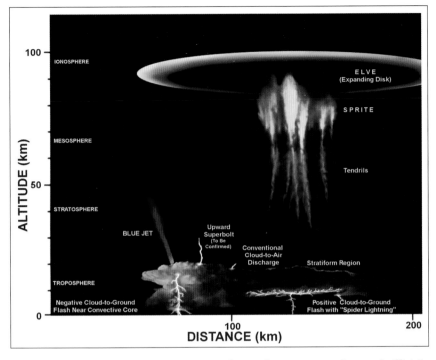

ALTITUDE (km)

DISTANCE (km)

IONOSPHERE

ELVE
(Expanding Disk)

SPRITE

MESOSPHERE

Tendrils

STRATOSPHERE

BLUE JET

Upward
Superbolt
(To Be
Confirmed)

Conventional
Cloud-to-Air
Discharge

Stratiform Region

TROPOSPHERE

Negative Cloud-to-Ground
Flash Near Convective Core

Positive Cloud-to-Ground
Flash with "Spider Lightning"

Sprites, Jets, and Elves—
This field guide to the menagerie of electrical phenomena seen in, around, and above thunderstorms only hints at the wide variety of lights that have been observed. WALTER A. LYONS, RUSSELL A. ARMSTRONG, E. A. BERING III, AND EARLE R. WILLIAMS, "THE HUNDRED YEAR HUNT FOR THE SPRITE," EOS, VOLUME 81, ISSUE 33, PAGES 373–377, 2000. COPYRIGHT 2000 AMERICAN GEOPHYSICAL UNION. REPRODUCED BY PERMISSION OF AMERICAN GEOPHYSICAL UNION.

for the storm situation. Experience shows that many coaches and officials are so involved in games that they are unwilling or unable to monitor the development of the storm situation at the same time. Follow the rules in the plan.

- Be aware of other storms in your area; if thunderstorms have formed on the mountain range next to where you are hiking, they may form where you are, also.
- Watch for signs of a thunderstorm that is starting to grow quickly. Storms can grow from the small towering cumulus stage to a lightning producer is less than half an hour.

WHEN THUNDERSTORMS DEVELOP

- Estimate distance to lightning using the flash-to-bang method: When you see the flash, count the seconds to the bang of its thunder, and divide by 5 for the distance in miles. Keep in mind that the next lightning strike could be 1 or 2 miles closer than the last one.
- Determine whether the storm is approaching your position.
- Know how long it will take to reach safe shelter from where you are. Then compare the time it will take to reach shelter with the time until lightning is expected to arrive at your location. If the storm is approaching faster

than it takes to reach shelter, it is already too late. The choice at this point is either to try to attain shelter as quickly as possible and be vulnerable to the flashes during the process of reaching shelter, or take a defensive posture away from safe shelter in less-than-ideal circumstances.

LIGHTNING NEARBY

- Go inside a building normally occupied by the public or used as a residence by people. A metal-topped building with stone or other nonconducting walls is not safe. In general, large all-metal buildings connected to the ground (not small sheds) are safe if a person stays low in the middle and keeps both feet together. Do not touch anything connected to the power, telephone, television cable, or plumbing entering from the outside.
- Go inside a vehicle with a solid metal top. Safe vehicles include a car, bus, van, or the cab of a truck. Do not contact any metal while lightning is nearby.
- Do not be the highest object. Do not be on a bicycle on an open road; do not be on top of a mountain or rock outcropping; do not stand in an open parking lot, on a roof, or in the water; do not be in a boat. Lightning seeks

Lightning Map of North America—The U.S. and Canadian Lightning Detection Networks use 187 electronic lightning sensors to locate nearly every lightning strike in North America. Three years (1998–2000) of data were averaged to produce this map of the annual lightning ground flash density, in strikes per square kilometer (multiply by 2.5 to get strikes per square mile). The highest values in the continent are found in Florida, while the West's highest lightning rates occur from southern Arizona into the Rocky Mountains of New Mexico and Colorado. The lowest rates are found along the Pacific coast and in the Arctic. RICHARD E. ORVILLE, TEXAS A&M UNIVERSITY

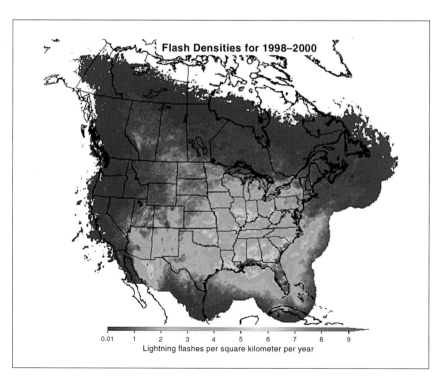

Flash Densities for 1998–2000

0.01 1 2 3 4 5 6 7 8 9
Lightning flashes per square kilometer per year

its ground contact point from an overhead thunderstorm in about a 50-yard search radius on the ground. Therefore do not stand in an open area such as a ball field, golf course, or large clearing between trees in the forest.

- Do not be connected to anything taller than its surroundings that will be attractive to lightning. Do not stand under or near a tree; stay away from poles, antennas, and towers that may be struck and transmit the charge to you.

- When hiking in a forest far from vehicles or buildings, there may be no better action than to seek a thick grove of small trees surrounded by tall trees, away from individual trees. In this situation, safety is a matter of taking the less risky alternative rather than finding a totally safe place.

LAST MINUTE

If you are out in the open with nearby lightning or your hair stands on end, do the following: crouch on the balls of your feet with your head down, don't touch the ground with your hands, and don't lie on the ground. This posture is based on the physical reasoning that is it best to minimize contact with the ground to avoid the strike's current traveling to the person from the ground, to be as low a target as possible, and to keep the head down to avoid critical injuries if struck. Although it is good to be as low as possible, lightning often enters the victim through the ground rather than from a direct overhead struck.

A LAST WORD

I suggest reading the "Last Minute" position described above, and then try it out in your living room. Imagine crouching like that in a thunderstorm, with lightning nearby and wind, rain, and maybe even hail lashing your body. Sounds pretty grim, doesn't it? Let this be an inspiration to follow the earlier parts of the plan, recognize the threat, and be in safe shelter before the storm is overhead.

LIGHTNING'S GREATEST HITS

July 22, 1918—A single lightning strike killed a flock of 504 sheep grazing in Utah's Wasatch Mountains.

April 7, 1926—Lightning struck an oil depot in San Luis Obispo, California, setting it aflame. When the fire was extinguished five days later, it had killed two people, burned 900 acres and consumed 6 million barrels of oil.

September 1, 1939—Another single lightning strike killed 835 sheep in Utah, this time in Box Elder County. The sheep were asleep on the wet ground when the nighttime storms struck. Fifteen sheep and the shepherd survived.

July 25, 1945—An early morning thunderstorm forced an hour and a half delay in the first test of an atomic bomb near Alamogordo, New Mexico. For obvious reasons, technicians were reluctant to perform adjustments on the device while lightning was striking nearby.

August 24, 1951—The construction site of Gross Reservoir Dam, in South Boulder Creek Canyon, 25 miles northwest of Denver, was busy with 250 workers—including "high scalers" drilling holes and installing dynamite charges in the canyon wall—when lightning struck the canyon walls. Thirty-two tons of explosives were ignited, and nine workers died in the tremendous blast.

August 15, 1967—Lightning touched off the 56,000-acre Sundance fire in Idaho's Selkirk Mountains. Intense flames generated tornado-like whirlwinds that blew burning trees around like matchsticks.

August 23–24, 1970—Dry thunderstorms ignited 100 separate fires in Washington's Cascade Mountains. The fires consumed 100,000 acres of forest and rangeland before they were finally controlled a week later.

July 12, 1984—A "bolt out of the blue" from a storm 3 miles away struck and killed a golfer in Tucson, Arizona.

July 6, 1985—Most of Utah was blacked out for several hours by a lightning strike to a generating station in Salt Lake City. The exploding transformer sent flames 200 feet into the air.

July 27, 1985—Lightning struck five hikers atop Half Dome in Yosemite National Park, California, killing two of them. The same day, lightning killed another hiker in Sequoia National Park, 100 miles away.

LIGHTNING'S GREATEST HITS, CONTINUED

April 5, 1992—One skier died and two were injured when lightning struck the chair lift they were riding in at a ski resort in Colorado. As often happens with spring thunderstorms in the mountains, there was a heavy fall of snow pellets at the time of the strike.

September 5, 1993—Lightning from a clear blue sky (possibly a positive lightning flash) struck and killed a farmer working in an alfalfa field near Blanding, Utah.

July 25, 2000—Lightning struck and killed an 18-year-old visitor who was exploring a boulder field at the summit of Pikes Peak in Colorado. The lightning was the first and only strike to come from a small, short-lived storm that was barely large enough to produce any lightning at all.

July 26, 2003—Six climbers were injured and one killed when lightning struck an exposed ridge below the summit of Wyoming's Grand Teton. Some of the injured began falling down the mountain, but were saved by their ropes.

VIOLENCE IN THE SKIES

CHAPTER

6

... a torrent of rain and hail fell more violent than ever I saw before, the rain fell like one voley of water falling from the heavens and gave us time only to get out of the way of a torrent of water which was Poreing down the hill in[to] the River with emence force tareing every thing before it takeing with it large rocks & mud, ... on arrival at the camp on the willow run met the party who had returned in great confusion to the run leaveing their loads in the Plain, the hail & wind being so large and violent in the plains, and them naked, they were much brused, and some nearly killed one knocked down three times, and others without hats or any thing on their heads bloody & complained verry much, I refreshed them with a little grog.

—William Clark, near Great Falls,
Montana, June 29, 1805

One of the many discoveries about the West made by the Lewis and Clark "Corps of Discovery" was the often violent nature of storms on the High Plains. But they were not the first; those who already lived on this land had made the discovery many times before. Years earlier, according to oral legend handed down by the Crow Indian tribe (and recounted in "Bear White Child and the First American Tornado Chase," by John Weaver, published in *Storm Track,* March 31, 1980), a young chief-to-be had an extremely close encounter on the same grassy plains of eastern Montana:

Shelf Cloud—A menacing "shelf cloud" bears down on the National Weather Service office in Rapid City, South Dakota on August 8, 2002. Shelf clouds result from powerful, concentrated updrafts feeding moisture into the leading edge of an advancing thunderstorm. This particular storm unleashed heavy rain and flash flooding in the Black Hills. BRIAN A. KLIMOWSKI

One day, as the young Bear White Child was sitting on a rock watching the setting sun, he noticed a black cloud, as if a storm were about to break. The cloud grew larger and more threatening. He felt strong gusts of wind and saw streaks of lightning. It began to rain and hail, and the boy was afraid the large hailstones would kill him. He was running for a place to hide, but a voice inside convinced him instead to remain with the storm.

The hail fell all around, but the boy was not touched. Again, he looked in the direction the storm had come; a black cloud hung in the middle of the hail. The cloud's center began taking shape, and he saw the head of Bear Up Above. At the moment the upper half of the bear's body appeared, the hail stopped. The bear sang a song as it reached down to embrace the boy. It lifted him into the air, and when it had finished singing, put him down. This occurred four times without apparent harm to the boy. The account ends as the storm passes, leaving behind a clear blue sky.

When Bear Up Above visited Earth, he didn't skimp on the effects—lightning, rain, gusty winds, hail, and, apparently, even a tornado accompanied his encounter with the boy Bear White Child. The future chief was fortunate, having survived the variety of forces thrown at him (his experience actually enhanced his status when he became chief); not all westerners have been so lucky with the weather in the centuries since.

HAIL AND HIGH WATER

As the Corps of Discovery, Bear White Child, and many others have found out, thunder and lightning aren't the only mischief thunderstorms can make. Thunderstorms can also be prodigious rainmakers, and when too much rain falls too fast in too small a place, the result is a flash flood. Lightning is quick, tornadoes are awesome, but no weather-related disaster kills more westerners than flash floods.

The first requirement for a thunderstorm to cause a flood is the obvious one—that it produce an exceptional amount of rain. However, this is not enough. Most thunderstorms move along at a sprightly 10 to 40 miles an hour, which means the storms last half an hour or so at any one place. Flash flood storms, on the other hand, stand still for hours. Tremendous amounts of rain can dump on one valley, while the next valley—within earshot and hearing thunder throughout—gets a sprinkle.

Why do a select few thunderstorms stand still while most of their peers move? The motion of thunderstorms is not a simple process. To some extent, it is controlled by upper-level winds, which continually nudge along the top portions of thunderclouds. Thunderstorms may also move because they're growing faster on one side than on the other, and the cloud mass shifts in that direction. Remember the wave of thunderstorms that sweeps off mountains? This is much the same thing—cold downdrafts spreading out at the base of the storm give moist air an upward shove, and new towers of cumulus build up on the side of the thundercloud. The building cumulus towers tap fresh supplies of water vapor, keeping the thunderstorm alive.

It may seem contradictory to have a stationary thunderstorm produce lots of rain, since cold air collecting at the base of the storm should cut off its moisture supply. But what if a wave of thunderstorms tries to move, say, east into the face of a westward blowing wind? If the speeds match, the wave stands still. The thunderstorms also stand still, while easterly winds feed fresh, moist air into their hungry jaws.

Thunderstorms are more likely to stay put if there's a mountain nearby, since sloping terrain encourages the storms' growth by forcing moist wind upward. That's why

Costly Cloud—The skyline of downtown Denver nearly disappears in a haze of hail pouring from the turbulent base of a massive supercell thunderstorm. Damage from the July 10, 1990, storm totaled two-thirds of a billion dollars, making it the costliest hail storm in Western history.
RICHARD A. KEEN

Hail Holes—This hail-damaged windshield of the author's Subaru, along with the egg-carton dents on the hood and roof, helped make Denver's 1990 hailstorm the most destructive to ever hit the West. RICHARD A. KEEN

many of the West's heaviest thundershowers occur in the mountains, and these thunderstorms become problems because much of the population of mountainous areas lives in the valleys. Of course, you don't need a mountain to make a flash flood, since places like Kansas City and Houston have been struck. But in the West, a thunderstorm sitting over the head of a valley with a ready supply of moist air is the prime ingredient for a flash flood.

Not all of the water falls as rain. We saw in the last chapter how strong updrafts can blow raindrops back into the frozen parts of the cloud. These frozen drops grow into hail. There's not much more to say about hail here, except that the stronger the updraft, the bigger the hailstones can grow. Strong updrafts also feed water vapor into the cloud at a faster rate, stepping up the production of raindrops. So hail and high water very often go together.

GUST FRONTS

Cheyenne Hail—For several hours during the evening of August 1, 1985, an intense thunderstorm sat motionless over Cheyenne, Wyoming. Up to 7 inches of rain drenched the city, causing street and stream flooding that took 12 lives and caused $65 million damage. Two-inch diameter hailstones accompanying the rain were washed into piles 8 feet high along roads and 5 feet deep in basements. Floodwaters washed hail and cars into roadside heaps. FEDERAL EMERGENCY MANAGEMENT ADMINISTRATION, PHOTO BY MICHAEL MEE

At its peak of vigor, a healthy thunderstorm has both updrafts and downdrafts. Each has its role: upward currents lift moist air to the condensation

level, and downward currents carry the load of rain and hail earthward. The core of the downdraft may be several miles wide, but as it approaches the ground it has no choice but to spread out horizontally. The leading edge of the expanding outflow of cold air is known as a "gust front," which may spread over an area 10 or 20 miles wide.

Parting Shot—Lightning punctuates a departing cumulonimbus cloud (complete with mammatus formations) at the end of a day spent chasing storms.
ELKE EDWARDS

Gust fronts are often more than breezes; they have been known to flatten trees and buildings, sink boats, and send cars off the road with their 100-m.p.h. winds. They have broken up everything from picnics to airplanes. Later in this chapter we'll see how gust fronts can spawn small whirlwinds strong enough to be called tornadoes.

The passage of a gust front is marked by a sudden rush of wind and a drop in the temperature, often by 20 or 30 degrees in as many minutes. If the ground is dry and dusty, the gust front may actually become visible as a 1,000-foot-high, dust-laden wall of air. Dusty gust fronts are known as "haboobs," a word which, all jokes aside, comes from the Sudan, where such things are commonplace. They are also common in the desert regions of the West, and some spectacular ones have passed across Phoenix. In moister climates, such as the High Plains, ragged bands of low clouds may form along the gust front. Sometimes these low cloud bands form in layers and rotate like a log rolling on the ground; the respective names are "shelf" and "roll" clouds.

To meteorologists, any difference of wind speed or direction between two places is called a "wind shear." Usually it's nothing to worry about, but during the 1970s and 1980s the sharp wind shears along gust fronts caused several major aircraft disasters, in some cases killing 100 or more people. These tragedies led to research projects such as the Joint Airport Weather Study (JAWS) project near Denver in the summer of 1982. JAWS was followed a few years later by CLAWS—Classify and Locate Airport Wind Shear. These and other programs helped develop wind shear detection technologies (such as Doppler radar) that are now operational at most major airports and which have greatly reduced the number of tragedies.

Close Call—A microburst kicks up a cloud of dust near the end of a runway at Denver, as seen from the window seat of a passenger jet. The landing was bumpy, but the pilot successfully avoided the strongest tubulence.
RICHARD A. KEEN

DOWNBURSTS

Using such sophisticated equipment as Doppler radar, which can measure wind speeds throughout the interior of a storm, along with more basic techniques, such as observers in the field with binoculars and cameras, researchers have discovered a diminutive downdraft that may cause the most dangerous wind shears. The narrow streams of air are less than a mile across and may only span 100 yards or so. As the stream hits the ground, its 50-m.p.h. downdrafts may turn into spreading winds of 100-m.p.h. or more, similar to water from a faucet splattering onto the sink. The resulting sudden, nearly explosive winds have earned these intense downdrafts the name "downbursts."

Strong downbursts have felled trees in radial patterns, with all the lumber pointing away from the center; sometimes the damage area is only a few hundred feet across! Park chairs have been sent flying, while outside the downburst, picnickers watch in disbelief. Sometimes downbursts are visible as expanding

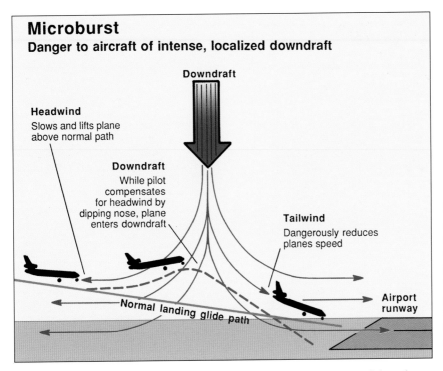

Microburst
Danger to aircraft of intense, localized downdraft

Downdraft

Headwind
Slows and lifts plane
above normal path

Downdraft
While pilot
compensates
for headwind by
dipping nose, plane
enters downdraft

Tailwind
Dangerously reduces
planes speed

Normal landing glide path

**Airport
runway**

Downburst Danger to Aircraft—The spreading air currents as a strong downdraft reaches the ground causes rapidly changing winds that can prove fatal to unwary aviators. DIAGRAM COURTESY NATIONAL CENTER FOR ATMOSPHERIC RESEARCH/ NATIONAL SCIENCE FOUNDATION

rings of dust picked up by the winds. Look fast, though—the typical downburst lasts only 2 or 3 minutes.

The brief but high winds of a downburst can down trees and houses, but their greatest havoc is wreaked upon airliners. Airplanes are kept in flight by the lift of the air flowing over their wings; the faster the airspeed over the wings, the greater the lift. Every plane has a specific airspeed, called the "stall speed," below which there's not enough lift to keep the plane flying. Airspeed is the speed across the wings, and is the combination of the plane's ground speed plus the speed of a headwind (or minus the speed of a tailwind).

Airplanes are most susceptible to downbursts right after takeoff and just before landing, when they are closest to the ground, flying the slowest (just barely above stall speed), and where the strongest downburst winds occur. Encountering a downburst, a jetliner may see a 30-m.p.h. headwind change to a 30-m.p.h. tailwind in 10 seconds. If the sudden loss of lift occurs at too low an altitude, the plane has no chance to recover. In 1982, a jetliner with 144 aboard was downed by a downburst 30 seconds after taking off from New Orleans; there were no survivors. There have been several incidents of downburst-caused jetliner crashes and near crashes in the West, but, fortunately, without any deaths.

A Wheel Within a Wheel—A debris-filled funnel drops from a wall cloud, the swirling base of a rotating "supercell" thunderstorm, near Fort Morgan, Colorado, on July 21, 2000. Supercell tornadoes are relatively rare in the West, but those that do occur are found mostly on the high plains.
REED COVELLI

Downdrafts in thunderstorms are usually accompanied by brief heavy rain. It might then seem odd that most of the downbursts studied in the JAWS experiment did not have any rain, and that some of the strongest bursts were on hot, dry days. These dry downbursts are excellent raisers of dust, but how do they get their winds? It turns out that dry downbursts begin as rain showers, but the rains never reach the ground. As the rain-laden downdraft drops below the cloud, raindrops start evaporating. Cooled by evaporation, the downdraft air becomes heavier and falls faster—the exact opposite of condensation and convection.

Most people have probably seen downbursts in the making, in the form of thin, dark streamers of rain dropping from a cloud. If the shaft of rain disappears before reaching the ground, it's called "virga," and beneath it there's probably a stiff downdraft. If the cloud doesn't make a lot of rain, the downburst may fall as a bubble of cool air; when it lands, its winds might last only a few seconds.

Downbursts are small, brief, and scattered. Some fall from thunderstorms, but others come out of the most inoffensive-looking cumulus clouds. This makes them difficult to detect while they are occurring and virtually impossible to predict even minutes in advance. Fortunately, there are downburst detection devices, including Doppler radar and networks of wind gauges, that are making landing and taking off a bit safer.

There is one practical step you frequent flyers can take to reduce your odds of being ruined by a downburst. The JAWS experiment found that downbursts in the Denver area usually occur between 1 and 6 P.M., when the sky contains the highest concentration of cumulus and cumulonimbus clouds. Other airports in the arid regions of the West also probably get their downbursts in the afternoon. The moral is: fly early!

TORNADOES

Big whirls have little whirls
that feed on their velocity
and little whirls have lesser whirls,
and so on to viscosity
—Meteorologist L. F. Richardson

Richardson's Rhyme, as this little ditty is called, is well known in the weather business, because it so succinctly sums up (as only poetry can!) how the

Salt Lake City Tornado—The August 11, 1999, tornado is caught in the middle of downtown Salt Lake City in this video frame. The bright flash is probably an exploding power transformer. IMAGE COURTESY KTVX NEWS 4 UTAH

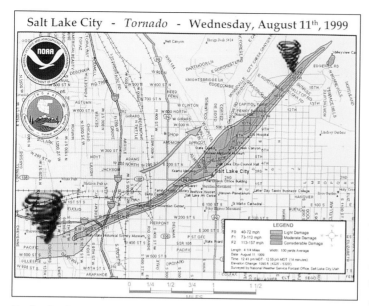

Path of Salt Lake City Tornado—The swath of destruction left by the tornado that cut through Salt Lake City. NATIONAL WEATHER SERVICE

atmosphere works (we won't get sidetracked into a discourse on viscosity here). The message is particularly true for tornadoes. Spun from rotating thunderstorms embedded in the turning winds of cyclones, themselves generated by the spinning Earth, tornadoes themselves may spin off lesser whirls a few feet across.

The concentrated motion—and power—in tornadoes make them a very special form of weather. Nowhere else does the atmosphere show its stuff in a more visual and dramatic style. Folks who would otherwise never look up at a cloud will take note of a tornado. But let's make it clear right here: few people will ever see a tornado, and fewer still will be injured by one. When they strike, it's news.

Like downbursts, tornadoes have powerful winds. However, in tornadoes, most of the air is going up! Tornadoes are picky, too, and happen only when there's a very special set of weather conditions. First, the air has to be moist enough to feed a growing thunderstorm. Next, the atmosphere has to be highly unstable in order to get some extremely strong updrafts going. It also helps to have a strong jet stream aloft—most tornado-producing thunderstorms are

Tree Damage—Although most tornadoes occur in the open country of the Great Plains, they occasionally plow across mountainous terrain. These lodgepole pines near Rockerville, in South Dakota's Black Hills, were all neatly snapped off 20 feet above the ground by a tornado in 1966. RICHARD A. KEEN

movers. Finally, the tornado needs to get its spin from somewhere, so the lowest layers of air must already be turning. If the jet stream is blowing in a different direction than the winds lower down, the shifting currents can give some extra spin to the growing thunderstorm.

Meteorologically speaking, the favorite haunts for tornadoes are the warm sectors of strong cyclones, where all the above ingredients are found to one degree or another. Hurricanes have no shortage of moisture, instability, and rotation, and have been known to unleash tornadoes—as many as 115 in one Texas hurricane. Occasionally a hurricane remnant brings a few small tornadoes to the Southwest. Even isolated thunderstorms can whip up a tornado, if the air currents are just right enough to get a little spin going.

Small Western Twister—A small tornado whips the high plains near Lamar, Colorado. Unlike many western twisters, the air was moist enough for a complete funnel cloud to form. IAN WITTMEYER

When a thunderstorm develops in these unusual situations, its powerful updrafts draw in the slowly rotating air. This concentrates the spinning motion, like water swirling faster as it approaches a drain. As the updraft strengthens, the spinning speeds up, until the updraft becomes a narrow, rotating column—a tornado.

In exceptional cases, the whole thunderstorm cell may start rotating, becoming a parent cloud that may spawn tornadoes every few minutes for an hour or more. These awesome "supercell" thunderstorms ravage the Midwest and Great Plains many times every year. Supercells are quite rare across most of the West, but east of the Rockies—in the high plains from New Mexico to Alberta—they bring several tornadoes every year.

Tornadoes come in many sizes, shapes, and strengths. The largest can be a mile or more across with 300-m.p.h. winds, and may scour the land along a 50- to 250-mile path before dissipating. Fortunately, these mile-wide monsters are exceedingly rare in the West, although a few have visited the high plains. At the other extreme, tiny twisters may touch down for a few seconds, damaging a single tree or part of a roof before disappearing. I saw one leave a neat but narrow 30-foot-wide path in a cornfield near Greeley, Colorado, and another with winds barely strong enough to pick up cardboard boxes from a

Killer Tornado—The West's deadliest tornado struck Edmonton, Alberta, in 1987, and is seen here plowing through the city's refinery row. ROBERT CHARLTON

White Tornado—A small tornado makes a big spectacle as it whips up tons of gypsum dust from the dunes at White Sands Missile Range, New Mexico. U.S. ARMY, WHITE SANDS MISSILE RANGE

landfill east of Denver (although it sent newspapers spiraling thousands of feet up into the base of the thunderstorm!). The typical tornado, based on nation-wide statistics, has winds of 150 m.p.h. swirling around a 700-foot-wide funnel, and moves at 40 m.p.h. over a 5-mile-long path during its 5- or 10-minute lifetime. Like the 1.9-child family, though, this "typical" tornado is actually the rarest of them all.

The appearance of a tornado can vary as much as its size, ranging from fat cylinders to thin, coiling ropes. The famous funnel cloud comes from the condensation of water vapor inside the rotating column, where the pressure and temperature are lower. When the funnel cloud fails to touch the ground, the odds are the rotating tube of air doesn't go all the way down either, or if it does, its winds are very weak. Powerful tornadoes often look like ice-cream cones, and in extreme storms the base of the thundercloud itself may appear to simply dip to the ground. Miniature, snake-like whirlwinds, a few feet across and lasting only seconds, might be seen along the fringes of the main funnel. Often the funnel is surrounded by rain, and not visible at all. The classic "Wizard of Oz" elephant trunk funnels are photogenic and popular in weather books, but they're not all that common, especially in the West.

Many western tornadoes don't even look like tornadoes. The funnel cloud comes from the condensation of water vapor inside the rotating column, where the pressure and temperature are lower. In the dry climate of the West, the funnel cloud often fails to fill the whirlwind. The typical western tornado has a stubby funnel protruding from the cloud and a whirlwind full of dust and debris on the ground. As in any tornado, the rotating

Killer Cloud—The cloud that unleashed a lethal flood in Colorado's Big Thompson Canyon in 1976 grows from a small thundershower into a monster storm. John Asztalos snapped this sequence of photos from Mitchell Lake, about 25 miles from the flood zone. After a day of hiking in off-and-on rain, he was setting up camp near the lake when the brilliant, sun-lit cloud caught his attention. By measuring the photographs, John determined that the cloud reached an exceptional height of 70,000 feet. The storm reached its peak size and intensity after dark, when another camper in the area described the lightning as so continuous that he could "read a book without getting eye strain"! JOHN ASZTALOS

Waterspout—A diaphanous waterspout—a tornado over water—skips across Bear Lake, Utah, on September 17, 1996.
NATIONAL WEATHER SERVICE, RYAN SHAUL

tube of air extends all the way from the cloud to the ground, but it's invisible. Some people prefer to call these tornadoes by their diminutive name, "twister."

So the West doesn't get the really big tornadoes, and the small ones often don't even look like tornadoes. Even these small ones aren't that common. Since 1953, the 12 western states have averaged 75 tornadoes per year, only 9 percent of the national total. Of these, approximately 50 (or two-thirds of the West's total) touch down on the High Plains from Montana to New Mexico. The plains of Alberta add another 16 tornadoes per year to these totals. In an average year, fewer than 25 tornadoes occur west of the Continental Divide.

By American standards, tornadoes are rare in the West. However, three-fourths of the world's twisters touch down in the United States, making the tornado as American as apple pie. Canada hosts another 5 percent of the global total (including 5 or 10 that crossed the border from the States), leaving only one tornado in five for the rest of the world. Therefore, although the West catches only a small fraction of the 800 tornadoes in the United States and Canada during an average year, the yearly quota of 25 twisters west of the divide turns out to be fairly impressive by global standards. For comparison, the entire continent of Australia has reported an annual average of 14 tornadoes, and relatively tornado-prone Japan has averaged 11 twisters per year. Probably the only countries that are comparable to the West are Great Britain and Nevada-sized New Zealand, each averaging 25 or so a year.

Small, rare, and invisible they may be, but no tornado should be sneezed at. In the eight decades since 1916, tornadoes have killed about 60 residents of the western U.S., almost a third of whom were Coloradans. No one in Alaska, California, Oregon, or Nevada has ever been dispatched by a twister. But the West's most lethal tornadoes have occurred in Canada, with 39 people losing their lives in two separate Alberta tornadoes in the past two decades.

TORNADO WARNING

Tornado prediction is no longer a mere possibility, but in many respects may be considered an accomplished fact. By this I do not mean absolute perfection, but reasonable success.

—John Finley, "Tornadoes" (1887)

The smaller and briefer a weather phenomenon is, the harder it is to predict. The problem is multiplied with tornadoes because of their lethal nature. John Finley's estimation of the tornado forecasts issued by the U.S. Army Signal Corps was written in 1887, but despite vast advances in our understanding of tornadoes and their causes, they could have been written yesterday.

Over the century since Finley issued his first warnings, forecasters have improved their skills at recognizing the proper conditions—moisture, instability, and so on—in which tornadoes are likely to break out. When these conditions occur, the National Weather Service issues a "Tornado Watch" stating that tornadoes are possible in an area 100 or so miles across sometime during the next few hours. Until recently, however, they couldn't issue a Tornado Warning, meaning a twister *will* strike a certain place at a certain time (in other words, "Duck!"), until someone had actually seen the funnel cloud or the tornado was already on the ground. In the 1990s, the latest in meteorological technology, Doppler radar, became operational across the United States. By virtue of its

Rope Stage—Tornadoes often stretch into contorted, ropelike vortices before dissipating, as seen in this fantastic funnel north of Cheyenne, Wyoming. IAN WITTMEYER

ability to sense wind motions in the atmosphere, and in particular little swirls that may become tornadoes, Doppler radar can provide up to 20 minutes advance notice of developing twisters. It might seem that 20 minutes is not a whole lot of time, considering it takes 5 or 10 minutes just to get the warning out to the public, where it will do some good. However, the remaining 10 minutes is still sufficient to get a school full of kids into the basement or hallway.

Tornado Days—This map, produced by National Severe Storms Lab, shows the frequency of tornadoes across the United States. In the salmon-colored centers of activity in central Florida and eastern Colorado, tornadoes occur within 25 miles of a given point about 1.8 times per year, on average (1980– 1999). However, in both locations the tornadoes tend to be small and short-lived. When the map is redrawn to show only the stronger tornadoes, the center of peak activity moves to Oklahoma. NATIONAL SEVERE STORMS LAB

TORNADO ALLEY

There is no other place in the world like the area from the mouth of the Mackenzie River in Canada to the mouth of old Missip in the Gulf of Mexico. This area between the Rockies and the Appalachians can cook up more different kinds of weather in less time than any other area in the world.
—President Harry S. Truman, addressing the American Meteorological Society in 1957

Some locales seem more prone to tornado strikes than others. Western "tornado alleys," like everything else related to tornadoes, are smaller than their Midwestern counterparts. In the Midwest, tornado alleys are measured in states; western tornado alleys extend across counties. Some of the West's favorite tornado hangouts are the Columbia River Basin from Portland to Spokane, the Los Angeles Basin, the Gila Desert around Phoenix, the Snake River Plains of Idaho, and several swaths across the High Plains.

All of these tornado alleys are wide, flat areas where storms can spin undisturbed by mountains. Over the High Plains, the swaths may follow zones of eddies downwind from mountains and ridges (see more on this subject in chapter 8, "Whirlwinds, Walliwaws, and Washoe Zephyrs"). Most of the alleys are in populated farm country or even cities, where residents notice tornadoes. Many twisters probably go undetected as they tumble sagebrush across some uninhabited desert.

As the population of the West increases, so does the number of tornadoes. Consider the words of Lorin Blodget in his 1857 *Climatology of*

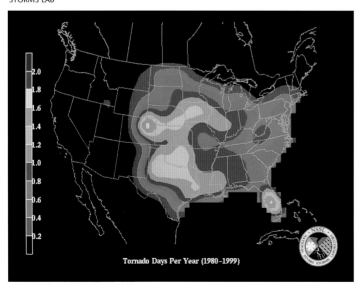

Tornado Days Per Year (1980–1999)

the United States: "The frequency and distribution of these tornadoes is a subject of practical interest. There are none on the Great Plains so far as known. They are most numerous in the Mississippi Valley." But that was back when the Great Plains had few people to notice tornadoes; we now know that the area breeds fully half the tornadoes in the United States, and that it has more tornadoes per square mile than any other place in the world. As tornado reports continue to rise in the West, we can expect to hear a lot of discussion about changing storm patterns. It may really be changing people patterns.

GHOST TWISTERS IN THE SKY

Unless you are one of those people who goes out of his way to seek such things, the odds are that you'll never see a tornado—and for most folks, that's just fine! However, almost every day you can spot a smaller, weaker, and usually harmless cousin of the fearsome funnel from the comfort of your back porch. All you need is a pair of binoculars and an airplane passing overhead, and if you look closely, you'll often see two narrow, parallel strings of cloud following the airplane. These are "wing tip vortices," caused by air on the underside of the wings spinning upward around the tips of the wings. This motion is a necessary consequence of the way wings work: as the airplane flies along, air streaming across the curved top side of the wing creates a partial vacuum (or low pressure), while the air beneath the wing is slightly compressed (high pressure). The difference in pressure creates "lift," the force that holds airplanes up when they are flying. Because air will move from high to low pressure, some of the air curls around the wing tip, creating little vortices in the wake of the airplane. The combustion of fuel produces water vapor, which gets caught in the vortices, condenses

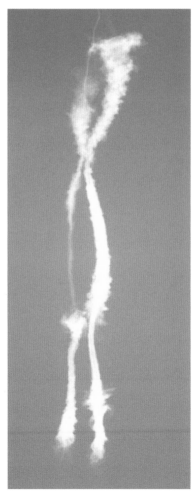

Double Trouble—Twin twisters—wing tip vortices created by a passing jetliner—dance in the sky, 30,000 feet up.
RICHARD A. KEEN

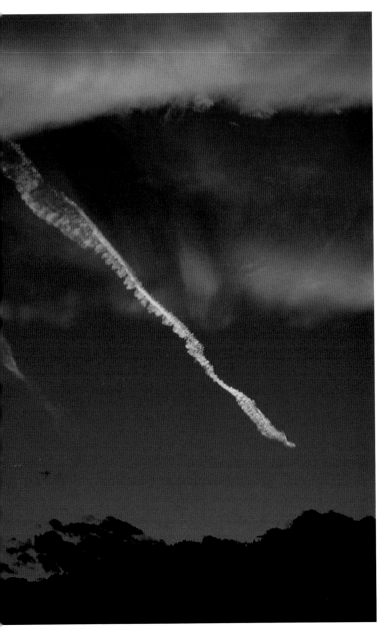

into cloud and makes the whole thing visible from the ground. The bigger the plane, the stronger and longer-lived the vortices are, and sometimes they are visible for several minutes after the plane has passed.

Looking through binoculars, you can see these vortices spinning, breaking up, and eventually dissipating. Often, the vortices from each wing tip (which spin in opposite directions) connect to each other, creating vortex rings (like smoke rings) that undulate and distort until they too dissipate.

While wing tip vortices pose no danger to anyone watching them with binoculars, they are not entirely harmless. The vortices from a large aircraft (such as a jumbo jet) can be strong enough to flip a smaller plane that happens to get caught in them; as a result, aviation rules mandate minimum spacing (in time and distance) between aircraft during take-off and landing, as well as in the air. Even with these rules, the vortices may linger longer than is normally possible, and these twisting winds have been implicated in several major airline disasters.

Contrail—Short for condensation trail, this contrail, an artificial cloud made of condensed water vapor expelled by airplane engines, extends from a lenticular cloud.
RICHARD A. KEEN

THE BIG STORMS

December 27, 1866—A tornado in Nevada County, California, may be the first ever reported in the West.

July 29, 1883—The snail's pace of geology speeded up briefly, as a flash flood dug a 50-foot-deep gorge along Kanab Creek, Utah.

June 14, 1903—A cloudburst unleashed a 40-foot "wall of water" that washed away Heppner, Oregon, with a loss of 247 lives.

August 7, 1904—Eighty-nine passengers drowned as a train trestle, weakened by a flash flood, collapsed near Pueblo, Colorado.

August 10, 1924—The western United States' most lethal tornado in recorded history struck Thurman, in northeastern Colorado, killing 10 occupants of a single house.

June 19, 1938—Another train disaster caused by a flood-weakened trestle. The "Olympian" bound from Chicago to Tacoma, plowed into Custer Creek, near Miles City, Montana, with a loss of 49 lives.

August 12-13, 1967—Five inches of rain—a biblical deluge by subarctic standards—filled the Chena River to record flood levels at Fairbanks, Alaska. The flood rose higher than any ice-jam flood (the usual cause of flooding in Fairbanks), and 90 percent of the buildings in town suffered some damage.

December 2, 1970—A "white tornado" swept across Timpanogos Divide, Utah, snapping trees and lifting snow 1,000 feet up into its funnel.

April 5, 1972—A quarter-mile-wide tornado touched down in Portland, Oregon, and crossed the Columbia River to Vancouver, Washington, where it devastated a shopping center and killed six people.

June 9, 1972—A stationary thunderstorm dumped up to 15 inches of rain on the Black Hills of South Dakota, sending torrents of water into Rapid City and other towns. It was South Dakota's worst disaster, with 236 people killed, 2,900 injured, and nearly 1,000 homes destroyed.

August 7, 1975—A Continental Airlines 727 jet encountered a downburst as it took off from Denver. The plane fell back to the runway and skidded into a field, injuring 15 passengers.

July 31, 1976—On the eve of its 100th anniversary of statehood, Colorado suffered its worst natural disaster. A stationary thunderstorm, very similar to the Rapid City storm, flooded the Big Thompson River. Of the estimated 3,000 people (many of them vacationers) in the canyon at the time, 139 died in the flood.

THE BIG STORMS, CONTINUED

August 26, 1976—North America's northernmost tornado touched down for a few minutes near Kiana, Alaska, just north of the Arctic Circle.

May 18, 1977—A huge, cone-shaped tornado cut a 42-mile-long path from Oklahoma into extreme southeastern Colorado. Most of its track was over open country but the storm struck several farms, tossing trucks, farm machinery, and cattle up to one-half mile away. Fortunately, no people were injured. Damage patterns indicated peak winds exceeding 260 m.p.h., making this the most powerful tornado ever known to have struck a western state.

March 4–5, 1978—Six tornadoes in two days touched down around the north end of Sacramento Valley, while waterspouts churned waters off Santa Monica. Damage was limited to several barns and chicken coops.

July 16, 1979—A tornado cut across the northern part of Cheyenne, Wyoming, destroying planes and hangars at the airport and more than 150 houses and trailers. Thirty minutes later a much weaker twister touched down in eastern Cheyenne.

June 3, 1981—Three tornadoes touched down from a powerful thunderstorm that swept northward across Denver. The second tornado destroyed 87 homes in the northern suburb of Thornton, but thanks to timely warnings there were no deaths.

November 9, 1982—A Pacific storm spawned seven tornadoes in the Los Angeles area. One twister cut a 10-mile-long path against the Los Angeles River through Long Beach, another blew a catamaran 100 feet into the air at Malibu, but in general the damage was minor.

March 1, 1983—Another Los Angeles tornado came within a mile of the Civic Center, damaging 50 homes and injuring 30 residents. Two more twisters in September 1983 brought the 12-month total in the Los Angeles Basin to 11 tornadoes!

August 17, 1984—A short-lived tornado was sighted above timberline on Colorado's Longs Peak in Rocky Mountain National Park. At 11,400 feet elevation, it may be the highest ground ever crossed by a twister.

June 18, 1987—While participating in a NOAA-sponsored severe storm research project, I spotted my first tornado—a small one that scurried across the south side of Castle Rock, Colorado. The only damage was a downed stop sign.

July 21, 1987—A mile-wide tornado flattened 15,000 acres of lodgepole pine trees on a 24-mile-long path from Wyoming's Teton Wilderness Area into

THE BIG STORMS, CONTINUED

Yellowstone National Park. The monster tornado crossed the Continental Divide at an elevation of 10,170 feet; its peak winds of 225 m.p.h.—F4 on the Fujita scale—made toothpicks out of 2-foot-diameter tree trunks (see Appendix 3, "Wind Speed Scales," for more information).

July 31, 1987—Canada's third most deadly tornado in history (and the deadliest anywhere in western North America) roared through the northeast part of Edmonton, Alberta, killing 27 and exacting $250 million damage.

June 6, 1990—One of the most powerful tornadoes in Colorado history plowed right down Limon's main street, wrecking more than half the buildings in town. Thanks to timely warnings, there were no major injuries.

October 29, 1992—Another "white tornado" (see the entry for December 2, 1970) struck the West. This time the twister whipped across the White Sands Missile Range in southern New Mexico and was whitened by clouds of gypsum sand, rather than snow.

July 16, 1993—Microburst winds from a supercell thunderstorm ripped through Morgan and Washington counties in northeastern Colorado. Gusts as high as 150 m.p.h. demolished a mobile home, killing one occupant. The high winds were initially thought to be from a tornado, but a damage survey revealed the cause was straight-line winds.

August 12, 1997—A distant thunderstorm sent a 50- to 80-foot-high wall of water down Antelope Canyon, a narrow slot canyon near Lake Powell, Arizona. Eleven hikers, all visitors from Europe, were swept to their deaths.

September 26, 1998—At least half a dozen waterspouts danced across the northern end of Lake Tahoe, causing no harm but putting on quite a show. The largest spout was 250 feet in diameter.

August 11, 1999—A 200-yard-wide tornado ripped right through downtown Salt Lake City, narrowly missing the State Capitol and Temple Square. One person was killed.

July 14, 2000—Twelve campers were killed and more than a hundred injured, as a half-mile-wide tornado demolished a crowded campground on Pine Lake, in southeast of Red Deer, Alberta. Three weeks later, as people were gathering for a memorial service for those who died, another tornado passed over the same campground.

Hurricanes

*Warmest climes
but nurse the cruelest fangs ...*

—Herman Melville, *Moby Dick*

To the Indians of the Caribbean they were known as Huracan—the "Storm Devil." The Indians of India call them *cyclones,* a word of Greek heritage passed on by the British. In Chinese the name is *typhoon,* or "great wind." And Australians, for some peculiar reason, have been heard to call them "Willy Willies." We call them hurricanes, and in any language they are the greatest storm on Earth.

THE GREATEST STORM ON EARTH

Frightful stories of hurricanes' power and destruction abound in the annals of history. Columbus lost two ships to a hurricane during his second voyage to the New World in 1494. Four-and-a-half centuries later, on December 18, 1944, the U.S. Third Fleet was attacked by a small but intense Pacific typhoon named Cobra. In a few hours, the tempest had claimed 3 destroyers, 146 aircraft, and 790 sailors. It was one of the greatest disasters inflicted on the American Navy during the final year of World War II. Many a survivor of a hurricane at sea shares Shakespeare's account of Casca's stormy premonition of Caesar's death: "I have seen the ambitious ocean swell, and rage, and foam, to be exalted with the threat'ning clouds ..."

It is when hurricanes leave the sea and come ashore that they unleash their greatest wrath on humanity. A hurricane from the Bay of Bengal drowned 300,000 people in 1737, and as recently as 1970, another hurricane killed half a million citizens of the then-soon-to-be nation of Bangladesh. The greatest natural disaster ever to befall the United States was the devastation of Galveston, Texas, by a

Hurricane Linda—the eastern Pacific's most powerful hurricane on record, threatens Baja California on September 12, 1997. Linda later threatened southern California, but fortunately, no land was impacted by this massive storm. This perspective image was created by NASA's Marit Jentoft-Nilsen from NOAA satellite data. NASA GODDARD SPACE FLIGHT CENTER

hurricane in 1900. One sixth of the city's 40,000 residents perished when the storm pushed the Gulf of Mexico several miles inland. The power of storm waves striking shore is so great that seismographs—designed to measure earthquakes—in Alaska detected the rumble of crashing seas from the New England hurricane of 1938. Hurricanes are truly earth-shaking storms!

Galveston, New England, and Bangladesh are a long way from the West, and it might seem that hurricanes are not part of the West's varied weather. It is true that in the past century no full-force hurricane has ever directly struck any western state. But tropical storms with winds just below hurricane force (74 m.p.h.) have, on several occasions, wreaked considerable damage to western towns and cities. Almost every year, the West's weather is affected by dying remnants of hurricanes whose lives began in such distant places as Micronesia and West Africa. Before we can appreciate the impact of hurricanes on western weather, we must first understand what a hurricane is, and what makes them so different from the multitude of other storms that darken western skies.

Hurricanes are creatures of the sea. Their breeding grounds are the warm oceans of the tropics, and they grow as long as their travels continue to take them over the tepid seas. Unlike mid-latitude cyclones, which draw their power from the temperature differences across frontal boundaries, hurricanes thrive on undiluted warmth. Warm water feeds tremendous volumes of water vapor into the tropical atmosphere. This moisture-laden air is the fuel that drives hurricanes; without it, the great storms weaken and die. Like many other sea creatures, hurricanes soon expire when they leave the sea and go ashore.

The hurricane season begins in late summer, when the tropical (between 10 and 30 degrees north latitude) Atlantic and Pacific Oceans warm to their highest temperatures of the year. Several months of nearly overhead sun has heated the water to 85–90° F. At these temperatures, water readily evaporates into the overlying atmosphere. The dew point of the tropical atmosphere may rise above 80° F. Such oppressive humidity is rarely experienced anywhere in the western United States. The huge volume of water vapor in tropical air contains a tremendous amount of energy in the form of latent heat stored in molecules of water vapor when they evaporated from the ocean surface. When vapor condenses back into liquid water, the latent heat is released back to the air.

The air overlying just 1 square foot of the tropics may hold enough energy as latent heat to drive an automobile 2 miles. Multiply this by tropical oceans that cover tens of millions of square miles! In the tropics, latent heat is normally released back into the atmosphere by the same process of convection that powers thunderstorms. The moist air of the tropics needs to rise only 1,000 or 2,000 feet before condensation creates cumulus clouds. The release of latent heat warms the air, and the clouds grow into towering cumulus and then go on to become cumulonimbus clouds. The cycle of evaporation, rising streams of air, and condensation is the driving force behind hurricanes. Similar to the ignition of gasoline vapor inside the cylinders of an automobile engine, hurricanes use their fuel to create motion.

For months, from late summer well into the autumn, vast reaches of the tropical atmosphere are ripe for the formation hurricanes. But hurricanes are relatively rare, and every year only a few dozen are born worldwide. It takes more than hot, muggy air to give birth to a hurricane. Something needs to lift the air to its condensation level. Even this lifting is not enough, though, since cumulus clouds are commonplace in the tropics. Although many cumulus clouds grow into thunderstorms and even huge masses of thunderstorms hundreds of miles across, these thunderstorm masses usually lack the intense, swirling winds of a hurricane. Early in the life of a hurricane, conditions must be just right or the great storm will never develop. Hurricanes need some sort of "seed" disturbance—a slight swirl in the

Cross-Section of a Hurricane—Moist air spirals into the storm at low levels, then corkscrews upward near the center. The rising currents near the center form enormous, rainy clouds that surround that bizarre feature of all hurricanes—the clear eye.
NOAA

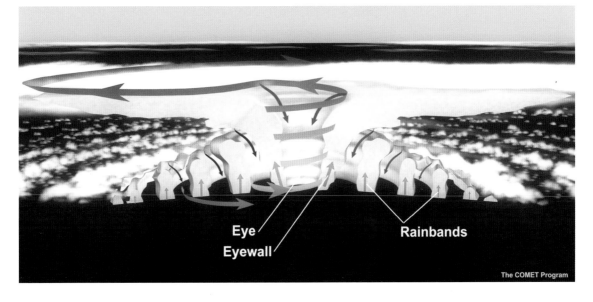

Eye
Eyewall
Rainbands

The COMET Program

Rocky Mountain Hurricane Remnant—
The remnants of Hurricane Polo, a Pacific storm that came ashore in Mexico, spin across the Rocky Mountains in October, 1984. The storm brought several inches of rain to the foothills of the Rockies, and snow to the higher elevations. NOAA

atmosphere—to get things going on the right track. If the upper level winds were too strong or blew in a direction different from the low-level winds, however, the developing thunderstorms could be torn apart as they reached the upper atmosphere. Hurricanes, indeed, have difficult childhoods.

Sometimes a twist in the trade winds or a weakening cold front from the north provides the initial impetus. The "seed" may be an exceptionally intense mass of tropical thunderstorms. Whatever its origins, the incipient hurricane starts as a collection of slow-rotating thunderstorms. Warm, moist air from outside the disturbance spirals slowly in, replacing the air that rose upward in the thunderstorms. The Coriolis effect assures that this spiral will, in the Northern Hemisphere, turn counterclockwise. Like an upside-down version of a draining bathtub, the inward flow spirals faster and rises as it approaches the center. On their way to the storm center, the winds evaporate more moisture from the ocean surface; this moisture then drives the convection at the core of the spiral. The cycle continues to accelerate until the swirling winds reach gale force (39 m.p.h.), and the tempest becomes a "tropical storm." When the winds reach 74 m.p.h., their circular motion becomes so strong that a calm spot—the eye—forms at the center. The storm is now a hurricane.

A fully grown hurricane is a marvel of natural engineering. In a continuous, mechanical cycle it extracts latent heat energy from the ocean, releases the energy in the towering thunderclouds surrounding the eye, and exhausts the spent air at the top of the storm. The amount of energy involved in a hurricane is almost beyond comprehension, and renders humanity's most awesome efforts—nuclear weapons—feeble by comparison. The heat energy contained in the combined nuclear arsenals of the United States and Russia at the peak of the Cold War would not keep a large hurricane going for one day. Many will recall photographs of the 1946 underwater nuclear explosion in the Pacific, which tested the effects of the blast on captured Japanese warships. That detonation heaved 10 million tons of water into the air. A good-sized hurricane can evaporate that much water from the ocean in 40 seconds.

Such tremendous energy releases give hurricanes their purpose in life. In the global atmospheric ecosystem, the prime function of all storms is to equalize the great heat imbalance that builds up between the equator and the poles. At higher latitudes, it is the familiar mid-latitude cyclone that does the job. In the tropics, hurricanes are particularly efficient at moving heat. They extract latent heat from the oceans, convert it to sensible heat, and lift it to the upper atmosphere, from where the heat is blown poleward.

Most hurricanes wither and die when they encounter cold water. Cold water evaporates less readily than warm water and, without a continuous supply of water vapor, hurricanes soon "run out of steam." Some hurricanes are deprived of their needed vapor supply when they pass over land, but the effect is the same—oblivion. When hurricanes die, however, there is always something left over. Remnants may take the form of a mass of moisture-laden air, a slight residual swirl in the upper atmosphere or both.

HURRICANE ALLEY

Some parts of the tropics are more amenable to hurricanes than others. There are seven regions around the globe—the North and South Indian Oceans, the seas northwest of Australia, the South Pacific, the western and eastern North Pacific Oceans, and the western North Atlantic—where hurricanes and tropical storms can develop. None has ever formed over the cool waters of the tropical South Atlantic or southeastern Pacific. The western North Pacific Ocean is the most active region, with one-third of the globe's average of 79 tropical storms per year. Surprisingly, the second-busiest hurricane alley is the eastern North Pacific, averaging 13 storms per year. Most of these storms form off the west coast of Mexico and move west toward Hawaii (but few ever reach the islands). This reach of the Pacific has few islands and sparsely traveled shipping lanes, so many hurricanes went undetected in the days before weather satellites. It wasn't until the 1960s, with the advent of regular satellite coverage of the world's weather, that the importance of this hurricane alley became fully appreciated.

Mexicans living along the west coast from Acapulco to Guaymas and southern Baja California have long appreciated these storms.

Hurricane Alley— The tracks of ten hurricanes (or tropical storms) that have affected the West are shown on this map. Most are "Cordonazo" type storms that moved up the west coast of Mexico, while a few have stormed up the Rio Grande Valley from the Gulf of Mexico. The remains of one western Pacific typhoon, Freda, crossed the ocean to become the Columbus Day storm in 1962.

RICHARD A. KEEN

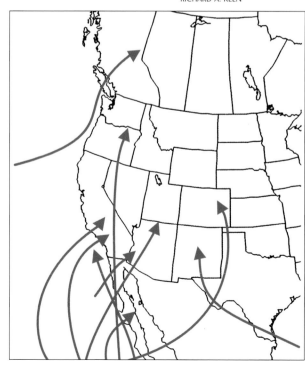

Hurricane Linda—A "conventional" satellite view of Hurricane Linda on September 12, 1997, reveals the boiling tops of thunderstorms swirling around the clear, dark eye. NOAA

Once every few years a hurricane sweeps northwestward along the coast before turning inland, wreaking havoc among fishing fleets and their home villages. Peak season for these coastal storms is September and October, centering around the Feast of Saint Francis on October 4. This has earned the storms the local name *el Cordonazo de San Francisco*—"The Lash of Saint Francis." The southwestern United States has also suffered from el Cordonazo, and indeed most, but not all, of the tropical storms to strike the western states are of Mexican birth. Hurricane remnants from the Gulf of Mexico sometimes reach into the western states, and on one occasion the remains of a western Pacific typhoon inflicted heavy damage to the Pacific Northwest.

From the moment a hurricane is born, its movement is guided by prevailing winds. While still in the tropics (10 to 30 degrees latitude), hurricanes usually move westward with the easterly trade winds. Once north of the 30th parallel, the storms encounter the prevailing westerlies of higher latitudes and tend to turn eastward. The typical path of a well-behaved hurricane is a sweeping arc, at first heading west, then turning north, and finally heading northeast toward the cooler waters of the northern oceans. These guiding winds, called "steering currents," are not always well behaved. Hurricanes have been known to backtrack, loop, and even stand still for days on end. Sometimes the steering currents bring tropical storms into the western states. Take el Cordonazo, for example. Steering currents carry most of the storms northwest to cooler waters. A few turn north and move inland over Mexico. Fewer still move as far north as southern California, where chilly coastal waters quickly sap their vigor. Once in a blue moon, tropical storms race north into the United States before losing their strength, and the normally dry early autumn in southern California or Arizona suddenly turns windy and wet.

No full-force hurricane has directly struck the western states in nearly two centuries. However, twice in this century el Cordonazo storms of near-hurricane intensity damaged cities of the southwestern United States. The first was the tropical storm of September 1939, which stormed straight into Los Angeles with gales and torrential rains, claiming 45 lives. In 1976, Hurricane Kathleen, which had just been downgraded to tropical storm status, lashed Yuma, Arizona, with 76 m.p.h. gusts. Remnants of this remarkable storm were tracked as far north

Toppling Tower—
Photographer Wes Luchau of Western Oregon University caught the 1962 "Columbus Day storm" in the act of toppling the tower on Campbell Hall on the college's campus in Monmouth, Oregon.
WES LUCHAU, WESTERN OREGON UNIVERSITY

as Oregon and Idaho. Every few years the fading remains of a tropical storm drift into the southwestern states, dumping heavy rains onto normally dry deserts and mountains. And nearly every year, the counterclockwise circulation around one or two hurricanes off the West Coast drives moist air into the Southwest, triggering tropical downpours that occasionally develop into floods.

Yuma— The West's "Hurricane Alley"

It may seem ironic that Yuma, Arizona, the driest city in the United States, has probably been affected by tropical storms more often than any town "west of the Pecos." A sizeable portion of Yuma's meager rainfall results from tropical storms passing nearby or from moisture brought in from more-distant storms. Yuma's annual rainfall averages just under 3 inches, and in one year (1956) it was just a tenth of that. It is not surprising that a large portion of the yearly total can arrive in one storm. When that happens, the storm is likely to be a hurricane remnant. Of the past 40 years, five—1963, 1967, 1972, 1977, and 1997—saw more than half the year's total rain fall from a dying hurricane. Hurricane Katherine dropped half of 1963's rain in just over one hour!

The other attendant of tropical storms, gale-force winds, visited Yuma in 1967, 1972, 1976, 1977, and 1997. That's about once every 5 or 10 years, nearly as often as many cities in Florida can expect tropical gales. Why does Yuma experience more tropical storms than coastal cities like Los Angeles or San Diego? It's the water. Although a desert city, Yuma lies just 70 miles north of the tepid waters of the Gulf of California, which can simmer at 90° F in the summer. Tropical storms approaching Yuma can therefore get a last quick fix of water vapor before reaching land. On the other hand, any storm headed for southern California is sapped by chilly coastal water. As a result, Yuma's 43,000 inhabitants not only claim to live in the hottest, driest, and sunniest city in the United States, they also claim to live in the heart of western America's hurricane alley!

... gale-force winds, visited Yuma [Arizona] ... about once every five or ten years, nearly as often as many cities in Florida can expect tropical gales.

LOOKING ELLA IN THE EYE

Many superlatives can be applied to describe the power of a hurricane, but the surest way to appreciate the tempest is to encounter it personally. During World War II, the Navy experimented with flights into hurricanes to pinpoint their positions. The flights began in earnest following the Third Fleet disaster in 1944, and have since become routine. Few experiences impart a person with a greater sense of awe at nature's majestic might than a flight into the eye of a hurricane. In 1978, I had the good fortune to fly on a National Oceanic and Atmospheric Administration (NOAA) flight into Hurricane Ella off Cape Hatteras.

The NOAA *Orion*—a four-engine propjet—took off from Miami as dawn was breaking. An hour after sunrise, the first squalls on the storm's fringe appeared on the horizon. Below, the ocean surface was an undulating pattern of long, rolling swells fleeing from Ella. A freighter wisely fled with the swells.

Minutes later the hurricane-hunting *Orion* began its bumpy journey through these outer fringes of Hurricane Ella. Viewed through the *Orion's* panoramic bubble windows, the squalls appeared as long bands of billowing cumulus clouds, curving in toward the storm's center, now 100 miles away. The many scientific instruments on board the $8 million flying laboratory went into action, recording temperature, humidity, wind, even the size of the droplets in the clouds. Scientists strapped with seat belts in front of consoles pushed buttons and flicked switches; charts and numbers appeared on computer screens.

On radar, the entire hurricane was in clear view. Its spiral pattern could have been a telescopic view of some distant galaxy, except for its closeness and the hole in its center. The *Orion* drove on toward Ella's core, sweeping in and out of the spiral rainbands; 700 feet below, turquoise streamers of underwater foam—churned by the furious winds—stretched to the horizon.

Several severe jolts announced the plane's entry into the ring of 8-mile-high rain clouds surrounding the eye of the storm. Winds of 100 m.p.h.—momentarily gusting to 150 m.p.h.—whipped an almost-solid sheet of foam across the surface of the sea. It seemed as if the waves were being flattened by the very winds that had created them.

Suddenly—within seconds—the jolts ceased. The *Orion* had entered the calm eye of Ella. Below, only a few whitecaps marred the blue waters of the sea. Above, the sun occasionally peeked through thin clouds. As the *Orion* darted in and out of puffy gray clouds, hurricane hunters on board caught occasional glimpses of the eyewall itself—an awesome amphitheater of massed clouds, dimly visible through the mists.

The respite in the 10-mile-wide eye lasted only two minutes. The plane plowed back into the violent winds of the eyewall and for the next half-hour bounced its way back to the relatively calm fringes of Ella. When the *Orion* was safely on its way home to Miami, the old-timers on board began telling their tales of lost wingtips, ruptured gas lines, and disabled navigational equipment.

A Tempest in a Teacup

It's easy to demonstrate how hurricanes work by doing a little experiment right in your kitchen. Make a cup of tea using loose tea or a torn open tea bag. This gives you plenty of tiny leaves on the bottom of the cup. Stir the tea with a spoon in a counterclockwise direction. If you stir it hard enough, a dip forms in the center of the cup. Satellite photos of hurricanes show that the clouds around the eye have the same shape as the tea surface around this dip. Now look at the tea leaves. They are piling up in the middle of the cup, thanks to a current of tea moving toward the center along the bottom, just like the low-level flow into a hurricane. The lighter tea leaves swirl up around the center toward the surface, mimicking the rising air currents near the eye of a hurricane. Near the surface, the tea leaves spiral away from the "eye" and sink back down near the edge of the cup. These currents of tea are virtually identical to the motions of air in a hurricane, with one important difference. Hurricanes keep themselves going by releasing latent heat in their centers. Tea leaves contain no latent heat, so the energy must come from the stirs of the spoon.

Several severe jolts announced the plane's entry into the ring of 8-mile-high rain clouds surrounding the eye of the storm. Suddenly—within seconds—the jolts ceased. The Orion *had entered the calm eye of Ella.*

WESTERN HURRICANES

August 23, 1838—The then-tiny town of El Pueblo de Nuestra Señora la Reina de los Angeles de Porciuncula (now known as Los Angeles) was devastated by a hurricane that brought winds which, by some accounts, exceeded 100 m.p.h. It is the only time in recorded history that a full-fledged hurricane has struck the West coast of the United States.

September 25, 1939—A long-lived Cordonazo that formed south of El Salvador on September 14 came ashore over Los Angeles. Gales exceeding 50 m.p.h. damaged boats, buildings, and power lines along the coast to the tune of $1.5 million. Forty-five lives were lost. Torrential rains—5.42 inches in Los Angeles and 13 inches on Mount Wilson—ruined half a million dollars worth of crops. This was the third—and strongest—Cordonazo to ruffle southern California in 18 years.

September 1, 1942—The remains of a powerful Gulf of Mexico hurricane crossed Texas and stalled over eastern New Mexico. Rains in excess of 6 inches flooded the Pecos River near Roswell.

October 12, 1962—The "Columbus Day storm," with hurricane-force winds and heavy rains, ripped Washington, Oregon, and British Columbia at a cost of 56 lives and $250 million in damages. Wind gusts of 170 m.p.h. were reported along the Oregon Coast. The storm originated as Typhoon Freda, born nine days earlier near Wake Island in the western Pacific. Freda merged with a cold front over the North Pacific to become an intense mid-latitude cyclone, which raced eastward into the Pacific Northwest.

September 4–6, 1970—Although Tropical Storm Norma remained hundreds of miles to the south, her circulation pumped enough moist air over the Southwest to trigger the deadliest flooding in Arizona's history. Flash flooding in canyons and streams across Arizona and neighboring sections of Utah, Colorado, and New Mexico drowned 25 people and washed out numerous roads and bridges. Thunderstorms also brought small tornadoes to Scottsdale, Arizona, and Cortez, Colorado.

September 29, 1971—The remnants of Hurricane Olivia brought generally welcome rains to Arizona and New Mexico. Olivia originated as Hurricane Irene, born 800 miles east of Barbados in the Atlantic, and was renamed when the storm crossed Central America and entered the Pacific. This long-lived storm endured 19 days.

WESTERN HURRICANES, CONTINUED

September 10, 1976—Hurricane Kathleen, weakening but still strong, came ashore south of Ensenada, Mexico, and raced north over Calexico and Death Valley, California, and into western Nevada. Up to 10 inches of rain flooded the deserts of southern California, unleashing a 15-foot wall of water that roared into the small town of Ocotillo, killing six people. Hurricane-force (76 m.p.h.) gusts inflicted $2 million in damages to Yuma. The next day, rains and gusty winds moved as far north as Oregon, Montana, and Idaho, flooding basements in Boise. Before it was all over, this remarkable storm had dumped heavy rains in every state in the West.

August 14–17, 1977—While tracking northward along the Baja California coast, Hurricane Doreen brought flash floods to Imperial Valley, California, and southeastern Arizona. Several irrigation canals were breached, inundating crops and the town of Niland, California. In Yuma, Arizona, 3-inch rainfall was accompanied by 56-m.p.h. winds. Los Angeles, where August is normally rainless, received 2.47 inches from the storm.

September 6, 1978—Ex–Hurricane Norman dissipated near San Clemente Island, off the southern California coast, after causing local flooding in the deserts. This marked the third year in a row that this area sustained flooding.

August 14, 1980—One of the most intense Atlantic storms in history, Hurricane Allen, came ashore in Texas and moved up the Rio Grande Valley toward New Mexico. Five inches of rain flooded streets and homes in the northeast section of Albuquerque. Allen originated as a disturbance off the west coast of Africa and tracked 5,000 miles to dump its rain on Albuquerque. At one point its winds reached 190 m.p.h.

September 26, 1982—Remains of Hurricane Olivia came ashore near Santa Barbara, California. Heavy rain soaked half of California's raisin crop, and agricultural losses totaled more than $300 million. Moisture streamed into Utah, flooding parts of Salt Lake City.

September 30–October 3, 1983—Although its center remained well to the south, Tropical Storm Octave pumped moist air into the Southwest, triggering Arizona's most destructive flood in history. Thirteen people died in the deluge. The same moist air mass bred two tornadoes that struck the Los Angeles area, but damage was comparatively minor.

WESTERN HURRICANES, CONTINUED

September 10, 1984—Moisture from Hurricane Marie, 300 miles south of Los Angeles, triggered street flooding in Las Vegas and Phoenix. Five people drowned when their pickup truck was washed away.

October 1–4, 1984—Remains of Hurricane Polo came ashore north of Mazatlán, Mexico, and tracked northward across New Mexico into Colorado. Heavy rains caused minor flooding along the east slopes of the Rockies. A foot of snow fell at Summit Lake at the base of Mount Evans, west of Denver.

September 12, 1997—Hurricane Linda became the most powerful eastern Pacific hurricane ever when its winds grew to 185 m.p.h. (with gusts estimated to 220 m.p.h.!). At the time, Linda was about 300 miles south of the southern tip of Baja California. Some early forecasts had Linda tracking across the El Niño–warmed ocean into Los Angeles, possibly as a full hurricane, but fortunately, she stayed far out at sea.

September 25, 1997—Hurricane Nora, now a tropical storm as it entered Arizona, deluged the summit of Harquahala Mountain, with 11.97 inches of rain in 24 hours, a state record.

WHIRLWINDS, WILLIWAWS, AND WASHOE ZEPHYRS

This was all we saw that day, for it was two o'clock, now, and according to custom the daily "Washoe Zephyr" set in; a soaring dustdrift about the size of the United States set up edgewise came with it, and the capital of the Nevada Territory disappeared from view. Still, there were sights to be seen which were not wholly uninteresting to new comers; for the vast dust cloud was thickly freckled with things strange to the upper air—things living and dead, that flitted hither and thither, going and coming, appearing and disappearing among the rolling billows of dust-hats, chickens and parasols sailing the remote heavens; blankets, tin signs, sage-brush and shingles a shade lower; door-mats and buffalo robes lower still; shovels and coal scuttles on the next grade; glass doors, cats, and little children on the next; disrupted lumber yards, light buggies and wheelbarrows on the next, and down only thirty or forty feet above the ground was a scurrying storm of emigrating roofs and vacant lots.

—Mark Twain, *Roughing It*

Mark Twain first encountered the fantastic variety of western climates during a stagecoach trip from Missouri to Nevada in 1862. In the above passage from *Roughing It,* he recounts the approach of a "Washoe Zephyr" during his first day in Carson City, Nevada. Along with chinooks, lee waves, williwaws, Santa Ana winds, sea breezes, valley winds, and those little whirlwinds called dust devils, Washoe Zephyrs are one of the multitude of local winds that color western weather. In a sense, there are as many local winds as

Lenticular Cloud—So named because of its smooth, lens-shaped appearance (although this one looks more like a sausage), this lenticular cloud marks a ripple in the air flow over the Continental Divide in Colorado. RICHARD A. KEEN

there are hills and valleys, plus a few more. Many of these winds have a lot in common, though, and fortunately there is no need to describe each one individually. Instead, we'll look at the main types of local winds that occur and point out some of their local characters.

CHINOOKS

Mountain Waves—Like ripples in a creek, waves form downstream from mountain ranges. NATIONAL WEATHER SERVICE

Once you get away from the coast, there's hardly a place in the West that doesn't get a chinook once in a while. The name comes from the Chinook Indians of coastal Oregon, who called the warming southwest winds off the ocean "snow-eater." Now the name is usually given to warm westerly winds that eat the snow in the valleys of the Sierras, Cascades, and Rockies.

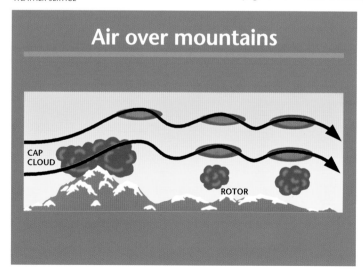

Snow-eaters can be a welcome treat in the winter. Chinooks can lift temperatures 20 to 80 degrees in a few hours and melt half a foot of snow in an afternoon. A chinook at Kipp, Montana, reportedly ate 30 inches of snow in half a day. But chinooks can also tear roofs from houses and blow trains from their tracks. They are truly mixed blessings. Whether you like them or not, however, they are as much a part of the West as cowboys and rattlesnakes.

Most of the West's mountain ranges run roughly north to south, while, most of the time, winds blow from west to east. This is why chinooks are so common. When a west wind meets a long range of mountains blocking its flow, it has no choice but to go up and over. When conditions are right, which they often are, the air continues to go up and down after it has passed the mountain ridge. The best way to visualize this is to watch what happens in a shallow stream when the water runs over a rock. The water goes up and over, and downstream there is a series of ripples. Air does the same thing. As far as the laws of physics are concerned, air is a fluid, just like water. Air may be lighter, and water wetter, but they're both still fluids.

These ripples of air are known as "mountain waves" or, by virtue of their position downstream from mountains, as "lee waves." Similar to the creek waves, they stand still while the air flows through them. And, like the creek, the air flows fastest at the bottom—or trough—of the waves, especially in the first trough. These features are very important for the kind of weather these waves can bring.

Chinook Winds—Power line poles in Boulder, Colorado, were toppled like falling dominoes by the chinook windstorm of January 17, 1982.
JOSE MEITIN

Mountain waves are a lot larger than anything in a creek. Ripples can be 10 miles apart, and the air going through them may rise and fall a mile or more. Mountain waves can also extend upward through the atmosphere—they have been measured as high as 15 miles above the ground, where the air is only 5 percent as dense as at sea level. Glider pilots love them because they often provide a reliable, stationary, and strong upward current of air—great for hitching a soaring ride! Many gliding records for altitude and duration came from pilots successfully "catching a wave," and their exploits have contributed greatly to our knowledge about mountain waves.

If chinook means "snow-eater," what makes these winds so warm? One common explanation is that air cools as it goes up one side of the mountain, and its water vapor condenses, releasing latent heat into the air. Since the air has gained a certain amount of latent heat, it's warmer when it comes back down the other side of the mountain. If air blowing off the Pacific Ocean has a lot of moisture, it can warm as much as 10 degrees as it crosses the Sierras and Cascades. Over most of the West the air is simply too dry, and the release of latent heat warms the air only a degree or so. Usually, though, there is enough moisture for "cap clouds" or "crest clouds" to form right on the mountain ridge.

Lenticular Clouds—The streamlined features of these lenticular clouds over Mount Evans, Colorado, are strongly suggestive of the strength of the winds (blowing right to left) that created the clouds.
RICHARD A. KEEN

The main reason chinooks are warm is very simple—their air comes from a relatively warm place! The westerly winds that bring chinooks also bring mild air off the Pacific Ocean. The air further warms by compression as it blows downhill in a mountain wave. Inland, the winter air masses are usually a bit colder than this temperate Pacific air—and sometimes much, much colder. Some spectacular temperature rises have happened when chinook winds replaced arctic air masses. In the next chapter you'll see exactly how rapidly a chinook can warm things up.

There's no law that says chinooks *must* be warm. If the westerlies drive a cold air mass into the West, the chinooks are cold. When the new air is colder than the air mass that's being blown away, the wind is properly called a *bora*, originally a Yugoslavian word for the cold winds that pour through their mountains. Usually, however, chinook winds are warm.

The welcome warming a chinook brings can exact a high price at times. Remember that the air flow through a mountain wave is fastest at the bottom of the first trough east of the mountains. These "downslope winds" often exceed 100 m.p.h. Since the mountains don't move, the troughs don't either, and their powerful winds ventilate the same place year after year. The highest winds nearly always occur in a narrow band within 10 or 20 miles of the foothills.

The Ute Indians of Colorado knew this and would not set their tepees at certain places just east of the Rockies. White pioneers didn't know this, or ignored it if they did, and in 1859 settled at the mouth of Colorado's Boulder Canyon. Every few years since then, the town (now city) of Boulder has been raked by chinook winds strong enough to raise roofs and down power lines. A windstorm in 1969 did $1 million in damages, and just three years later another tripled the damage toll. A 1982 chinook cost the insurance industry $17 million.

The same story can be told in Livingston, Montana; Sheridan, Wyoming; Calgary, Alberta; Bishop, California; and Carson City, Nevada—home of the

Washoe Zephyr. Salt Lake City can be whisked by chinook winds, even though its nearby mountain range, the Wasatch, is to the *east*. This happens when a strong low-pressure system moves south of Utah, with high pressure to the north. The winds then come from the east, and the mountain wave develops west of the Wasatch—right over Salt Lake City. Although rare, these easterly chinooks have been every bit as strong as their more common westerly cousins.

Easterly chinook winds are more common along the Pacific Coast of Alaska, particularly in Anchorage and Juneau, both of which have ice-covered mountains to their east. As with the Salt Lake City chinooks, these Alaskan winds howl when there is a strong Low over the Gulf of Alaska, a frequent occurrence in the winter. But when the air originates from the interior of Alaska and the Yukon, the winds are not particularly warm. Although these cold winds are more like a Yugoslavian "Bora" wind than a snow-eating chinook, they have their own names—"Williwaw" in Anchorage and "Taku wind" in Juneau.

Besides melting snow and wrecking cities, chinooks also make for the most spectacular sunsets on earth. As the air streaming through a mountain wave rises from trough to crest, its moisture condenses into little clouds that sit atop the waves. Because of their smooth, rounded, lens-shaped appearance, these clouds have earned the name "lenticular clouds," although others prefer to call them "grindstone" clouds. These weird clouds will stand still for

Banner Cloud—High winds produce a banner cloud that forms in the lee of Mount Rainier, Washington.
RICHARD A. KEEN

Up in Smoke—Santa Ana winds emanating from a high over Idaho fan the flames of widespread wildfires over southern California and sweep the smoke hundreds of miles out to sea. Santa Catalina and other offshore islands are dimly visible through the smoke, while the cities of Los Angeles and San Diego are almost completely obscured. In addition to the smoke and the landscape, heat sensors aboard NASA's Terra satellite also show areas where the fires are burning. NASA

hours, even though the wind is ripping through them at 100 m.p.h. or more. Look at one with binoculars; tiny shreds of cloud form on the upwind edge, blow through the lenticular, and dissolve on the downwind edge.

The brilliant sunsets come just before the sun dips behind the mountains to the west. The descending air flow between the mountains to the first wave trough leaves a wide clear slot, allowing the sun to illuminate the wall of lenticular clouds that rises to the east. Many a winter day comes to a crimson close in chinook country.

SANTA ANA WINDS

Another wind that charges a high price for the good it does is the Santa Ana wind of southern California. These hot, blustery gales are very similar to chinooks, but since they whip through the palms of Los Angeles, they never get a chance to eat much snow. The meteorological setting calls for high pressure to settle over the Great Basin, with lower pressure to the south. With the help of upper-level winds out of the north, the winds stream up and over the San Gabriel, San Bernardino, and Santa Ana Mountains, and descend into the vast basin occupied by Los Angeles and environs.

These northerly or northeasterly winds can blow any time of year, but they prefer late fall and winter. Like chinooks, they have unroofed homes and downed trees and power lines. Their good side is that they blow the smog far out to sea.

By the time the winds reach Los Angeles, they have dropped several thousand feet from the Great Basin. Thanks to compressional heating, the temperature goes up and the humidity goes down, which, combined with the gusty winds, makes for serious fire danger. Nearly every year, especially in the fall when foliage is dry, fires break out during spells of Santa Ana winds. At times these fires have turned into major disasters, consuming hundreds of homes and thousands of acres of forest.

Other places along the coast can also get these desiccating gales, although not nearly as often as Los Angeles. This is probably because Los Angeles gets struck when the wind is from the north, while most of the coast needs a rarer east wind. But San Francisco and San Diego have seen their own versions of the Santa Ana, and sometimes with the same results—fire! Probably the most devastating was the weak, but still dry, easterly wind that swept fire across San Francisco on April 18, 1906—the day of the great earthquake.

Guadaloupe Eddy—Lee eddies form in the clouds downwind from Guadaloupe Island, in the Pacific Ocean 300 miles south of San Diego. These eddies are similar to the Catalina Eddy that develops off southern California, but are much more photogenic because of the isolation of the island. NASA/GODDARD SPACE FLIGHT CENTER

LEE EDDIES

No, these aren't the names of a couple of good ol' boys. These are eddies, or swirls, of air that form in the lee of mountains. They're not mountain waves or even lee waves. Picture a stream again, this time with a bigger rock or shallower water, so water flows *around* the rock, not over

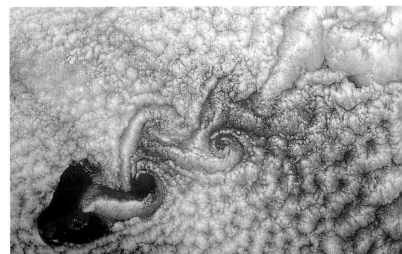

Changing Wind—A light wind blowing around a house-sized rock generates a very small lee eddy whose presence is revealed by two anemometers pointing in different directions. RICHARD A. KEEN

it. See how the water whirls around the backside of the rock? That's a lee eddy. Kayakers know these well and take great pains to avoid the greater pain of getting caught in one.

Lee eddies come in many sizes. The largest are the cyclones that redevelop east of the Rockies, described in chapter 2, "Fronts, Jets, and Cyclones." Next down in size are the county-sized swirls that develop downstream from county-sized mountain ranges. Meteorologists at the University of Washington have discovered that little cyclones, 20 miles or so across, develop east of the Olympic Mountains when the wind is from the west or southwest. These little cyclones are no laughing matter—one of them took down the Hood Canal Bridge.

Researchers at the NOAA labs in Boulder, Colorado, have found that a similar but weaker cyclone often develops north and east of Denver. This "Denver cyclone" happens when southerly winds curl around a low ridge south of town. Its cyclonic winds are only about 10 m.p.h., but the rotational motion encourages the growth of thunderstorms. The developing thunderstorms then start spinning themselves, and many of these storms spawn small tornadoes. In spring and summer, the Denver cyclone is Colorado's favorite breeding grounds for tornadoes, and helps make the counties to the north and east of Denver the most tornado-prone area in the West (as measured by the number of tornadoes per square mile). A similar phenomenon has been noted east of Flagstaff, Arizona, where the Mogollon Rim spins off eddies that contribute to a relatively high number of tornadoes in the Painted Desert region.

Another weak cyclone sometimes spins off southern California, as northwest winds pass Point Conception and turn toward land. The center of the counterclockwise swirl is often near Santa Catalina Island, giving it the name "Catalina Eddy." Winds around this eddy don't blow any trees down, but they do tend to push the smog inland.

The smaller a mountain, the smaller the eddies. Hills may kick off eddies just a few feet across. These little swirls are commonplace on windy days in the mountains, picking snow off the ground and spinning it around for a few seconds. Usually, these "snow devils" aren't very strong; however, the eddies get their energy from the wind that creates them, and if these winds are hurricane-force, the eddies may be even stronger. Chinook windstorms have spawned swirls powerful enough to lift sheds and small planes off the ground.

Eddies big and small doubtlessly form downwind from every mountain and hillock in the West. Only the lucky few that pass through a populated area or over a wind gauge ever get to tell their story. Keep your eyes and ears open as you watch the weather—these swirling winds are everywhere.

DUST DEVILS

They dance and twirl across dry valley floors, frightening jackrabbits and spinning dust around and around. Sometimes they look like tornadoes, but in some ways they're more like midget hurricanes. This is why dust devils are so fascinating to watch. Where else can you see a miniature storm system, compressed so small that you can run right through it?

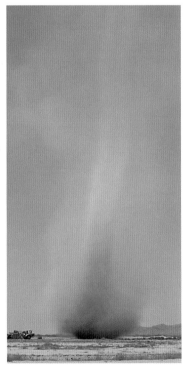

Arizona Dust Devil—A giant dust devil in the Gila Desert near Phoenix, Arizona. The land grader in the foreground gives some idea of the scale. Clouds of dust are swirling around a tubular-looking core, where the winds are strongest. The air is nearly calm at the center of the tube. SHERWOOD B. IDSO

Nature's Merry-Go-Round—The photographer's children cavort near a snake-like dust devil, inadvertently giving a sense of scale to the whirlwind. SHERWOOD B. IDSO

Oregon Dust Devil—A delicate dust devil picks up dust from a roadside field in Oregon's Willamette Valley. The core of this whirlwind is only a few feet across, but the corkscrew pattern of upward swirling dust is clearly visible. DAVID O. BLANCHARD

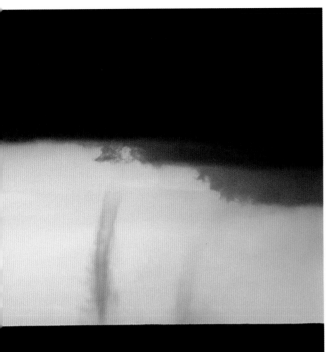

Gustnadoes—A pair of "Gust Front Tornadoes," or "gustnadoes" for short, sweep the high plains of Colorado. These short-lived and generally weak funnels are not considered true tornadoes by most meteorologists and are not included in tornado statistics. DAVID O. BLANCHARD

A flat bit of ground and a sunny, calm day are the main ingredients to make a dust devil. The stage is set a few hours before noon, particularly during the late spring or early summer, when the sun beats mercilessly from a cloudless sky onto the parched earth.

Air warms up during the day because of the heat it gets from the sunlit ground. So it's not surprising that the ground heats up earlier and eventually gets hotter than the air above it. It also helps to have dry ground, so solar energy is not wasted through evaporating moisture. At noon, when solar heating is at its greatest, the ground may get as much as 80 degrees hotter than the air. In 1972, a ground temperature of 201° F was measured in Death Valley, while the air was a brisk 128° F. One should always wear shoes in Death Valley.

Right next to the ground—1 or 2 inches above the surface—the air can get nearly as hot as the ground. Farther up, the air gets less hot, and so on. So, there is a thin layer of extremely hot air near the ground and cooler air aloft. At some point, a bubble of this hot air rises up into the cooler layer. More hot surface air rushes in to take the place of that pioneering hot bubble, and an upwardly mobile stream of hot air develops. These currents can go up thousands of feet, where glider pilots (once again) know them as "thermals." Thermals are also the favorite haunts of hawks and other birds looking for a lift.

Some thermals go straight up, while others—for a variety of reasons—start to spin. Thermals are much too small to be twisted by the same Coriolis effect that instigates the spinning action of larger cyclones; more likely, rising currents pick up small eddies downwind of small bumps in the ground (little lee eddies). It has even been suggested that coyotes and rabbits start the small swirls that grow into dust devils. In any event, as more hot air gets sucked into the base of the thermal, the spinning grows faster. Mix in some dust, leaves, or any other debris, so you can see the swirling column of air, and a dust devil is born!

A typical western dust devil may be 20 feet across and 100 feet tall, but in extreme desert areas, such as Death Valley and the Gila Desert near Phoenix, the dust column may rise half a mile high. Most dust devils last a few minutes at most, but the giant ones can live much longer. Some 2,000 footers have been followed for up to seven hours as they wandered 40 or so miles across Utah's Bonneville Salt Flats. These occasional giants are probably about as large as dust devils ever get—on Earth. The deserts of the West pale in comparison to the eternally rainless plains of Mars, where orbiting spacecraft have spotted monster dust whirls half a mile wide and three miles high.

The funnel of dust may look like a tornado, but its winds are rarely destructive. Tornado winds have been measured at over 200 m.p.h., while typical dust devils spin at one-tenth that speed. Winds have reached as high as 90 m.p.h. in some desert giants, but that's about tops for a dust devil. Upward wind speed is likewise smaller. While tornadoes have been known to lift cows and cars off the ground, dust devils prefer smaller game, such as tumbleweeds and kangaroo rats. Yes, kangaroo rats have flown in dust devils. To keep such critters airborne requires a minimum vertical wind of 30 m.p.h.

At the same time dust and kangaroo rats may be swirling around the edge of the dust funnel, it's quite calm inside. In the calm center, air may actually be sinking slowly back to the ground—a feature strongly reminiscent of the "eye" of a hurricane! Another resemblance between the humble dust devil and the greatest storm on earth is the spiral of warm air into the center, where it rises and streams out the top of the whirlwind. Of course, there are differences. Dust devils are dry, while hurricanes thrive on moisture. Then, there's the obvious fact that billions of large dust devils can fit inside a small hurricane.

While tornadoes have been known to lift cows and cars off the ground, dust devils prefer smaller game, such as tumbleweeds and kangaroo rats.

Another class of dust devils can get a bit more serious than the little whirligigs that dot desert valleys on summer afternoons. These whirlwinds are often triggered by gust fronts from thundershowers. Acting much like a cold front, a gust front runs into hot air and gives it an upward shove. The resulting whirlwind—do we really want to call them dust devils?—can grow 1,000 or more feet high, and pack the wallop of a minor tornado. However, they lack the funnel-shaped cloud that tornadoes are famous for. More of a cross between tornadoes and dust devils than anything else, these hybrid creatures have been called "eddy tornadoes" and "gustnadoes." Souped-up dust devils have been spotted by weather watchers across Colorado's High Plains, the Arizona desert, and no doubt many other spots in the West. Just remember to be careful with "dust devils" if there's a thunderstorm nearby, because that "dust devil" might turn out to be something a bit more dangerous!

Now we turn to some local winds, which, while they lack the drama of chinooks and dust devils, can still strongly affect the weather of the West.

SEA BREEZES

The most remarkable phenomenon of the weather there is the summer coast wind and its attendant mists. This seems to be due solely to the proximity of the districts of great heat and sudden rarefaction on the land, to the cold mass of waters off this coast, and its refrigerated surface atmosphere. A maximum day temperature of 110 degrees is often experienced at Fort Miller, a point in the San Joaquin Valley, when at the same time off Monterey and San Francisco the sea and sea wind are at 55 degrees. Such extreme contrasts existing at sea level and not far apart must be expected to originate violent winds, and it is only wonderful that they are not more severe at the passes giving access to the interior.

—Lorin Blodget,
Climatology of the United States, 1857

Lorin Blodget was well aware of the incredible contrast of temperature between California's coast and its Central Valley when he wrote *Climatology of the United States* in the mid-19th century. Nowhere else in the United States, and possibly the world, do such extreme differences occur with such regularity. Blodget correctly supposed that this contrast would drive a wind inland from the sea—a "sea breeze."

The persistent heat of the Central Valley virtually assures that sea breezes will cool the City by the Bay from May through August, when most parts of the country are suffering their hottest weather.

Sea breezes blow Blodget's "refrigerated" coastal air inland to replace the hot air that rises over the interior—by now a familiar cycle to readers. This refrigerated air layer is rarely more than a few thousand feet deep and has a hard time getting past the 2,000- to 4,000-foot-high coastal ranges. There's only one place where the chilly air can pour relatively unimpeded into the Central Valley—the Golden Gate. This gives San Francisco its famous natural air conditioning in the summer.

The cooling effect fades rapidly as the oceanic air streams inland and spreads northward and southward into California's Central Valley. On a typical July afternoon, downtown San Francisco averages only 64° F, but by the time the cool air reaches the city's airport—only 7 miles inland—it has warmed to 72° F. Twenty-five miles inland, Walnut Creek averages 87° F, and when Tracy, 50 miles from shore at the edge of the Central Valley, gets the sea breeze, it has warmed to a tepid 95° F. Deep into the valley, beyond the reach of the cooling breeze, Red Bluff and Fresno average a full 100° F on a July afternoon.

The persistent heat of the Central Valley virtually assures that sea breezes will cool the City by the Bay from May through August, when most parts of the country are suffering their hottest weather. By September, the heat of the Central Valley begins to moderate, and the sea breeze abates. Easterly winds from the land break through to the coast, and seaside towns even experience occasional heat waves. As most locations are feeling the first hints of autumn, September and October usually bring San Francisco its warmest weather of the year!

Sea breezes on a smaller scale also ventilate the Los Angeles basin. Milder water leads to a weaker cooling effect, but it's still enough to chill a July afternoon on the pier at Santa Monica to 75° F, while 15 miles inland, Canoga Park averages 95° F. Wind from the sea also clears smog from the coastal points, but, unlike the Santa Ana, wafts it back up the valley to places like San Bernardino, Riverside, and Cucamonga. As a result, these communities at the eastern end of the Los Angeles basin frequently suffer the worst smog in the area.

The opposite of a sea breeze is a land breeze. At night, when the land may get colder than the ocean, the winds blow out to sea. One effect of this change is to bring more bugs to the beach at night—yet another reason the crowds leave when the sun goes down!

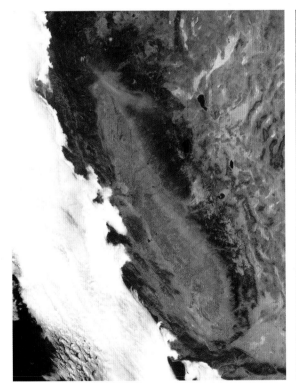 

California in the Summer—Cool, foggy air that persists all summer along the California coast seeps inland through the Golden Gate, but evaporated quickly in the 100-degree heat of the Central Valley. NASA/GODDARD SPACE FLIGHT CENTER

California in the Winter—Winter brings a flip-flop in the weather pattern, with the fog now occupying the Central Valley. Cool air settling into the valley creates an inversion that keeps the fog around for weeks on end, while offshore winds keep the coast clear. NASA/GODDARD SPACE FLIGHT CENTER

MOUNTAIN AND VALLEY WINDS

Those who live far from the ocean can take heart—they too have their version of the sea breeze. These winds are driven by the uneven heating and cooling of mountain slopes and valley floors, and so we call them "mountain and valley winds." Because these winds are as varied as the shapes of the terrain that cause them, let it suffice here to point out a few generic features.

Mountain and valley winds rely on the way air close to the ground heats up faster by day and cools off faster at night than air farther off the ground—similar to dust devils. During the day, warm, light air near the ground drifts up hills and the sides of valleys, to be replaced by cooler air that sinks down the center of the valley. The warm air currents rising above the hills can lead to clouds and, sometimes, thunderstorms.

Los Angeles's famous smog is kept in by the shallow layer of cool air that drifts in from the sea.

At night the opposite happens. Layers of cool air that form on hillsides slide into the valleys, creating air currents commonly called "drainage winds." If the hill is steep enough, drainage winds may start right after sunset, but on gently sloping terrain the cold air may have to build up for several hours before it starts moving. Being heavier, the cold air eventually finds itself in the lowest place around, which is the valley floor. This is why night temperatures are almost always colder in valleys than on mountain tops.

If you live in a valley or near a mountain, take note of how the wind direction changes from day to night. No matter where you live, the surest way to appreciate these fickle little winds is to camp in the mountains. When that first cool breeze slides down the valley during your evening meal, you'll know it.

KATABATIC WINDS

No, these winds are not caused by cats or bats. They are caused by cold air near the ground sliding downhill, much like the "drainage winds" described above. The word "katabatic" means "downward" in Greek and often refers to downslope winds that form over glaciers and ice sheets (upslope winds would be called "anabatic," but for some reason, that name has never caught on). The world's largest and strongest katabatic winds are found along the edges of the Antarctic plateau, where they drive incessant ground blizzards. Greenland's katabatic winds aren't too shabby, either. In the West they occur intermittently over most of the mountain glaciers, and more persistently over the larger glaciers and ice fields of Alaska and British Columbia.

I've spent several summers measuring katabatic winds on the 100-mile-long Juneau Ice Field in Alaska, and found this normally invisible stream of glacier-chilled air to be blowing nearly constantly, day and night, day in and day out, from the highest parts of the ice field down the glaciers to the sea. Katabatic winds occur in a shallow layer, typically 50 or 100 feet deep. They blow no matter what the weather is doing a few hundred feet higher up. This gives the surface of the glacier a completely different climate than that of the hills and valley sides a mile away and 100 to 200 feet up. On a glacier, reflected sunlight from all directions can make even a cool day feel like summer in the Sahara, and it's actually quite refreshing to ski from calm, sunny, 70-degree conditions at the edge of the glacier into the breezy (but still sunny) 40-degree katabatic airstream!

Katabatic Wind—A shallow layer of glacially chilled air flows from right to left, down the gently sloping, 4-mile-wide Taku Glacier on the Juneau Ice Field in Alaska.
RICHARD A. KEEN

INVERSIONS

The end result of nighttime valley breezes (and katabatic winds, if there's a glacier nearby) is often a valley full of cold air. If the breezes are doing their job, the coldest air is right at the bottom. This is an inversion, from the Latin word roughly meaning "upside down." Since air cools as it rises, in most situations the atmosphere is colder aloft than it is near the ground. With inversions, however, the atmosphere gets warmer with altitude.

This inverted atmosphere has one particularly nasty feature: If you give the cold heavy air near the ground an upward kick, it will come right back down. It's not easy to get cold air out of a valley. Whatever we put into the air—exhaust, smoke, dust, and the like—stays right there with us. Virtually all episodes of heavy pollution come from the concentration of pollutants in a thin, inverted layer of air near the ground.

Inversions don't just happen in valleys at night. Los Angeles's famous smog is kept in by the shallow layer of cool air that drifts in from the sea. In places like Denver and Salt Lake City the cold layer can be the remnants of an arctic cold wave, while up north where arctic cold waves originate, the inversion that pervades Fairbanks, Alaska, persists for most of the winter. North or south, inversions remain until either the sun heats the cold layer into oblivion or a strong wind blows the mess away.

SOME BIG LOCAL WINDS

May 29, 1902—An intense dust devil, perhaps one of the tornado–dust devil hybrids, destroyed a livery stable in Phoenix. The next day another whirlwind unroofed a store.

April 21–23, 1931—Dry easterly winds downed trees on the western slopes of the Cascades, in a Pacific Northwest version of the Santa Ana. Chinook winds from the same storm system blew 11 freight cars off their tracks in Utah.

September 8, 1943—An inversion led to the first widespread smog in the Los Angeles basin.

October 30, 1959—A Wasatch chinook, with gusts exceeding 100 m.p.h., caused millions of dollars' damage in Utah.

November 5–6, 1961—Extremely dry Santa Ana winds following a record hot summer fanned brush and forest fires across the Bel Air section of Los Angeles.

January 25, 1962—A Montana Air National Guard C-47 airplane crashed near Wolf Creek, killing six, including the state's governor, Donald Nutter. Severe mountain wave turbulence had torn one wing off the plane.

April 3, 1964—Easterly chinook winds along the Wasatch Mountains blew trucks over between Salt Lake City and Ogden, Utah; turbulent winds aloft flipped over a crop duster. Fortunately, the pilot regained control of his plane.

March 12, 1968—A Washoe Zephyr swept the eastern slopes of the Sierra Nevada, damaging buildings and trees in Reno, Nevada.

January 7, 1969—Chinook winds gusting to 130 m.p.h. in Boulder, Colorado, sent roofs and parked airplanes into flight, and damaged half of the city's houses. Inside one of these houses, I measured a 70-m.p.h. gust after the windows were blown out.

September 22–29, 1971—Hot, dry Santa Ana winds led to widespread fires from southern California to the Oakland–Berkeley area. More than 500 homes and half a million acres were consumed.

March 6, 1972—Powerful chinook winds, gusting from 90 to 100 m.p.h., blasted Lander and Cheyenne, Wyoming, and Livingston, Montana, with $1 million in damages to roofs, airplanes, and other targets.

November 12, 1973—Strong winds, intensified and localized by mountain waves, toppled 10,000 trees in a narrow, 15-mile swath east of the Grand Teton Range in northwest Wyoming.

SOME BIG LOCAL WINDS, CONTINUED

January 8, 1975—"Taku" winds from the northeast pounded the Alaskan capital, Juneau. Fortunately, the most extreme winds (estimated to have exceeded 200 m.p.h.) hit a sparsely settled ridge south of town, knocking down some power lines. Taku winds reaching 180 m.p.h. raked the same ridge a few months earlier in March 1974.

July 4, 1978—Out of a clear blue sky, a potent dust devil tore the roof off a mobile home in Salida, Colorado, sending rafters flying 200 feet into the air.

February 13, 1979—Southwesterly winds from an offshore storm spawned a lee eddy east of the Olympic Mountains. The localized 100-m.p.h. winds sank the Hood Canal Pontoon Bridge.

December 4, 1979—From Montana to Colorado, chinook winds as high as 119 m.p.h. rolled over airplanes and mobile homes. Twenty-three freight cars were blown off the tracks near Cheyenne.

April 1, 1980—Wild Williwaw winds walloped the east side of Anchorage, Alaska, as winds that may have exceeded 130 m.p.h. descended from the Chugach Mountains. Most of the buildings in the area suffered roof damage, some homes lost their upper floors, and many mobile homes were destroyed. The total damage was $25 million. It was the third notable windstorm to hit Anchorage that winter, with only slightly weaker chinook-type winds occurring earlier, on January 18 and November 15, 1979.

January 17, 1982—Powerful chinook winds, measured as high as 140 m.p.h., raked the eastern foothills of the Colorado Rockies. In Boulder, utility poles were snapped in half, and damage totaled $17 million. The high winds raised Boulder's temperature from 2° F to 50° F in just one hour. A week later, another windstorm generated tornado-force eddies, one of which popped the windows out of 100 cars parked at a shopping center.

October 9, 1982—Santa Ana winds measuring 60 m.p.h. fanned flames that destroyed almost 100 homes near Los Angeles. One fire burned a 15-mile path across the Santa Monica Mountains to the sea.

April 4–5, 1983—Two days of chinook winds raked the western slopes of Utah's Wasatch Mountains, blowing down high-tension power lines, overturning mobile homes, and rolling trucks off Interstate 15. Damage totaled $8 million.

SOME BIG LOCAL WINDS, CONTINUED

December 24, 1983—Cold "bora" winds as strong as 100 m.p.h. descended the western slopes of the Cascades, flattening several homes near Enumclaw, Washington, while easterly gales funneling through the Columbia Gorge downed trees and power lines. Total damage reached $27 million.

February 25, 1986—Chinook wind gusts reached 103 m.p.h. in Lethbridge, Alberta's "windy city."

February 26, 1988—Chinook winds lifted the temperature at Calgary, Alberta, to 65° F. The pleasant temperatures were an unwelcome visitor to the 1988 Winter Olympics in Calgary!

May 14, 1991—The anemometer at the Albuquerque, New Mexico, airport logged a 70-m.p.h. gust as a dust devil passed directly over the weather station.

Winter 1997–1998—Winter temperatures measured by Rick Thoman, a National Weather Service forecaster living in hills above Fairbanks, Alaska, averaged 16 degrees warmer than those recorded by a colleague living 1,000 feet lower in the Goldstream Creek Valley. Thoman estimated that his home heating costs were 20 percent less that those of the valley dweller, an example of the subtle but sizeable economic costs of an inversion.

September 14, 2000—A hurricane-force (75-m.p.h. winds) dust devil plowed through the Coconino County Fairgrounds in Flagstaff, Arizona, flattening tents and damaging permanent structures. The dust devil's strength may have been enhanced by eddy winds spinning off the Mogollon Rim.

How Hot? How Cold?

CHAPTER 9

Records are made to be broken.

—Anonymous

The West has long been renowned for its diverse weather. In *Roughing It,* Mark Twain recounts with pithy eloquence his impression of the first desert he had ever seen, the Great Salt Lake Desert:

> The sun beats down with dead, blistering relentless malignity; the perspiration is welling from every pore in man and beast, but scarcely a sign of it finds its way to the surface—it is absorbed before it gets there; there is not the faintest breath of air stirring; there is not a merciful shred of cloud in all the brilliant firmament; there is not a living creature visible in any direction whither one searches the blank level that stretches its monotonous miles on every hand; there is not a sound not a sign—not a whisper—not a buzz; or a whir of wings, or distant pipe of bird—not even a sob from the lost souls that doubtless people that dead air.

Twain's comment that "if you don't like the weather, wait a minute," was said about the climate of New England, but others have noted the rapid changes that can occur in the West. During the course of his transcontinental survey for the Central Pacific Railroad in 1853, Captain Beckwith remarked:

> Several times during the day (Sept. 5) we experienced very sensibly the sudden changes of temperature to which high altitudes in mountain regions are subject from a passing storm or a change of wind—our thick coats being at one moment necessary to our comfort and the next oppressive.

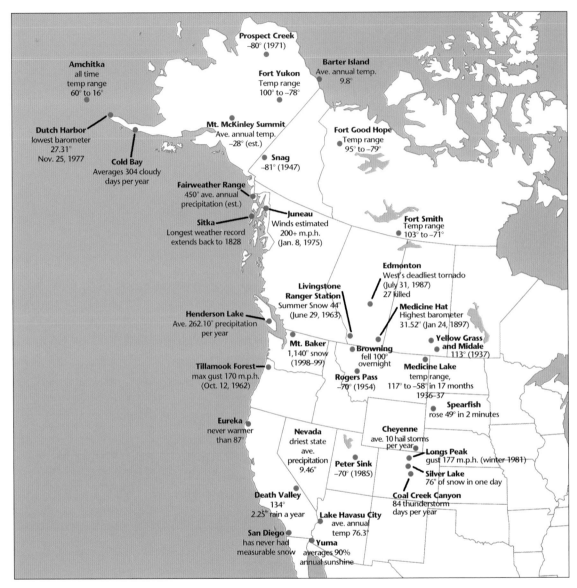

Prospect Creek
-80° (1971)

Barter Island
Ave. annual temp.
9.8°

Amchitka
all time
temp range
60° to 16°

Fort Yukon
Temp range
100° to –78°

Dutch Harbor
lowest barometer
27.31"
Nov. 25, 1977

Mt. McKinley Summit
Ave. annual temp.
–28° (est.)

Fort Good Hope
Temp range
95° to –79°

Cold Bay
Averages 304 cloudy
days per year

Snag
-81° (1947)

Fairweather Range
450" ave. annual
precipitation (est.)

Juneau
Winds estimated
200+ m.p.h.
(Jan. 8, 1975)

Fort Smith
Temp range
103° to –71°

Sitka
Longest weather record
extends back to 1828

Edmonton
West's deadliest tornado
(July 31, 1987)
27 killed

**Livingstone
Ranger Station**
Summer Snow 44"
(June 29, 1963)

Medicine Hat
Highest barometer
31.52" (Jan 24, 1897)

Henderson Lake
Ave. 262.10" precipitation
per year

Mt. Baker
1,140" snow
(1998–99)

Browning
fell 100°
overnight

**Yellow Grass
and Midale**
113° (1937)

Tillamook Forest
max gust 170 m.p.h.
(Oct. 12, 1962)

Rogers Pass
-70° (1954)

Medicine Lake
temp range,
117° to –58° in 17 months
1936–37

Spearfish
rose 49° in 2 minutes

Eureka
never warmer
than 87°

Nevada
driest state
ave.
precipitation
9.46"

Cheyenne
ave. 10 hail storms
per year

Longs Peak
gust 177 m.p.h. (winter 1981)

Peter Sink
-70° (1985)

Silver Lake
76" of snow in one day

Death Valley
134°
2.25" rain a year

Lake Havasu City
ave. annual
temp 76.3°

Coal Creek Canyon
84 thunderstorm
days per year

San Diego
has never had
measurable snow

Yuma
averages 90%
annual sunshine

**Western Temperature
Extremes** RICHARD A. KEEN

These narratives were written before there was much in the way of actual weather records in the West. Lewis and Clark and Zebulon Pike made weather observations during their explorations of the West in 1804–1806. The first western weather station was managed in 1821 by the British at Fort George, near the present-day town of Castle Rock, Washington, but the records from this and other early weather stations in the western United States and Canada were spotty and short-lived. Between 1826 and 1828, the Russians began weather observations at several far-flung sites in Alaska, including Illoolook (in the Aleutian Islands), Kotzebue (north of Nome and above the Arctic Circle), and Sitka (in the temperate rainforest of the Alaska Panhandle). Although the Sitka weather station has changed hands several times (from the Russian Physical Observatory, to the U.S. Army Assistant Surgeon, to the U.S. Geological Survey Magnetic Observatory, to the U.S. Federal Aviation Administration, and the National Weather Service), the weather records there have continued to this very day. The climate record at Sitka is the longest in the West, and we'll take a look at it later in the book.

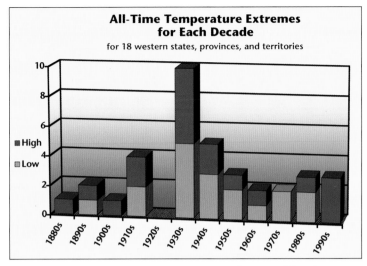

Weather data from a network of consistently reporting stations didn't begin until after 1846, when much of the West became U.S. territory and the army began taking observations at its newly emplaced forts and posts. It didn't take long for these record keepers to realize how extreme their climate could be.

During the summer of 1853, a high temperature of 121° F was recorded at Fort Miller, in California's San Joaquin Valley. At the time, this was probably the hottest temperature ever recorded in the world—the Old World record being 117° F at Esna, Egypt. Up north in Montana in 1885, the alcohol (mercury freezes at –40° F below, so alcohol thermometers are used) plunged to a frigid –63° F at Poplar River. The army beat that three years later with a –65° F reading at Fort Keogh (near Miles City). Before these Montana low temperatures, the record cold readings for the United States had been in Vermont, New Hampshire, and Maine. From 1885 on, the all-time temperature extremes for the United States belonged to the West. All these extremes have been exceeded in the past century. We'll get to these later.

The weather of the West holds more surprises than simple highs and lows of temperature. Some changes of temperature are equally remarkable—not just changes that occur over time, but also differences between places just a few miles apart (vertically and horizontally). There are locations where the degree of moderation in climate is as notable as the extremes are elsewhere. We'll go through these climate oddities one at a time and give some explanation as to why they occur.

State and Province Extremes by Decade— This graph shows how many of the all-time high and low temperatures for 18 western states, provinces, and territories occurred in each decade. Half of these extremes occurred between 1933 and 1954, and ten occurred in just five years—1933 through 1937.
RICHARD A. KEEN

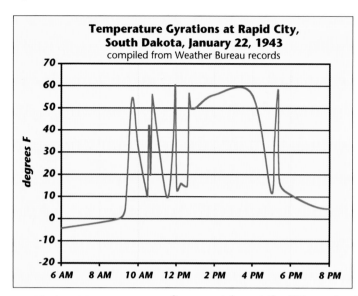

Temperature Gyrations at Rapid City, South Dakota, January 22, 1943
compiled from Weather Bureau records

Rapid City Chinook—
Spectacular temperature gyrations recorded in downtown Rapid City, South Dakota, on January 22, 1943. RICHARD A. KEEN

HOW HOT?

Since the 121° F reading at Fort Miller, California, several other states in the continental United States have reported readings as high or higher. Nevada has recorded 125° F, and Arizona a blistering 128° F. During the Dust Bowl summer of 1936, highs of 121° F seared Kansas and even North Dakota. The honors go to Death Valley, California, which recorded 134° F on July 10, 1913. As a new world record, though, it didn't last long. Just nine years later, a 136° F reading was taken at the little oasis of Azizia, Libya. But Death Valley's 134° F day remains the nation's hottest, and its annual average of 76° F is the highest in the country.

On the other end of the heat scale, a 14-year-long record of temperatures (1874–1888) atop Pikes Peak, Colorado, showed a maximum of only 64° F. This is the highest western weather station with a record lasting more than a few years. Incidentally, the average yearly temperature on that famous mountain is 20° F, the lowest in the "Lower 48" states. Doubtless there are places—such as the top of Mount Rainier, Washington or Mount McKinley, Alaska—where the maximum would be even lower had somebody been fool enough to stay up there keeping records for several years. (Temperature extremes for Death Valley, Pikes Peak, and other locations in the West, along with other climatic data, are listed in Appendix 1, "Climatic Data.")

The reason for the dramatic temperature difference between Death Valley and Pikes Peak is obvious. The Pikes Peak weather station stood at 14,134 feet above sea level, while the Death Valley station sits at 178 feet below sea level. Air that is taken from Death Valley and lifted 14,312 feet to Pikes Peak cools by 79 degrees due to the pressure drop alone. The observed difference of 70 degrees is basically what one should expect based on the altitude difference. This means that equally hot air can reach into most parts of the West at some time during the summer. It is primarily the altitude of the weather station that determines the extreme highest temperatures.

But what of Eureka, California? This coastal city in northern California has never been hotter than 87° F, and yet it is only a few feet higher than

Death Valley. Much hotter readings (100° F!) have been observed at Fort Yukon, Alaska, above the Arctic Circle, and I have personally recorded higher temperatures at 9,000 feet in Colorado. These latter two places are far from any ocean; Eureka, on the other hand, sits right next to the Pacific and owes its moderation to the chilly offshore currents.

An interesting feature of the West Coast south of Alaska is that the coldest offshore water is around northern California near Eureka. Water here averages about 55° F, colder than to the south or north along the coast. The cold water results from the south-bound California Current. Remember the Coriolis effect (see chapter 2, "Fronts, Jets, and Cyclones")? It works on ocean currents as well as on winds, and tries to make the California Current turn to its right (i.e., offshore). As the current peels away from the coast, cold water comes up from below to take its place in a band extending out anywhere from 25 to 50 miles. This phenomenon, called

Pyrocumulus—Heat, smoke, and moisture given off by burning trees created this massive thunderhead above the 130,000-acre Hayman Fire in central Colorado on June 9, 2002. A hot and dry spring and summer led to Colorado's worst fire season ever.
RICHARD A. KEEN

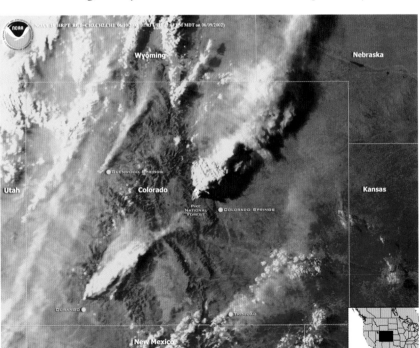

Hayman Fire from Space—Even from hundreds of miles in space, the Hayman pyrocumulus was an impressive spectacle. The smoke plume extended into Nebraska, and the fire cloud's shadow spread 50 miles across the plains.
NOAA

Pikes Peak Weather Station—The highest weather station in the United States was occupied from 1874 to 1888. NWS ARCHIVES

"upwelling" by oceanographers, brings a continuous supply of chilly deep water to the surface and maintains the low temperatures near Eureka. In turn, the cold water chills the lowest 1,000 or 2,000 feet of atmosphere. Eureka sits in the cold layer all summer long, and its temperature rarely rises above 70° F.

Even colder ocean water is found along the Pacific Coast of Alaska. Far out near the end of the Aleutian Island chain, the foggy town of Amchitka has never warmed over 60° F. Along the north coast of Alaska, where Arctic Ocean ice is never far offshore, one might think that the warmest readings are even lower. But such is not the case, as mild breezes from the landmass to the south has brought readings as high as 79° F to Barrow.

How Cold?

The last we looked, Fort Keogh, Montana, had seen a record national low of –65° F. Records, like rules, are meant to be broken. In 1933, the national low left Montana and moved into Wyoming (just barely), when the thermometer at Yellowstone National Park's Riverside Ranger Station dipped to –66° F. That record stood until January 20, 1954, when 5,470-foot Rogers Pass, Montana, 40 miles northwest of Helena, saw the temperature dip to –69.7° F. Let's call it –70° F; it is still the national record for the "Lower 48." Even lower temperatures have been

Death Valley Weather Station—The lowest— and hottest—weather station in the United States is equipped with many standard meteorological instruments. The white box in the far left contains the thermometers, and the vertical cylinder along the back fence is the rain gauge. The white instrument on the right measures solar radiation, while the tank of water (which looks like a cattle watering tank) is used to measure evaporation.
RICHARD A. KEEN

seen in Alaska (–80° F in 1971), and the all-time record for the North American continent is –81° F, measured on the runway at Snag in Canada's Yukon Territory.

In world competition, the West doesn't do as well in the cold category as it does in the hot one. The continental record at Snag is still 46 degrees shy of the world record of –127° F, recorded at Russia's Vostok station, 11,000 feet up on the Antarctic Plateau.

On the high end of the low-temperature scale, Los Angeles has never chilled below 28° F. This means that every city in the West has experienced subfreezing weather. Even on the pier at Avalon, on Santa Catalina Island 26 miles offshore from Los Angeles, the mercury has dipped to the freezing mark. The only city in the mainland United States (outside of Hawaii) that has never frozen is Key West, Florida (which is actually an island).

It takes more than elevation to explain the difference between Rogers Pass and Los Angeles. The 5,400-foot separation in altitude accounts for only 29 degrees of the 98-degree observed difference in minimum temperature. Unlike the situation with extremely hot air in the summer, which at times may spread fairly uniformly across the West, there is an important difference in the cold air masses that reach the two locations. The air that invades Montana in winter is much colder than the air that moves into southern California.

Cold air masses responsible for the low temperatures at any location in the West form over the arctic regions of northwest Canada, Alaska, and Siberia. While these areas receive virtually no sunlight during winter, their snow-covered

Mount McKinley—At an elevation of 20,320-feet, the summit of Mount McKinley (also known as "Denali"—the Great One) in Alaska is the highest place in North America. It is also the coldest place on the continent, and the temperature has never reached the freezing point.
RICHARD A. KEEN

surfaces radiate heat off into space. As a result, any air that passes over the Arctic finds itself losing heat and becoming colder. The longer the air stays, the colder it gets. Eventually, these refrigerated air masses are taken south by cyclones forming along their southern boundaries.

The normal west-to-east flow of jet streams across the western states brings a stream of relatively mild air from the Pacific Ocean, and keeps arctic air from moving south. As the arctic air continues to chill, however, the temperature difference grows between the Arctic and the tropics. With this temperature difference, the strength of the jet must also increase. When the jet blows too fast, it starts to buckle. The buckling takes the form of troughs and ridges in the upper atmosphere and of fronts, cyclones, and anticyclones in the lower atmosphere. And the frigid mass of arctic air begins to move southward.

The path of the cold air outbreak depends on where the buckles form on the jet. A common pattern is for the ridge to develop over the Yukon and the trough over the Great Lakes. This pattern brings the cold wave into the Midwest and East. Less frequently, an Alaskan ridge and Rocky Mountain trough deliver the arctic air into the Rockies. If the trough forms over the West Coast, the cold wave strikes the Pacific Northwest and perhaps moves into California. This last pattern is the rarest of all, which explains why winters are so mild along the coast.

Once a cold wave has overrun the West, local terrain may play some tricks with the temperature. At the Pikes Peak weather station, the lowest recorded temperature was –39° F. Yet 85 miles away and 5,000 feet lower, Taylor Park has been down to –60° F. Three thousand feet lower—nearly 2 miles below Pikes Peak—the town of Maybell, Colorado, has recorded the state's low of –61° F. So, does it really get colder at lower elevations?

The answer is yes and no. Cold air is heavy, and extremely cold air tends to hug the ground. The coldest air masses moving south from the Arctic often extend upward only 2 or 3 miles. Within the depth of the air mass, air near the top is colder than that near the surface, due to the familiar drop-off of pressure. Once the cold air settles in over the mountains and valleys of the West, however, locally chilled air has a habit of sinking into the valleys at night. If the valley has a thick blanket of snow on the ground (which effectively insulates the air from the residual heat in the ground, and vice versa), a thin layer of air near the ground can cool off extremely rapidly after sunset, leading to very low overnight temperatures. The day of its –70° F reading, Rogers Pass had 5 feet of snow on the ground. The next morning, as the sun heated the shallow surface layer of cold air, temperatures rose as fast as they had fallen the night before, and by afternoon Rogers Pass had warmed back up to near zero.

A shallow cold air mass may sweep into the lowlands, but leave the mountaintops in mild Pacific air. A deeper air mass engulfs mountains and valleys alike. During the day, the mountains, being higher up, are colder than the valleys. At night, air locally cooled by radiation sends the valley bottoms into the icebox. A high valley gets colder air to start with, leading to even colder readings at night. The ideal conditions for extreme cold temperatures are clear, calm nights in high-altitude, mountain-rimmed valleys with deep snow on the ground.

UPS AND DOWNS

Temperatures in the West have ranged from –81° F to 134° F, an incredible 215-degree spread. But Death Valley is a long way from Snag, Yukon. What are the greatest (and smallest) temperature ranges ever recorded at one place? What are the quickest changes ever recorded?

Many of these extreme temperature-change records come from northeastern Montana. Montana's fame stems from its location relative to the average positions of the fronts and air masses that affect the West. Northeastern Montana is closer to the main track of the arctic air masses that invade the United States from the north, and thus is subject to the coldest of these air masses. In winter, western Montana usually remains in the mild air blowing in from the Pacific Ocean. Northeastern Montana is therefore the frequent battleground of the two contrasting air masses, and the battles can lead to some spectacular temperature changes. In summer, Montana is subject to the same extremely hot air mass that covers the rest of the West. While Montana's extreme highs may equal those recorded elsewhere, its extreme lows can be much lower.

Temperatures in the West have ranged from –81° F to 134° F, an incredible 215-degree spread.

GREATEST ALL-TIME TEMPERATURE RANGE

"LOWER 48" STATES
175 degrees—Medicine Lake, Montana, from –58° F in February 1936 to 117° F in July 1937.

ALASKA
178 degrees—Fort Yukon, from –78° F to 100° F.

170 degrees—Tanana, from –76° F to 94° F, and Manley Hot Springs, from –77° F to 93° F.

CANADA
174 degrees—Fort Good Hope, Northwest Territories, from –79° F to 95° F, and Fort Smith, Northwest Territories, from –71° F to 103° F.

179 degrees—North America's largest all-time temperature range lies not in the West, however, but in Ontario, where Iroquois Falls has experienced everything from -73° F to 106° F.

OTHER "GREATS"
Smallest all-time temperature range—44 degrees, Amchitka, Alaska, from 16° F to 60° F.

Greatest range in one year—171 degrees, Glasgow, Montana, in 1936, from –59° F in February 15 to 112° F in July 18.

Greatest range in one day—100 degrees, Browning, Montana, January 23–24, 1916. Temperature fell from 44° F to –56° F in less than 24 hours with the passage of a cold front.

Greatest temperature rise in one day—75 degrees, Deeth, Nevada, September 21, 1954. The thermometer shot from a morning low of 12° F to an afternoon high of 87° F.

Greatest warming in two minutes—49 degrees, from –4° F to 45° F, at Spearfish, in the Black Hills of South Dakota, from 7:32 to 7:34 A.M. on January 22, 1943.

The most remarkable temperature fluctuations occur east of the Rockies when the thermometer is situated near the top of a shallow cold air mass. The dense, cold air may act like water on a beach. As it washes in and out, the temperature jumps up and down almost as fast as the thermometer can record it. At Great Falls, Montana, on January 11, 1980, the mercury rose from

–32° F to 15° F—a 47-degree change—in seven minutes. Havre, Montana, once reported a warming of 26 degrees in 45 seconds.

The most-celebrated case of wild temperature fluctuations began with the record two-minute warming at Spearfish. An hour and a half later, the temperature had slowly risen to 54° F. Suddenly, the arctic air sloshed back in, dropping the temperature 58 degrees—from 54° F to –4° F—in 27 minutes. A similar event at Pincher Creek, Alberta, on January 6, 1966, sent the temperature soaring from –12° F at 6 A.M. to 33° F an hour later, only to fall back to –7° F the next hour. Later that same day, the mercury rocketed up again from –10° F to 36° F. Imagine trying to dress for days like that!

Less dramatic are the records for the smallest changes of temperature. There have been many instances of 24-hour temperature fluctuations of zero degrees—no change all day. But for a small range of all-time extremes at any one location, we return to that moderate city by the sea, Eureka, California. In 100 years of record, the temperature has never exceeded 87 degrees or fallen below 20 degrees, a spread of only 67 degrees. In the 48 states, only Key West, Florida, with a range of 56 degrees, has a more uniform climate. However, as is often the case, we can find an even more (or less?) extreme climate in Alaska. In 44 years of record at Amchitka, the temperature has never risen above 60° F (four degrees lower than Pikes Peak's maximum) and has never fallen below 16° F (Phoenix, Arizona, has been just as cold)—a range of just 44 degrees. In two minutes, Spearfish has experienced a greater change of temperature than Amchitka has seen in four decades!

FROM HERE TO THERE

Some of the temperature differences between places a few miles apart can be as impressive as the changes over short periods of time. Differences exceeding 40 degrees are common between Pikes Peak and Colorado Springs, 12 miles east and 8,100 feet lower. If there were a weather station on Mount Whitney in California, we might see temperature differences of 70 or 80 degrees over the 80 miles and 14,600 vertical feet that separate it from Death Valley. However, this is cheating. We expect it to be much colder on mountains.

The largest horizontal temperature differences occur along fronts. On the eastern plains of Montana, Wyoming, Colorado, and Alberta, as well as along the eastern slope's of South Dakota's Black Hills, temperature changes of 40 to 50 degrees over as many miles happen several times each winter. The wildly gyrating temperatures at Spearfish were caused by slight shifts in the location of an incredibly sharp front. At times, this front cut towns and even city blocks

The most-celebrated case of wild temperature fluctuations began with the record two-minute warming at Spearfish (49 degrees). An hour and a half later, the temperature had slowly risen to 54° F. Suddenly, the arctic air sloshed back in, dropping the temperature 58 degrees—from 54° F to –4° F—in 27 minutes.

At times, this front cut towns and even city blocks in half. In Rapid City, South Dakota, ... "on the east side of the Alex Johnson Hotel, winter was in all its glory, while around the corner on the south side, not 50 feet away, spring held sway, only to be swept away in a flash by the sting of winter, and then to return.'

in half. In Rapid City, South Dakota, during the famous 1943 event, weatherman Roland Hamann reported that "at 11 A.M., on the east side of the Alex Johnson Hotel, winter was in all its glory, while around the corner on the south side, not 50 feet away, spring held sway, only to be swept away in a flash by the sting of winter, and then to return." Motorists driving across town reported fogging, frosting, and even cracking of windshields as they drove between the air masses. In one gully, the temperature on the bank was measured as 40 degrees warmer than at the creek bed, just 20 feet below.

At one moment, the Black Hills town of Lead reported 52° F, while Deadwood, not more than 2 miles away, froze at –16° F! Fortunately, this remarkable front spent the day in an area populated by weather enthusiasts, so it was well documented. Generally, however, weather stations in the West are spaced too far apart to catch such incredible temperature differences.

Large temperature differences usually don't last very long because cold fronts and warm fronts are continually moving. One front that sits around for months on end is the separation between the cold, foggy air along the California coast and the hot, dry air inland over the San Joaquin and Sacramento Valleys. This front is a near-permanent feature during the summer, and the temperature changes across it can be every bit as large as those in a wintertime cold front in Montana. When Fort Miller, in the San Joaquin Valley, recorded its world-record 121° F in July 1853, Monterey, on the coast 130 miles to the west, never got above 70° F. For the entire month, Monterey averaged 45 degrees cooler than Fort Miller.

More than a century later, in August 1981, the town of Red Bluff, at the northern end of the Sacramento Valley, recorded its all-time high temperature—also 121° F. At the same time, the city of Eureka shivered in the fog and in the heat of the day only reached 61° F. That's a 60-degree difference only 100 miles apart. The boundary between these vastly differing air masses moves very little and from June to September can usually be found somewhere in the Coast Ranges of California. With its 50-degree temperature contrasts, it may very well be the most persistent front in the world.

The coastal front is found all up and down the Pacific shoreline, but farther north it is more a wintertime feature—and the temperature contrast is reversed. For much of the winter, sub-zero arctic air sits over the Yukon and inland reaches of Alaska and British Columbia, sometimes extending into eastern Washington and Oregon. Offshore, moist and mild air—with temperatures in the 30s, 40s, and 50s—works its way through the islands, straits, and sounds and fjords of the Northwest. The front separating the two contrasting air masses is often found just inland, straddling the Coast Mountains, but its slightest movement can exact huge changes in local temperatures.

It may be academic, perhaps, but the greatest temperature difference ever recorded across the entire western United States probably occurred at 2 A.M. on January 20, 1954. The weather observer at Rogers Pass read –70° F from his thermometer. At that same moment in the balmy desert Southwest, Yuma, Arizona, read 55° F—a temperature difference of 125° F over a distance of 1,000 miles.

What is the least temperature difference the West has ever seen? The far corners of the region, San Diego, California, and Fort Yukon, Alaska, have exactly the same average daily maximum temperature—76 degrees—during July. Consequently, we could expect that during summer afternoons, the difference between these two points, 2,600 miles apart, often amounts to precisely nothing!

In the region called the West there are places where the temperature has fallen 100 degrees in a day and places where it hasn't nudged a degree. The West harbors the hottest and coldest places in all of the United States and Canada, as well as the most and least variable climates. At any moment the weather may range from arctic to tropical across its 15 states and provinces, or it may be identical at locales 2,000 miles apart. This, in a nutshell, is the varied weather of the West.

Following is a list of some of the extremes of heat and cold that have visited the West over the past century. The selection was a difficult one, since nearly every year someplace in the West gets a memorably hot or cold spell. The events chosen here are based as much on their extent as on their severity.

San Diego, California, and Fort Yukon, Alaska, have exactly the same average daily maximum temperature—76 degrees—during July.

GREAT WESTERN HEAT WAVES

Summer 1913—In July, Death Valley baked at 134° F, the hottest temperature ever recorded in North America at the time (and still the hottest ever measured in the Western Hemisphere). Two months later, coastal San Diego reached 110° F. Death Valley's 134-degree reading has been officially accepted by the National Weather Service as the nation's highest temperature reading. However, there are some doubts about the accuracy of that temperature—the thermometer at Death Valley was having problems at the time. If we choose to discard that reading, and we'll never really know if we should, the next hottest record is 129° F, also in Death Valley, on July 18, 1960 and again on July 17, 1998.

July 1934—Idaho and New Mexico recorded their hottest days to date, at 118° F and 116° F respectively.

Summer 1937—Yuma, Arizona, broiled at or above the century mark for 101 days in a row. In July, the heat reached into Montana, hitting 117° F at Medicine Lake, just 35 miles from the Canadian border. Across the border, the mercury soared to 113° F at Yellow Grass, Saskatchewan, an all-time high for Canada. This was in the middle of the Dust Bowl years, 1933–1939, the worst drought of record in the Great Plains. The heat extended into the West, and many places had their hottest days, months, or summers during this period. Amazingly, many of these same places recorded their coldest winters during the same decade. It was a period of extreme variability of western weather.

July 1941—British Columbia's greatest heat wave (97° F at Victoria and 112° F at Lytton, Chinook Cove, and Lillooet) extended into the Northwest Territories, where Fort Smith logged a reading of 103° F, the highest temperature ever reported north of the 60th parallel in North America.

June–July 1954—In one of the most extensive hot spells ever to scorch the nation, coast-to-coast, six states saw their hottest days ever, including 122° F at Overton, Nevada. In the West, records were broken as temperatures soared to 99° F at Ely, Nevada; 100° F at Cheyenne, Wyoming; 104° F at Boulder, Colorado, and Casper, Wyoming; and 106° F at Sheridan, Wyoming.

June–September 1955—Torrid times continued, with another coast-to-coast heat wave. Seattle saw 100° F, an all-time high for the city. Los Angeles withered under an eight-day spell of 100° F-plus weather, with the mercury reaching 110° F on September 1. For the next six years, unusually hot summers were the rule for southern California.

Summer 1959—Desert heat at its finest. Death Valley lived up to its reputation, with 126 days in a row at 100° F or hotter, topping out at 125° F.

GREAT WESTERN HEAT WAVES, CONTINUED

July–August 1961—A searing summer in the North, Lewistown, Montana, soared to 115° F and, at inappropriately named Ice Harbor Dam, Washington, a reading of 118° F reading was a record for the state. Even on the coast, Astoria, Oregon, topped out at 100° F, and 106° F was reached at San Francisco's airport. Widespread forest fires broke out all across the West. As the heat continued into November, fires struck the Los Angeles area.

August 1969—Another hot one in Montana—Helena's hottest day (105° F) and a toasty 110° F at Havre. Havre's high is all the more impressive considering that residents shivered at –52° F half a year earlier.

August 1981—The red-hot conclusion to a searing summer. All-time high temperatures were recorded at Red Bluff, California (121° F), Portland (107° F), Olympia, Washington (104° F), and Quillayute, on the Pacific shores of Washington's Olympic rain forest (99° F). The persistent heat made it Phoenix's hottest summer ever.

June–September 1988—A summer reminiscent of the Dust Bowl days scorched the country from coast to coast. Two cities recorded their hottest days ever—Cleveland (104° F) and downtown San Francisco (103° F), while Death Valley peaked at 127° F (not a record). In August, dozens of lightning strikes ignited forest, and range fires broke out across the West, with the largest fires consuming approximately one million acres of Yellowstone National Park. Smoke from the Yellowstone fires rose to 30,000 feet and dimmed the sun across several states.

June 1990—Temperatures more appropriate for a cookbook than a weather report seared the Southwest. Phoenix topped out at 122° F, 4 degrees higher than the previous record, and Tucson reached 117° F. Other records included 112° F in downtown Los Angeles, and 108° F in Pueblo, Colorado. The hot weather in Phoenix forced the closing of the international airport—airplanes couldn't take off in the heat-thinned air!

June 1994—A late June heat wave baked the Southwest and set state records for Arizona (128° F at Lake Havasu City), Nevada (125° F at Laughlin), and New Mexico (122° F near Lakewood). The 128° F reading at Lake Havasu and at Death Valley, California, set a national record for the month of June. However, at Badwater (the lowest place in Death Valley and in the United States), an "unofficial" thermometer soared to 131° F degrees. There was also an overnight minimum of 101° F at Death Valley.

Summer 1998—Across Canada, it was the warmest summer on record, capping the driest year ever recorded in the Yukon and northern British Columbia. The heat peaked at Osoyoos, British Columbia, at 109° F on July 27. Heat and drought led to a record fire year in Canada, with 10,567 wildfires reported.

GREAT WESTERN COLD WAVES

December, 1804—"The weather today was colder than any we had experienced, the thermometer at sunrise being 45 below zero... ." This observation by Lewis and Clark as they wintered over near what is now Bismarck, North Dakota, matches the modern-day low record for that city.

January 1854—Cold engulfed the entire West, sending the temperature to –1° F at Steilacoom (near Tacoma), Washington, and 25° F at San Francisco.

Winter 1886–1887—More than half of Montana's cattle population froze to death during a bitter winter that brought several blizzards and temperatures reaching –60° F. The disaster put an end to open-range cattle raising in the state.

January 1888—One of the Pacific Northwest's greatest cold waves, with –2° F in Portland, Oregon, and –65° F in Montana, and all-time lows in Spokane, Washington (–30° F below), and Eureka, California (20° F). Portlanders could walk across the frozen Willamette River for 10 straight days.

January 1893—Another Northwest cold snap, with downtown Seattle's all-time low of 3° F and 7° F offshore at Tatoosh Island, Washington. In Canada, record lows were set at Calgary (–49° F), Edmonton (–57° F), and Prince Albert, Saskatchewan (–70° F).

February 1899—The most severe and widespread cold wave ever to freeze the United States. Subzero readings were reported from every state (except Hawaii, of course), ranging from –61° F at Fort Logan, Montana, to –2° F in Tallahassee, Florida. All-time records were set at such diverse locations as Billings (–49° F) and Miles City (–49° F), Montana; Greeley, Colorado (–45° F); Brownsville, Texas (12° F); and Washington, D.C. (–15° F).

January 1913—Freezing weather swept into the normally mild Southwest, setting all-time lows at San Diego (25° F), Phoenix (16° F), and Tucson (6° F).

January 1930—Temperatures fell to –52° F in Oregon and Montana, and to –57° F in Wyoming. The Columbia River was frozen for two weeks. It was Wyoming's coldest January ever, but was followed by the warmest February on record.

February 1933—Extreme cold over the northern Great Basin and Rockies set all-time lows for Wyoming (–66° F, which remained a national record for 21 years), Oregon (–54° F at Seneca, where it was 99 degrees warmer the next day), and Salt Lake City (–30° F).

February 1936—A series of cold waves over the Plains east of the Rockies set all-time record minimum temperatures at Denver (–30° F); Lander, Wyoming (–40° F); and Great Falls (–49° F) and Glasgow, Montana (–59° F).

GREAT WESTERN COLD WAVES, CONTINUED

January 1937—The Southwest shivered as all-time cold records fell from Elko, Nevada (–43° F), to Yuma, Arizona (22° F). Cold records for the state were set in Boca, California (–45° F), and San Jacinto, Nevada (–50° F).

January 1943—A state record for Idaho of –60° F was set. The return of mild Pacific air following the cold outbreak led to the spectacular gyrations of temperature at Spearfish, South Dakota.

January 1947—A bitterly cold spell set low records in Alaska (–38° F at Anchorage) and British Columbia (–74° F at Smith River), and at the little town of Snag, in the Yukon, a reading of –81° F set a record for North America.

January 1949—In terms of average temperature, it was the coldest winter much of the West has ever seen, and right in the middle of it, a sharp cold snap set record low temperatures from Pocatello, Idaho (–30° F), to downtown Los Angeles (28° F). Even on the pier at Santa Catalina Island, off Los Angeles, the temperature fell to 32° F.

January 1950—This time it was western Canada's turn for a memorable winter, with record low average temperatures across most of British Columbia and Alberta. Extreme lows ranged from –60° F at Banff to 0° F at Vancouver and 4° F at Victoria.

January 1954—A new national record (Alaska wasn't a state yet) of –70° F was set at Rogers Pass, but the cold was short-lived. At nearby Helena, where the low was –36° F, temperatures soared to 54° F, a recovery of 90 degrees in just two days. Statewide, the winter as a whole averaged 4 degrees warmer than normal.

January 1963—The first of a series of arctic blasts to strike the Rockies this month was the worst. West Yellowstone saw –60° F, and Denver recorded an afternoon maximum of –15° F. Las Vegas froze at an unprecedented 8° F.

December 1968–January 1969—A late December cold wave struck the Northwest with –50° F at Moscow, Idaho, and 11° F on the coast at Astoria, Oregon. In northern Montana, the entire winter—December through February—averaged only 1° F, the coldest winter ever observed anywhere in the western United States. Similar records were set in Canadian cities like Calgary and Whitehorse. At Havre, Montana, the mercury remained continuously below zero for the last 17 days of January, and Edmonton, Alberta, saw 26 continuous days of below-zero weather. Hinsdale, Montana, dropped to –55° F, and Victoria, British Columbia, tied its record low of 4° F.

GREAT WESTERN COLD WAVES, CONTINUED

January 1971—Alaska's coldest night sent the thermometer down to –80° F at Prospect Creek, northeast of Fairbanks.

December 1983—Christmas was chilly this year with –52° F at Butte, Montana, where the entire month averaged –6° F. Denver's temperature remained below zero for nearly five days, while parts of Montana suffered twice as long. Meanwhile, the Southwest remained unusually warm all month.

February 1985—Polar air and light winds sent thermometer readings way below zero over the intermountain region. Maybell, Colorado, saw –61° F, a new record for the state. It was a classic case of rapid cooling of a shallow layer of air near the ground—Maybell's temperature recovered to a balmy 15° F by that afternoon. In Utah, another state record of –69° F was set at Peter's Sink, in the Wasatch Mountains. Five months later, Utah recorded its all-time highest temperature, 117° F at St. George!

September 1985—The Great Pumpkin Freeze struck eastern Colorado, destroying most of the year's pumpkin crop and causing a severe Halloween shortage. Temperatures fell into the teens across the eastern plains, and to near zero in the foothills.

February 1989—Alaska's second-coldest cold wave in history (–76° F at Tanana) poured south into Montana, where the town of Wisdom dipped to –52° F, and Colorado, where my backyard thermometer in Coal Creek Canyon read –36° F. At Boulder, Colorado, where a Global Warming conference was in progress, the mercury plunged to –24 ° F , the coldest in 26 years. Gale-force easterlies blew 7° F air into Seattle. After crossing the mild waters of Puget Sound, the cold air left 3-foot "sound-effect" snowfalls on the Olympic Peninsula. For much of the West it was the coldest February weather ever experienced.

December 20–25, 1990—Arctic air invaded central and southern California and stayed for five days, freezing crops, fruit, trees, and water pipes. In the San Joaquin Valley, daytime temperatures remained in the 20s for several days, and nighttime temperatures fell to all-time lows of 19° F at Bakersfield, 18° F at Sacramento and Fresno, and 17° F at Stockton.

August 25, 2002—A pre-dawn reading of 30° F was the lowest ever recorded on this date in the high valley town of Alamosa in southern Colorado. That low reading in itself was not horribly impressive, but the same afternoon, the mercury rose to 87° F—a record maximum for the same date!

SEA OF STORMS

CHAPTER 10

I claim this sea in the name of Spain
and call it "Pacific"

—Vasco Nuñez de Balboa, 1513

When Balboa first saw the Pacific Ocean from a hill above present-day Panama City, the watery expanse before him may have indeed appeared pacific, or peaceful. After all, Panama lies in the belt of the equatorial doldrums most of the year, and the flaccid winds of that zone often leave the ocean glassy smooth. However, if Balboa had stumbled upon his ocean at some other place—say, Hurricane Ridge, Washington, or inaptly named Mount Fairweather, Alaska, he may have chosen another name—perhaps "Ocean of Storms." But that name has since been given to the largest lava flow on the Moon (it's the big smile on the face some people see in the rising full moon), and so for the past 500 years, we have called the largest earthly ocean "Pacific."

The Pacific Ocean has its share of storms—perhaps no more than the Atlantic does, acre for acre, but since the Pacific is more than twice as large as the Atlantic (indeed, it is nearly as large as the world's other three oceans—the Atlantic, Indian, and Arctic—combined, and covers one-third of the entire earth's surface), it's a fair bet that it harbors more storms than any other ocean. And a large number of these affect North America, either directly or indirectly. We talked about the direct impact of Pacific storms in chapter 2, "Fronts, Jets, and Cyclones"; now it's time to describe some of the indirect, but longer-lasting, impacts of two stormy weather phenomena that occur far off the shores of North America. These two are "El Niño," which many of you are probably familiar with, and something called the "Pacific Decadal Oscillation," which many of you probably aren't familiar with.

EL NIÑO

El Niño is coming! It'll drown California!
It'll ruin the Olympics! It'll kill seals!

—Headline from an unnamed California newspaper,
quoted in the Bulletin of the American Meteorological Society

This headline, which appeared as the great El Niño of 1997–1998 was developing, illustrates some of the apprehensions—and misconceptions—that westerners have about the weather upheaval known as "El Niño." Recent history makes it clear that the Niño phenomenon is of great concern and interest to western weather watchers. The winters of 1982–1983 and 1997–1998 brought Niños that have been rated the biggest of the century (which of the two was bigger depends on which expert you listen to). Both winters, California was slammed by a relentless series of Pacific storms, with winds and pouring rains washing away the shoreline and sliding mounds of mud onto highways. Many will never forget the television images of houses and hot tubs floating away in the surf. Heavy snows choked the Sierras and Rockies, and even the cacti of northern Mexico were dusted several times. So what is this "dreaded" El Niño that strikes the West?

El Niño is the name given by fishermen of coastal Peru and Ecuador to a warm ocean current that shows up every so often.

Sometimes it is easier to tell what something isn't rather than what it is, and El Niño is not a storm that strikes the West Coast. As a matter of fact, the phenomenon that is correctly called "El Niño" happens far from western shores, and has little, if any, impact on western weather. Nonetheless, it's a catchy name, and in the absence of a better one, it appears that whatever it is that strikes the West will be called El Niño for some time to come.

In its original sense, El Niño is the name given by fishermen of coastal Peru and Ecuador to a warm ocean current that shows up every so often. Normally, the western coast of South America is swept by a northward current of cold water from the Antarctic. Along the immediate coast, the Southern Hemisphere Coriolis effect (which is the reverse of the northern effect) causes upwelling immediately offshore, keeping the water good and chilly. This is the Southern Hemisphere counterpart of the current that refrigerates the California coast, especially around Eureka, all summer long. The fresh supply of deep water brought to the surface by this upwelling is loaded with organic nutrients, which feed the plankton and, in turn, the swarms of anchovies that populate the area. As a result, these Peruvian and Ecuadoran coastal areas are among the richest fishing grounds in the world, although in recent years they have been severely depleted by overfishing.

The coastal current and its attendant upwelling vary according to seasons. In December, at the height of the Southern Hemisphere summer, the current usually weakens and the coastal water warms up a little. Some years the current ceases or reverses direction, and the water warms up a lot—as much as 10 degrees or more. In these years the nutrient-loaded upwelling ceases, dwindling the fish population. Since these warmings often begin around Christmas, the locals have dubbed the warm current El Niño, a Spanish word that means "The Child," referring to—without implying blame—the Christ child. Recent Niños began in 1957, 1965, 1972, 1976, 1982, 1987, 1991, 1994, 1997, and 2002; all of these continued into the following year. Combined with the over-fishing that has taken place, Niños have become increasingly disastrous for the local fishing industry, not to mention for the fish themselves and the birds that feed on them.

The phenomenon doesn't end with dead anchovies littering the beaches of Peru and Ecuador. The warm water may spread, reaching westward across the tropical Pacific and northward along the west coast of Mexico toward California and Oregon. At this point the warming becomes a global concern, since its worldwide climate effects can be enormous. However, out of due respect for the fishermen who coined the name, remember that the term "El Niño" really applies to the warming off the South American coast. It is, to say the least, stretching it a bit to apply the name to storms in California and the Rockies, but again, for lack of a better name, let's use it.

The variety and scale of the worldwide weather freaks that occurred during the particularly large 1982–1983 and 1997–1998 Niños are truly impressive. Elsewhere during those Niño years, hurricane-force cyclones pounded the

Disappearing Beach—A sequence of four photographs taken from October 1997 to February 1998 shows how El Niño spawned storms that progressively claimed the Santa Cruz Lighthouse Beach. BRUCE RICHMOND, U.S. GEOLOGICAL SURVEY

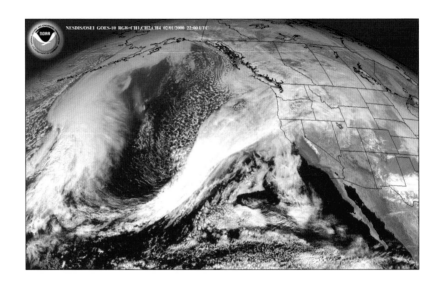

Pineapple Express—Jet stream winds send a plume of moisture streaming from the tropics into California and Oregon. Since these plumes often originate from the vicinity of the Hawaiian Islands (in the lower left corner of the picture), they've earned the nickname "Pineapple Express." Farther west, another plume extends all the way north into Alaska. The warm waters of El Niño often generate more of these northward surges of moisture and jet stream winds, bringing stormier than usual weather to the West Coast. However, these events also occur in non–El Niño years, such as these two plumes on February 1, 2000. NOAA

Gulf of Mexico and Atlantic coasts; however, in terms of temperature, the winters were exceptionally mild nationwide (especially 1997–1998). Around the globe, torrential rains flooded desert areas of Peru and Ecuador, while droughts struck Brazil, Africa, and Indonesia, and the life-giving rains of the Indian monsoon arrived late. Long, hot summers led to terrible brush fires that incinerated thousands of square miles of Australian bush, along with several small towns. Many meteorologists—not all, mind you—believe that these weather disasters were interrelated, and that the massive warming of the Pacific Ocean provided the common link.

CHANGING THE WIND

To paraphrase certain stockbrokers, when the Pacific warms up, the world listens. Indeed, a warmer-than-usual tropical Pacific Ocean can disturb the most fundamental forces that drive the world's weather. The most powerful and persistent winds of the world—the subtropical jets of the Northern and Southern Hemispheres—result from the upward and outward flow of air in the huge thunderstorm masses that cover Africa, South America, and Indonesia. North of the equator, air streaming north from the upper levels of these thunderstorms turns into an eastward-blowing jet stream, thanks to the slower speed of the underlying ground at higher latitudes. The predominant patterns of the subtropical jet result from the locations of the thunderstorm masses, with the jet being farther north and stronger in the vicinity of the storms. South American thunderstorms strengthen the jet over eastern North America and out into the North Atlantic. This Atlantic jet blows away from the western states, so it is the next jet to the west—the one north of Indonesia—that is the most important for western weather.

Normally, when the tropical thunderstorms are dousing Indonesia, New Guinea, and other islands at the western limits of the Pacific, the subtropical jet is strongest from eastern China to the western Pacific south of Japan. This jet stream is so persistent across most of the Pacific that during World War II, the Japanese used it to float balloon-borne bombs to the United States. However, the jet has a tendency to peter out by the time it reaches the West Coast, and often splits into two weak jets that skirt the northern and southern borders of the western United States. This kept most of the Japanese balloons from ever reaching the United States, although several did make it, causing several deaths and minor damage.

The thunderstorms that drive the subtropical jet are fed by latent heat evaporated from the surfaces of the warm tropical seas. These thunderstorms prefer to build up over the equatorial land masses, where the overhead sun is most effective at directly heating the ground and causing the rising currents of air that trigger the storms. Of the three major land masses along the equator, Indonesia is the smallest, being, in reality, a bunch of islands. Most of its surface area is water. Because Indonesia is surrounded by the most extensive and warmest of all the tropical ocean areas, it is the thunderstorm capital of the world.

When the tropical Pacific Ocean gets even warmer than usual, as happens during some Niños, a major shift in the position of the Indonesian thunderstorm mass can take place. Sensing the large supply of latent heat energy lying over the open ocean, and not feeling as bound to form over the islands as would its African and South American counterparts, this mass of storms may move east. The bulk of the thunderstorms can shift several thousand miles east. At the height of the 1982–1983 Niño, it strayed 5,000 miles from its normal location. When the largest source of energy released into the atmosphere moves one-fifth of the way around the world, things are bound to happen!

When the thunderstorms move east, the subtropical jet stream likewise extends farther east. At times, the jet may knife into the California coast at full strength, and the incessant rains that Mark Twain considered such a feature of San Francisco's climate are at their worst. Since the subtropical jet is usually at fairly low latitudes (hence its name), many of its attendant cyclones take the southerly storm track across the Southwest. Not only does the West Coast get more storms than usual, but these storms strike farther south than usual. Even San Diego gets treated to those incessant rains—their wettest year on record, 1941, was during a Niño.

… the subtropical jet is strongest from eastern China to the western Pacific south of Japan. This jet stream is so persistent across most of the Pacific that during World War II, the Japanese used it to float balloon-borne bombs to the United States.

NIÑO WEATHER

The classic pattern of Niño weather was followed in 1982–1983, with the coasts of California and Oregon receiving repeated batterings from November through March. The subtropical storm track continued across the southern United States, unleashing high winds, floods, and even some tornadoes along the Gulf of Mexico. Meanwhile, the northern United States was high and dry, well north of all the action; Wyoming had one of its warmest winters on record.

The arrival of spring brought no real relief from the ravages of the subtropical jet, just a change of targets. The jet performed its normal seasonal swing north, and frequent storms began dumping heavy snows on the Rockies. In May and June, snowmelt sent rivers of water through the streets of Salt Lake City. Floods devastated the banks of many rivers of the Southwest, particularly the Colorado River. Total losses from the flooding exceeded $1 billion.

The subtropical jet disappeared during the summer, as it usually does, but in a real sense the memory lingered on. The warm water of the tropical Pacific had spread up the West Coast, and the cooling effect along the coast weakened

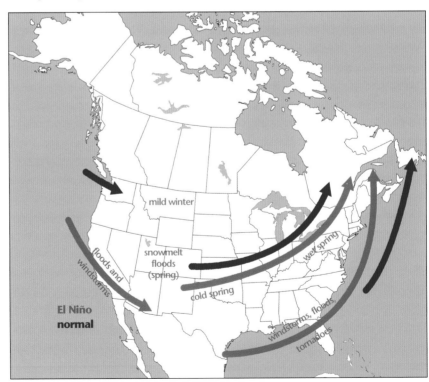

El Niño–Related Weather Anomalies— The weird weather of the big El Niños of 1982–1983 and 1997–1998 can, for the most part, be explained by shifted storm tracks. RICHARD A. KEEN

Salt Lake City Flood— Excess snowmelt runoff following the wet winter of 1982–1983 had to be channeled through downtown Salt Lake City.
FEDERAL EMERGENCY MANAGEMENT ADMINISTRATION, MICHAEL MEE

considerably. In September, the fog cleared off and Eureka, California soared to a sultry 86° F. At the end of September, moisture drawn from the exceptionally warm Pacific by Tropical Storm Octave led to Arizona's worst flood disaster in history.

The weather patterns of 1983 and 1998 were similar in many ways to those of 1878, 1941, 1958, and 1973—years with the largest Niños. Each of these years featured stormy winters in California and mild winters across the northern states, followed by snowy springs in the Rockies and warm summers along the coast. But there were important differences among these Niño years, particularly in the timing and duration of the unusual weather. Sometimes the stormiest weather started a year early!

Before you get the idea that El Niño is a totally bad thing that should be outlawed, or at least stiffly taxed, allow me to place a dollar value on the effects of the great El Niño of 1997–1998. Dr. Stanley Changnon, who has been doing climate studies for 60 years, pieced together this information and estimated that damages to the United States exceeded $4 billion, mostly losses to property from storms and flooding from California to Florida. However, he also estimated that the beneficial effects of that mild and relatively snow-free winter totaled nearly $20 billion! Across the northern United States (and probably most of Canada, as well), reduced heating costs, increased sales (people like to buy more when the weather is nice, especially in places where it's usually miserable), and the absence of snowmelt flooding contributed to the economy, while a hurricane-free summer along the Atlantic and Gulf Coasts (as often

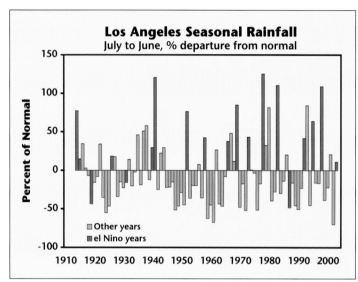

Los Angeles Seasonal Rainfall
July to June, % departure from normal

Percent of Normal

□ Other years
■ el Nino years

Los Angeles Seasonal Rainfall, 1915–2002—In the past 90 years, Los Angeles' seasonal (July to June) rainfall has ranged from 4.42 inches to 33.44 inches. A striking pattern in this variability is the overall wetness of El Niño years—of the 19 El Niño seasons, all but three had above normal rainfall. The wettest seasons of record, 1940–1941, 1977–1978, 1982–1983, and 1997–1998 were all El Niños.
RICHARD A. KEEN

occurs during El Niño) saved billions more in dollars. And while El Niño–related storms across the South took 189 lives that winter, an estimated 850 lives were saved due to the mild winter in the north (including fewer auto fatalities) and the absence of hurricanes. Dr. Changnon's summary didn't include the beneficial effects of a moist winter that filled reservoirs and wells all across the arid West (this was a particular benefit of the weak 2003 El Niño, whose storms effectively ended the previous year's drought across much of the West). So while Californians may have good reason to dread the arrival of El Niño, for many other North Americans, El Niño is something to welcome.

Not all Niños follow this plan, however. The Niño winter of 1976–1977 was nothing at all like its brethren of 1982–1983 and 1997–1998. The nation's bicentennial was the year of a great western drought, especially in California. Advertisements exhorted people to "shower with a friend" to conserve water. Ski areas from California to Colorado suffered snow shortages. Meanwhile, in the central and eastern states one of the bitterest winters in history featured the savage "Buffalo blizzard" in upstate New York and snow that fell south of Miami. Nationwide, it was the driest winter in recent history, while 1982–1983 and 1997–1998 were among the wettest.

The reason for the different behavior of the 1976–1977 Niño lies in the misuse of the term "El Niño." True, both years saw Niños off the coast of Peru. However, this relatively local phenomenon is not part of the global upheaval that strikes the West. Rather, it is the warming of large areas of the rest of the Pacific Ocean—and especially the tropical Pacific—that upsets western weather. In 1976–1977, the warm water off of Peru did not expand across the entire tropical Pacific as it does in a "classic" El Niño, so the Indonesian thunderstorms did not move far enough east to steer the subtropical jet into the West Coast. Instead, the jet veered far to the north, crossing into the Yukon before plunging back south into the heart of Dixie. This enormous bulge in the jet, with its western ridge and eastern trough, led polar air deep into the southeast, while leaving the West completely out of the storm track. The result: persistent drought. It turns out that the 1976–1977 event was so different that many Niño experts don't even include it in their lists of Niños.

A Niño Is Born

We have seen thunderstorms and ocean currents in places as distant as New Guinea and Micronesia can do strange things to the weather of the West. Accordingly, a few words are in order about the tropical Pacific Ocean and why its currents fluctuate. It begins with the sun heating the ocean's top layer. Being lighter than cold water, the warm water stays on top. Most of the time, winds in the tropics blow *from* the east—dubbed "trade winds" by sailors. The trade winds blow the warm water to the west, toward New Guinea, where it starts to pile up. This leaves cooler water in the eastern Pacific; this pattern of warm water to the west and cool water to the east is the normal situation in the tropical Pacific.

> ...why do the trade winds weaken? When this and other still-open questions are answered, we may be able to forecast winter weather patterns months in advance.

If the trade winds slacken, all that warm water piled up around New Guinea starts to slosh back toward Peru. Sometimes the trade winds actually reverse and blow from the west, giving the pile of warm water an extra push toward Peru. When this happens, the normally cool eastern Pacific gets overrun by warm water, and El Niño is in progress. Eventually, the easterly trade winds return, and the warm water heads back toward New Guinea.

This, in simplest terms, is the cause of El Niño. The real details are not so simple. The patterns of warming and cooling differ from one Niño to the next, as do the timing, duration, and strength of the events. One very basic question remaining for researchers is, why do the trade winds weaken? When this and other still-open questions are answered, we may be able to forecast winter weather patterns months in advance.

The Pacific Decadal Oscillation

Whatever is a Pacific Decadal Oscillation? It's an oscillation—a back-and-forth swing—of ocean temperatures and barometric pressure patterns across the Pacific Ocean. It can last for several decades, which explains the name (those who like acronyms refer to it as the PDO).

You might recall the Aleutian Low (described in chapter 2, "Fronts, Jets, and Cyclones"), a region of low pressure south of Alaska. It's where many storms from the coast of Asia end up spending the last days of their lives. Most days, one or more Lows can be found on the weather maps on this part of the Pacific. Let me remind you of a couple of relevant facts about Lows

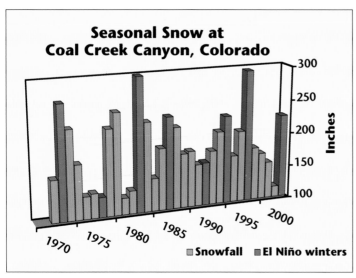

Seasonal Snow at Coal Creek Canyon, Colorado

Inches: 300, 250, 200, 150, 100

1970 1975 1980 1985 1990 1995 2000

☐ Snowfall ■ El Niño winters

Rocky Mountain Snowfall—The effects of El Niño reach far inland—in the middle of Colorado, the two snowiest winters in the past 32 years (1982–1983 and 1997–1998) at Coal Creek Canyon were also the two strongest El Niños of the century. RICHARD A. KEEN

(or cyclones) before we continue—namely, their winds spin a counterclockwise direction, and they get their energy from the temperature contrast between polar and tropical air masses. Around the Aleutian Low, the counterclockwise rotation means that west of the Low center, northerly winds draw cold polar air from Siberia around that side of the storm. Meanwhile, east of the Low, southerly winds bring warm winds (from the vicinity of Hawaii) up toward the Alaskan panhandle. This explains why southeast Alaska, say, Ketchikan, is so much milder than coastal Siberia at the same latitude.

Since the Aleutian Low is out there spinning most of the year, the cold and warm winds have plenty of time to chill the waters west of the Low, and warm the waters to the east. It takes a while for something as massive as the Pacific Ocean to change its temperature, but time is no problem for the Aleutian Low, and accordingly, the ocean west of the Low is normally colder than the water to the east. Now that it's there, this ocean temperature pattern "feeds back" into the atmosphere above. The temperature contrast adds energy to the storms that get sucked in to the Aleutian Low, either extending their lives, giving them new strength, or sometimes generating new storms. This "feed back" mechanism between the Aleutian Low and the Pacific Ocean is one reason the Low is so persistent and sticks around the Gulf of Alaska—like the ballast in a ship, the slowly varying bulk of ocean water keeps the Aleutian Low from straying too much from its home.

That is the normal situation for the Aleutian Low. Now, imagine what might happen if this Low is stronger than normal for a year or two (for whatever reason). It's spinning motion increases, the flow of cold and warm air increases, and the temperature contrast of the North Pacific increases. This, in turn, helps keep the Aleutian Low stronger, which, in turn, maintains the ocean temperature differences, and so on. This can keep the Aleutian Low persistently stronger for years, even decades (after all, this is the Pacific DECADAL Oscillation!), before it switches back to a normal, or even weaker, pattern. A weaker Aleutian Low means less east-to-west contrast in ocean temperature, which, of course, would tend to keep the Low weaker.

The ups and downs of the Aleutian Low have profound consequences on the climate of all of North America, especially the northwestern corner of the continent. When the Low is strong, the southerly winds that warm the coasts of Alaska and British Columbia increase, giving those areas mild weather, especially in the winter. The warm weather extends into the interior of Alaska and western Canada, but thanks to the rotation of the Earth, the large-scale winds turn to the south across the eastern parts of North America, bringing cold air deep into the southeastern United States. This pattern has held since 1977, when a weak Aleutian Low became persistently stronger. Before that, the Low switched from strong to weak around 1947, and there's some indication now that it's once again about to become weaker.

In the next chapter, there are some graphs of temperatures. When you get a chance, look at the one for Sitka, Alaska, and notice how Sitka's annual temperatures were much cooler from 1947 to 1977 (when the Aleutian Low was weak, allowing arctic air to reach the Alaskan coast) than they were during the decades before and since. You'll see a similar—but much less pronounced—story in the temperature graph for the entire western United States and Canada. This is the PDO in action; now, if we only knew how to predict what it will do next.

... southerly winds bring warm winds (from the vicinity of Hawaii) up toward the Alaskan panhandle. This explains why southeast Alaska is so much milder than coastal Siberia at the same latitude.

CHANGING CLIMATE

CHAPTER

11

A change in our climate however is taking place very sensibly. Both heats and colds are become much more moderate within the memory even of the middle-aged. Snows are less frequent and less deep.

—Thomas Jefferson
Notes on the State of Virginia, 1781

A NEW CENTURY

With everyone from presidents (like Jefferson) to meteorologists (like me!) talking about "global warming," and with a new century commencing, let's throw out the following hypothetical scenario:

Forty years after the first predictions that a "greenhouse effect," due to gases released into the atmosphere by factories and fires, would irretrievably alter the world's climate, there was still little solid evidence of any change in global temperatures. But after the turn of the century, numerous signs of the Warming began to appear and some brought calamity. Hurricanes killed thousands of Americans who had built their homes on exposed beaches, and in the West, extreme heat and drought led to firestorms that consumed entire towns and millions of acres of surrounding woodland. In California, temperatures rose to levels never before measured anywhere on Earth, and in Alaska, where 100-degree temperatures reached the Arctic Circle, some glaciers shrunk at the rate of 1 mile per year. But it wasn't until the third decade of the century came to a close that the Warming became unmistakable and undisputable. Global temperatures rose to their highest

165

levels on record, and nationwide, the United States experienced its warmest and driest years ever. Unprecedented numbers of hurricanes swept the Atlantic Ocean, with tropical storms straying far from their normal habitats to batter New England and California. Desert heat engulfed the United States and crept into Canada; in one summer alone, a third of the states set new all-time heat records. From Texas to Alberta, the Great Plains were subjected to higher temperatures—and lower rainfall—than normally seen in the deserts of Arizona. Before long, the combination of extreme heat and drought turned the fertile plains into dust, and high winds began blowing boiling clouds of soil eastward to the Atlantic Ocean.

Well, by now many of you old-timers—along with those youngsters who know their history—figured out that this apocalyptic upset of our climate is not something that may (or may not) happen in the 21st century, but a disastrous part of the 20th century. It was the Great Dust Bowl of the 1930s. (For the

Temperature trends over North America since 1930—North America has experienced a mixed bag of climate change over the past 70 years. Most of the western states have warmed by a fraction of a degree, and some arctic regions of Canada and Alaska have warmed as much as 2 degrees. Meanwhile, the eastern half of the U.S. has cooled by a degree or more. This general pattern—warmer in the Northwest, cooler in the Southeast—is what would be expected due to the Pacific Decadal Oscillation, with the Aleutian Low being unusually strong since the 1970s. NASA GODDARD INSTITUTE FOR SPACE STUDIES

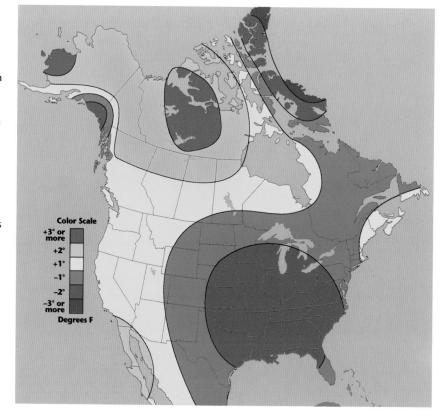

Color Scale

+3° or more	
+2°	
+1°	
−1°	
−2°	
−3° or more	

Degrees F

record, some of the other extreme events mentioned above are the Galveston, Texas, hurricane of 1900; the Idaho–Montana forest fire of 1910; Death Valley's record temperature of 134° F in 1913; 100° F at Fort Yukon, Alaska, in 1915; 121° F in North Dakota in 1936; the 1938 New England Hurricane; and Los Angeles' near-hurricane strength tropical storm in 1939.) In terms of its impact on the population at large, the Dust Bowl drought was the most devastating meteorological event in the history of the nation. To this day, the decade of the 1930s remains the warmest decade on record for much of the West and for the United States as a whole, and most of the heat records set during the Dust Bowl still hold.

In terms of its impact on the population at large, the Dust Bowl drought was the most devastating meteorological event in the history of the nation.

As for the greenhouse effect, the way in which our atmosphere can act like a greenhouse was first described by Jean-Baptiste Fourier (from France) in 1827, and in 1863, John Tyndall (England) proposed that variations in the concentration of carbon dioxide could trigger and terminate ice ages. In 1896, Svante Arrhenius (Sweden) predicted a 10-degree rise of global temperatures, due to increasing carbon dioxide levels, and in the 1930s, several scientists claimed that the warming was indeed occurring. However, for forty years after the Dust Bowl ended, a downturn in national (and global) temperatures put a damper on discussions of global warming, and the climate chit-chat turned to such things as incipient ice ages. Now that the climate appears to have warmed up a bit since the 1980s, the "greenhouse effect" has once again become a familiar term in newspapers, political debates, and even at social gatherings.

WHAT IS CLIMATE?

Inquiring minds want to know—is the "greenhouse effect" finally treating us to "global warming"? Along the same line, is the West, a region whose fortunes depend on the supply of water to make plants and people grow, wetter or drier now than it was in years past? Or is it all a bunch of cycles going round and round? These are interesting and important issues, but before we jump into the question of climate change, it makes sense to describe what climate is.

Climate is not the same as weather. Weather is the state of the atmosphere—temperature, pressure, wind, cloudiness, where it's raining and where it isn't, the positions of highs, lows, and fronts on the weather map, and many other factors—at any given moment. As Mark Twain noted once when asked what he thought about climate change, "Ma'am, the weather is *always* changing!" Climate, on the other hand, is the overall average of weather over an extended period of time. A complete description of the climate is not just a bunch of averages, but also includes a description of the variability of the weather from day to day, from summer to winter, and from year to year. For example, Denver's temperature can stray rather far from its annual average of 50° F, and nobody is surprised when one year averages several degrees warmer or colder than the previous year.

The most useful measurements for observing climate are the basics— temperature and precipitation.

It's trite but true that nothing is so constant as change, and climatologists recognize this. However, any definition that considers the Great Ice Age, the Age of the Dinosaurs, and the present as all being part of the same climate isn't very practical. While one exceptionally rainy spring, or bitter winter, or even decade-long drought, does not mean a permanent change of climate, the melting of mile-deep glaciers 12,000 years ago obviously does. The World Meteorological Organization, along with the U.S. National Weather Service, U.S. National Climate Data Center, and the Meteorological Service of Canada have concurred that averages taken over a 30-year period give the most useful definition of climate. The local climate data table in this book uses averages for 1971 through 2000. There's nothing magical about 30 years; many climatologists think 10 years works just as well. In either case, the averaging period is long enough to smooth out the large year-to-year fluctuations and reduce the impact of individual extreme years, but not so long as to mask important long-term changes of, say, rainfall patterns. Using the same statistical methods that pollsters use to predict your voting or buying habits, climatologists have deduced that a 10- to 30-year average of past climate gives a better guess as to what next year may bring than does a 5- or 50-year average. Nowadays we think of the most recent 30-year average of, say, temperature, as the current "normal" about which the weather fluctuates. However, these "normals" depend on the selection of years that go into them, and, like the weather, they are always changing. The truth is that there really is no exact normal.

There are many ways to express this thing called climate, depending on the information at hand. Lacking barometers, our ancestors used descriptive methods, recording crop successes and failures, freezes and thaws, and great deluges. This being the age of computers and weather instruments, the preferred method nowadays is to use numbers—lots of them. A bewildering variety of things in the atmosphere can be measured, and new ones are being thought up all the time. The most useful measurements for observing climate are the basics—temperature and precipitation. Long records of both are the cornerstone of climate studies; in the West they go back a century and a half. For earlier periods of time, we must rely on evidence supplied by tree rings, silt deposits in lakes, features gouged in the ground by now-melted glaciers, and even comments written by the earliest settlers.

WHAT A DIFFERENCE ONE YEAR MAKES

The shortest period of time that can be realistically called climate is a year, and the quickest kind of climate change is the variability between one year and the next. On the other end of the scale is the five-billion-year evolution of our planet's atmosphere, from a steamy soup of poisonous gases to the life-sustaining air of today. You can read about the history of the atmosphere in chapter 1; let's look at some of the things the climate has done since. For us mortals whose lives span less than a century, the most familiar and noticeable versions of climate change are the differences between one year and another. One summer may kill crops with drought, while the next drowns them with incessant rains. Some winters you may ski a trail, while other years is better suited for mountain biking. Winter temperatures averaged over the entire 11-state region of the western United States have changed as much as 11 degrees between one year and the next, and average temperatures for entire years have fluctuated by half that. Yearly rainfall totals for the region can be twice as high in wet years as in dry ones, and even greater contrasts are seen locally. In San Francisco, yearly rainfalls have ranged from 7 to 49 inches.

The year-to-year variability of climate in the West is enormous. In terms of averages, the changes are equivalent to moving from San Francisco to Seattle, or from Denver to Saint Louis. In fact, the changes are nearly as big as those that occurred during the Great Ice Age! The distinction, of course, is that the Ice Age went on for thousands of years, while the current fluctuations last a year or a season at a time. Nonetheless, we are talking about a rapid and large climate change.

Year-to-year climate fluctuations can have enormous economic consequences, due largely to the rapidity of the changes. Agricultural practices, for example, can adjust to the slower climate trends lasting decades or more. Nonetheless, imagine moving a California citrus orchard to Seattle for a year. It wouldn't do very well, would it? That's what an extremely cold year in California can be like.

In the previous chapter we saw the marked effects of El Niño on the climate of the West. However, Niños are relatively rare, and 10 or more years may pass between the really big ones. What happens the other nine years? There are all sorts of possibilities; the most plausible invoke some changes in the quantity and geographical distribution of heat entering and leaving the atmosphere. Remember, the need to carry excess heat from the tropics to the poles is what drives the weather in the first place. El Niño is an example of how huge shifts in the heat contained in the tropical ocean can affect climate.

The shortest period of time that can be realistically called climate is a year, and the quickest kind of climate change is the variability between one year and the next.

Similar shifts of warm and cold water can take place in the North Pacific, and no doubt affect the weather of the West. When the temperature contrast of the Pacific Ocean between Alaska and Hawaii is exceptionally great, the air tends to take on the same contrast, strengthening the jet stream. On the other hand, a weak temperature contrast weakens the jet. If the Pacific is cold to the west and warm to the east, the jet tends to follow the boundary by veering to the north. If it has nothing better to do, the jet tends to follow the boundaries between areas of warm and cold ocean water (this is similar to the Pacific Decadal Oscillation, but on a week-to-week or month-to-month, rather than decade-to-decade, basis). Sometimes it happens that way. However, from day to day the jet stream can, and does, stray far from its "expected" position.

Snow on the ground can also influence the heat balance of the atmosphere. Fresh snow is quite good at reflecting sunlight that would otherwise heat the ground. It is also an excellent radiator of heat out to space. Furthermore, a deep, insulating blanket of the white stuff prevents the residual warmth of the ground from seeping into the atmosphere. If Canada is covered with heavy snows early in the winter, polar air masses forming up north get a little colder than they would otherwise. Snow cover can affect the local climate too, particularly in the Great Basin. Cold air that pools in snow-coated valleys and basins may linger for weeks after it has left the nearby highlands. Cold pockets like this develop nearly every winter in valley locations such as the Salt Lake Valley, the basins of western Colorado, eastern Washington and Oregon, and the Snake River plain of southern Idaho. This can lead to marked temperature contrasts between the valleys and locations just 100 or 200 miles away.

Soil moisture is another possible culprit. In chapter 3, "Water for the West," we learned how damp soil from heavy rains can weaken the summertime ridge over the West and keep rain showers around. All these explanations have one problem in common—they don't really account for much of the variation that is actually seen from one year to the next. Every so often there is a winter or summer that looks like it suffered from one or another of these influences, but most years the weather acts in strange ways without any of these influences.

If the climate does not react frequently to outside forces, such as oceans and fallen snow, what is left? Can it be that it changes on its own whim? This may sound silly at first, but it is a possibility—which brings us to the elusive concept of "autovariability" (also known, less exotically, as "natural variability"). This has nothing to do with cars; it comes from the Greek prefix "auto," meaning "self." Our word translates to "self-changing." So what does it mean?

... the need to carry excess heat from the tropics to the poles is what drives the weather in the first place. El Niño is an example of how huge shifts in the heat contained in the tropical ocean can affect climate.

We know that tomorrow's weather pattern—the positions of highs, lows, jet streams, and other features on weather maps—depends very much on today's pattern. And today's weather pattern was determined by what happened yesterday. This concept is the essence of weather forecasting. By using the laws of physics and many calculations, we can predict what that change will be from one day to the next. Carrying this idea further, we realize that the weather pattern, say six months from now, will be affected by today's weather map. And so will every day between now and then. Certainly, the effect gets smaller as the interval gets longer, but it's still there. Remember, a single storm can be the most important feature of an entire winter, and a 100-mile difference in its track can make all the difference for your town. A severe winter may result from the weather "getting off on the wrong foot."

To put it in different terms, the whole sequence of fronts, cyclones, and anticyclones—the exact tracks they take and the specific dates and times they pass certain points—depends on their positions on the first day of the season (or any day). It's like rolling a boulder down a hillside. The law of gravity and the shape of the hill guide the path of the boulder once it is rolling, but the precise point of departure—the exact position of the rock when you shoved it—decides which of the infinite possible paths the rock actually takes and where it finally lands.

Unfortunately, our knowledge of the atmosphere isn't complete enough to allow forecasts to be made very far in advance. It's tough enough going five days into the future, much less six months. In effect, we know neither the shape of the hill nor the initial position of the rock, as it were, accurately enough to do better. This leaves us with the prospect that seasonal forecasts, those predictions of general weather patterns made a month to a year in advance, may never be as correct as we would like. It also leaves us with the uneasy prospect that a weather pattern, once it "gets off on the wrong foot," could linger for a year, or a century, or longer—in effect, a random climate change, self-inflicted by the atmosphere. Could a quick shift of the jet stream to a new and persistent pattern lead to another ice age? Next year, perhaps? As Ed Lorenz, a climatologist and mathematician at M.I.T., wrote in *Causes of Climate Change* (American Meteorological Society, 1968), "the atmosphere is neither a laboratory experiment nor a set of numbers in a computer, and we cannot turn it off and then set it in motion again to see whether a new climate develops." In other words, we won't know until—and unless—it happens.

Again, this "autovariability" is an elusive concept and difficult to understand. It's not as easy to deal with as some clear-cut, identifiable cause such as ocean temperatures or volcanoes. But it's there, and because of it, don't expect perfect long-range weather forecasts any time soon.

… tomorrow's weather pattern—the positions of highs, lows, jet streams, and other features on weather maps—depends very much on today's pattern. And today's weather pattern was determined by what happened yesterday. This concept is the essence of weather forecasting.

DROUGHT AND DELUGE

*There will come seven years of great plenty throughout
all the land of Egypt, but after them seven years of famine.*
—Genesis, 41:30

Cycles of rain and drought are nothing new. They plagued the pharaohs of Egypt, and today they plague the presidents and prime ministers of nations from Africa to North America. The United States had its share of problems during the great drought that scorched the central states during the 1930s. The drought area became known as the "Dust Bowl," and, curiously, it lasted seven years—from 1933 to 1940. The Dust Bowl combined with the Great Depression to make for the hardest times this country had seen since the Civil War. Many of the troubles were epitomized in John Steinbeck's 1939 novel, *The Grapes of Wrath,* describing the exodus of drought-ruined Oklahomans moving westward to California.

Dust Bowl—At the height of the Dust Bowl, a cold front whips up dirt into a boiling cloud descending on a ranch near Grenada, on the eastern plains of Colorado. BILL DODGE

The heart of the Dust Bowl extended to the eastern plains of Colorado and New Mexico, where huge volumes of dry topsoil were lifted from the ground and blown into the Atlantic by late winter cyclones. Farther west the drought

was much less severe, but dry conditions occasionally followed the Oklahomans into California.

Drought returned to the High Plains and mountain states in the mid-1950s. This time the conditions were not as severe as they were in the Dust Bowl, and with the agricultural lessons learned from that experience, crop yields stayed above the disaster level. In the mid-1970s, drought again struck the West. In February 1976, a dust storm reminiscent of the 1930s carried Colorado soil to the East Coast, although this one was less severe in the High Plains. It was a memorable dry spell on the West Coast, however (but note that while 1976 was a exceptional drought year in California and vicinity, up north the same year dumped 332 inches of precipitation on McLeod Harbor, Alaska—the most ever recorded in one year in the West. So droughts are regional, not global, events).

A glance at the dates of the great droughts shows what looks like a 20-year cycle. Indeed, from the mid-1850s up to the mid-1970s, drought has struck the Great Plains states with remarkable regularity. The similarity between this 20-year cycle and a 22-year cycle of storm activity on the surface of the sun, known as "sunspots," has led to speculation that sunspots may, in some way, cause the drought. However, this theory is very controversial. One problem is that after six drought cycles of 20 years each, the 22-year sunspot cycle is 12 years out of sync! Some recent droughts have occurred near the peak of the sunspot cycle, but in the 1800s they preferred the dips. And, at the appropriate phase of the solar cycle in the 1990s, the anticipated drought failed to occur at all—instead, the Great Plains (and much of the entire West) experienced some of their wettest years ever. It goes to show that while the sunspots cycle may load the dice in favor of drought, many other things are happening to our weather.

The droughts do occur, and if solar cycles fail to completely explain their timing, perhaps something else that punches the atmosphere every 20 years or so is responsible. One candidate is a thing called the Pacific Decadal Oscillation, or PDO (first discussed in chapter 10, "Sea of Storms"). Previously, I mentioned how year-to-year changes in the pattern of water temperatures in the Pacific Ocean can alter the wiggles of the jet stream as it blows into North America. Some recent research indicates that currents very deep in the ocean can cause the surface water temperature pattern to change more slowly, with certain patterns lasting for a decade or more. Meanwhile, the Atlantic Ocean has its own version called the North Atlantic Oscillation, or NAO. Perhaps the Great Plains, situated midway between these oceans, suffers (or enjoys) the effects of both of them, which, when you mix in a little bit of solar cycle

The heart of the Dust Bowl extended to the eastern plains of Colorado and New Mexico, where huge volumes of dry topsoil were lifted from the ground and blown into the Atlantic by late winter cyclones.

influence, can create a drought cycle that isn't quite regular. Research is being done on this question, and if it bears fruit, we may someday be able to predict these droughts.

The 20-year drought cycle, such as it is, doesn't always strike the same parts of the Plains. Farther west, in the Rockies and on the Pacific Coast, the 20-year cycle doesn't show up at all. Wet and dry spells appear to fluctuate more rapidly, and may be more influenced by the PDO, El Niño, and by that bane of climate forecasting, the natural variability of the atmosphere.

Terrible as the Dust Bowl was, history hints at more persistent and catastrophic droughts in the past. Some of the older pine trees along Colorado's Front Range contain records of an 18-year drought between 1729 and 1746 that was equal to three Dust Bowl droughts back-to-back! A record of tree rings (including growth rings measured from trees cut centuries ago and stored as beams in ancient ruins) has been counted from long-lived Douglas firs in the Mesa Verde region of southwestern Colorado. In this area the most intense drought appears to have occurred between 1573 and 1593. A less severe, but more persistent, 27-year-long drought from A.D. 1273 to 1300 has been linked to the disappearance of

Kliuchevskoy Volcano—
The Kliuchevskoy volcano, on the Pacific coast of Russia, spews ash, sulfur, water vapor, and carbon dioxide into the atmosphere in this view from the space shuttle *Endeavour* in 1994.
NASA

the Anasazi ("the Ancient Ones") from their pueblo dwellings all across the southwestern states. That drought appears to have extended into the Great Plains. The author of a study on ancient droughts, L. D. Bark, commented that "it is staggering to contemplate what effect such a drought would have today."

SOMETHING'S IN THE AIR

Now we get to some of the things that are more commonly thought of as causes of "climate change," such as the "greenhouse effect" due to carbon dioxide, and global cooling due to volcanoes. Compared to something as slippery as autovariability, the influences of dust and gases in the air are refreshingly simple to grasp. The theory behind these atmospheric pollutants, some natural and some man-made, rests on how they foul up the radiation balance of the globe. The Earth gains heat energy from sunlight striking the planet's surface and loses it by infrared radiation back out to space.

The current temperature of the Earth, averaged worldwide, results from the balance between heat gains and heat losses. Anything that changes the amount of incoming light or outgoing radiation, or both, should change the temperature of the planet. Yes, it's just like your checkbook—if you earn less, or spend more, or (especially) both, you go broke.

One way for planet Earth to earn less is to block out the sunshine. Volcanoes spew tremendous volumes of geologic gunk into the atmosphere, and these clouds can certainly blot out the sun. The ash cloud from Mount Saint Helens' cataclysmic eruption of May 18, 1980, kept towns from Yakima, Washington, to western Montana in the gloom for one or two memorable days. And these places did cool off from the lack of sunshine—afternoon temperatures were 10 degrees or more lower than they should have been. However, this was a local and short-term effect and qualifies more as a bizarre form of weather than as climate change.

To affect the climate, volcanic ash has to get high into the atmosphere and stay there for

Mount Saint Helens Ash Plume—The eruption of Mount Saint Helens on May 18, 1980, threw millions of tons of ash and gases into the atmosphere. In this satellite image, the plume of ash has spread across Washington into Idaho and Montana. By the next morning ash was falling on Colorado and Oklahoma. However, the long-term effect of the eruption on the climate, if any, was neglibible. NOAA

several years. Volcanic ash itself—those little particles of rock that gritted everyone's eyes after Mount Saint Helens—doesn't stay up all that long. Usually most of it falls from the sky after a few days and never has a chance to foul the climate. What does stay up are the clouds of sulfur dioxide gas shot into the sky from erupting volcanoes. Sulfur dioxide is the same noxious gas that comes from coal-burning factories and power plants. Saint Helens blew a half-million tons of the stuff into the atmosphere, equivalent to about five months' worth of emissions from all the industrial sources in the West.

Mount Saint Helens had relatively little sulfur, however, and much more of the stuff went skyward when the Philippine volcano Pinatubo blew in June 1991. The 1,000° F heat of the gases, combined with their muzzle velocities out the volcano's throat, sent tremendous amounts of sulfur dioxide into the stratosphere. The stratosphere is that part of the atmosphere approximately lying between 8 and 30 miles up. It is a pretty quiet place, and once gases get there, they stay for months or years.

The stratosphere is that part of the atmosphere approximately lying between 8 and 30 miles up. It is a pretty quiet place, and once gases get there, they stay for months or years.

As a gas, sulfur dioxide is transparent, but in the stratosphere it combines with water vapor to form little droplets of sulfuric acid—the same corrosive material that forms the clouds shrouding the planet Venus. Fortunately, Earth's sulfuric acid clouds never get as dense as Venus's, although after Pinatubo they were thick enough to block out 3 to 5 percent of the sun's rays. Pinatubo was the largest eruption since that of the Indonesian volcano Krakatoa in 1883. Other notable eruptions of the past century include Santa Maria in Guatemala (1902), Katmai in Alaska (1912), Agung, also in Indonesia (1963), and El Chichon in Mexico (1982). In 1815, yet another Indonesian volcano, Tambora, exploded with 50 times the force of Mount Saint Helens.

It's not hard to see these clouds of sulfuric acid if you look at the right time. At 15 miles up, they catch the last rays of sunlight long after the ground has slipped into darkness, resulting in brilliant lavender twilights about 20 minutes before sunrise and after sunset. Spectacular twilights went on for several years following all the big eruptions of the past century.

Theoretically, trimming the amount of sunlight by 3 or 4 percent should cool the surface of the planet. The amount of solar energy reaching the West also drops off by 4 percent every three days during autumn, due to the lowering sun angle. Over these three days, the West's average temperature normally cools about one degree, so we might expect a similar cooling following a big eruption. The volcanic cooling should last as long as the volcanic cloud—one or two years.

It's difficult to say whether these volcanoes really did cool the climate. Global temperatures appeared to dip by half a degree for a year or two following the blow-up of Pinatubo, and the summer of the following year (1992) was exceptionally cold in parts of the United States and Canada. On the other hand, worldwide average temperatures actually rose a bit following 1982's El Chichon eruption. This was, however, the same time El Niño was warming the Pacific Ocean. The global climate cooled about half a degree around the times of the Agung, Santa Maria, and Krakatoa eruptions, but some of these cooling trends seemed to start *before* the eruption! The detonation of Tambora was followed by all sorts of anecdotes about "1816, the Year without a Summer" in Europe and New England. While Philadelphia had its the coldest year in 250 years of records, farther south, Thomas Jefferson recorded a notably cool July at his home in Virginia.

Climate data for the West are equally noncommittal. There are no western weather records for 1816, and any changes following the more recent eruptions are mere fractions of a degree. However, global temperatures measured by satellites appeared to drop about one degree (as predicted) after the 1991 Pinatubo eruption. At my weather station in the Colorado Rockies, I recorded rare July snowfalls in consecutive years (1992 and 1993) following the eruption of Pinatubo, which is almost enough to make a believer out of me, although in 1982 I recorded no July snows following El Chichon. Probably the only way we'll ever know how much volcanoes can alter climate is to have another titanic eruption like Tambora or the 4,400 B.C. explosion of Mount Mazama (now Crater Lake, Oregon). It will be an expensive lesson to learn. When it went, Tambora took 92,000 souls with it.

Probably the only way we'll ever know how much volcanoes can alter climate is to have another titanic eruption like Tambora. … It will be an expensive lesson to learn. When it went, Tambora took 92,000 souls with it.

GREENHOUSES AND OUTHOUSES

We have found ways to keep the sunlight out. How about keeping the Earth's heat in? The way to do this, of course, is to block the escape of infrared radiation. Several trace constituents of the air, such as water vapor and methane (the flammable gas that rises from swamps, anthills, barnyards, and yes, outhouses), are quite effective at doing this. Being transparent, these gases let sunlight in; however, they do not let infrared radiation out. It works just like the glass covering of a greenhouse, and so the idea has been coined the "greenhouse effect," and the gases that cause this effect are "greenhouse gases." Another such gas is carbon dioxide, whose greenhouse effect on Venus has raised that planet's air temperature to 850° F.

Earth has carbon dioxide, too, but only 1/250,000 as much as Venus has. However, the amount of carbon dioxide in our atmosphere has been increasing over the past century, partly because of the burning of coal and oil, partly because of deforestation, and partly because of natural causes. The consumption of fossil fuels releases carbon dioxide that was removed from the atmosphere hundreds of millions of years ago when the coal and oil was formed. Deforestation of some parts of the planet, while offset somewhat by reforestation and fire suppression elsewhere, reduces the Earth's ability to remove carbon dioxide from the atmosphere. But even without human intervention, the oceans can release (or take up) tremendous volumes of carbon dioxide when the waters warm (as during El Niño) or cool. This process can be demonstrated by heating a pan of soda pop, seltzer water, or beer over a stove and watching the carbon dioxide bubbles being released to the atmosphere.

So far, human beings have burned up more than 10 cubic miles of oil, raising the amount of carbon dioxide in the atmosphere about 30 percent above its "natural" content of two centuries ago. Theoretically, this amount of additional carbon dioxide should warm the Earth about one-quarter of a degree Fahrenheit. This is the degree of warming that would happen if the greenhouse effect raised the temperature and left everything else in the atmosphere the same. It's not that simple, though. A warmer atmosphere evaporates more water from the oceans, and water vapor is also a greenhouse gas. As a matter of fact, water vapor is by far the main greenhouse gas in our atmosphere—there is 30 times as much vapor as carbon dioxide, and its contribution to the greenhouse effect is proportionately larger. So, in some theories, an increase in the vapor content of the atmosphere should further raise the temperature, changing that quarter degree warming to one or two degrees (or even more).

The greenhouse story gets even more complex due to the predilection of water vapor to condense into clouds. More moisture (due to the initial slight warming) should form more clouds. More clouds reflect more sunlight, reducing the amount of solar energy reaching the planet. At some point the reflected sunlight might outweigh the greenhouse effect, and limit the carbon dioxide warming. Another complication is that clouds form where air is rising, but since what goes up must come back down, there's going to be big holes between these clouds. These holes can let sunlight in, but they also let infrared radiation out. All of these factors are called "feedback" effects, and a positive feedback is one that would

Causes of Climate Change—The 150-year history of western temperatures are compared to slow changes in the brightness of the sun and with the increasing greenhouse effect. Notice that while temperature variations seem to follow the sun's brightness, the actual changes are much larger than what would be expected. The solar data is from *The Role of the Sun in Climate Change,* by Douglas Hoyt and Kenneth Schatten (Oxford University Press, 1997)

RICHARD A. KEEN

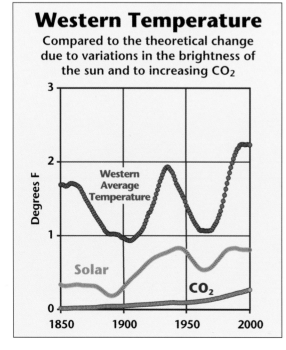

Western Temperature
Compared to the theoretical change due to variations in the brightness of the sun and to increasing CO_2

Degrees F

Western Average Temperature

Solar

CO_2

3

2

1

0

1850   1900   1950   2000

result in a larger warming than the initial quarter degree due to carbon dioxide alone. The point at which clouds cause the warming to level off, if at all, is a hot topic among researchers. Some forecasters put enough positive feedback mechanisms in their computer programs to raise the warming to 3 or 4 degrees, while others prefer to include negative feedbacks (such as reflective clouds) that virtually eliminate any warming.

As you read in the opening sentences of this chapter, the greenhouse effect was first predicted in 1863, and the hot Dust Bowl years convinced many that we were altering the climate (for the worse, of course). The subject was dropped during the cool years that followed—indeed, during the 1970s there were predictions that dust and soot from industry and farming would act like a perpetual volcanic cloud, and, outweighing the greenhouse effect, actually cool the planet. In 1972, the U.S. National Science Board concluded that "Judging from the record of the past interglacial ages, the present time of high temperatures should be drawing to an end ... leading into the next glacial age"! However, the warm 1980s rescued us from the incipient glacial age and revived the notoriety of carbon dioxide in scientific circles. Most recently, some hot years during the 1990s "elevated" discussion of "global warming" to political debates and bar rooms.

It's no coincidence that "greenhouse effects" seem to appear after warm spells, only to quietly disappear several years later. It's simple statistics. Scientists want to use the best and the latest data available. For studies of the global climate, this usually means looking at temperatures from 1870 or 1880 (the start of something resembling worldwide temperature records) up to the present. If the latest years in the temperature record are particularly warm, as they were in the 1930s and 1990s, the overall tendency for the whole period of record will be upward. This is especially true since the beginning of the record, the 1870s and 1880s, was relatively cool. The 1960s and 1970s were also on the cool side, and at that time it appeared that the climate was stable, if not cooling. You'll get a similar result if you roll dice a hundred times and keep a cumulative tab of your scores. The 1990s were a warm decade, but there's no convincing evidence that it was any warmer than the 1930s. With that kind of up-and-down variability in the climate, we just can't tell the greenhouse effect from everything else that goes on with the climate. A fraction of a degree is awfully small compared to the larger and more rapidly varying effects of El Niño and autovariability.

... human beings have burned up more than 10 cubic miles of oil, raising the amount of carbon dioxide in the atmosphere about 30 percent above its "natural" content of two centuries ago.

Caveat Emptor

This is a good time to warn you about climate data. It's tempting to gather as much temperature and rainfall data as can be found, compute a grand average, and look for minuscule differences to call "climate change." Statistically, there's safety in numbers—the more numbers you average, the more accurate that average is. That's only true if your data can be taken at face value, which in meteorology, unfortunately, is not always the case. Over the years, techniques and technology of weather observing have changed drastically. Thermometers are made differently now (they're electronic, not mercury), located differently, and often read differently.

... so many weather stations moved from downtowns to airports that some of the cooling observed after 1940 should really be called the "airport effect."

The favorite place for thermometers a century ago was atop the highest building in town, the idea being to measure the air free of obstructions by trees and other buildings. That all changed with the rapid growth in aviation during the 1930s and 1940s—pilots wanted, and needed, frequent weather reports from the places they were landing and departing. So, official weather stations began moving to airports, where the thermometers were placed on the grass between the runways. Temperatures can easily differ by several degrees between the top of City Hall and the airport. In fact, so many weather stations moved from downtowns to airports that some of the cooling observed after 1940 should really be called the "airport effect." In the decades since 1940, many cities have grown dramatically and some have grown so much that the airports are now engulfed in the urban sprawl—and the airport temperatures are now warmer. In California, for example, weather stations in the most populous counties (around the San Francisco Bay area and in the Los Angeles–San Diego area) warmed by 3 degrees since 1900, while those weather stations in the smaller, rural counties (population less than 100,000) showed no overall change over the same century. In general, the more populous the county, the greater the warming trend—a clear demonstration of the magnitude of the "urban warming" effect!

Even such a simple thing as the time of day the thermometer is read can affect a place's average temperature—this is discussed in more detail in chapter 13, "Watching the Weather." I have seen false "climate changes" of 2 to 4 degrees caused entirely by changes in location and reading time of the thermometer. Rainfall records are even worse, climatologically speaking, since the measured amount of rain and (especially) snow depends so much on the design of the gauge. When Canadians began using a new type of rain gauge in the 1950s, the annual precipitation (mostly snow) at many weather stations in the Arctic instantly doubled. The same goes for wind speed observations. A wind gauge commonly used decades ago is now known to read 20 to 30 percent too high. And so on.

Then there's the problem of computing a "global average temperature" from thousands of thermometers scattered around the world. It would be easy if all the thermometers were of the same type and placed uniformly (say, 10 miles apart) across the entire planet over big grassy fields (with the same kind of grass, of course). Furthermore, if you want to compare today's climate with the climate of one hundred or two hundred years ago, you'll want this same set-up of thermometers to have been in place one or two hundred years ago. The fact that 71 percent of the Earth is covered with oceans leaves the remaining 29 percent of the Earth to be covered with weather stations. In that 29 percent, there are large areas (deserts, Antarctica, Arctic forests, and tundra, etc.) that didn't have people taking temperature readings 50 or 100 years ago, and even now are sparsely settled. Some parts of the world—notably Russia and many tropical countries—have lost a large number of weather stations due to budget cuts. And there are very, very few weather stations that have been recording temperatures continuously for 100 years or more—so in the year 2000, you're not even averaging the same locations that you were in 1950 or 1850, for that matter.

What's the point of all this? Every January, several climate study groups around the world release their calculation of the average global temperature for the previous year. They usually pronounce last year to be a few tenths (or hundredths) of a degree warmer or colder than the previous year, and that the globe has warmed or cooled some fraction of a degree over the past 10, 50, or 100 years. I'd like to encourage you to think twice before believing that these tiny temperature changes are real.

There are other ways of measuring "global average temperatures," and each has its advantages and disadvantages. They are:

150 Years of Climate Trends across the West—Long-term trends in temperature for eight cities and towns across the West share some similar patterns—mild in the mid-1800s, cooling by 1900, warming back up by the 1930s and 1940s, a sharp cooling trend lasting into the 1970s, and warming into the 1990s. The heavy black line at the bottom of the chart shows a Western average temperature, based on these eight plus numerous other weather stations. RICHARD A. KEEN

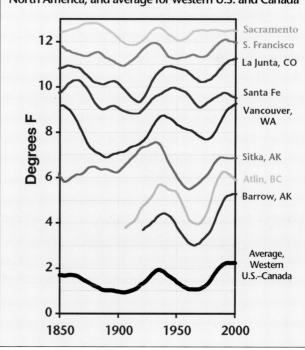

Weather Balloons—These are launched once or twice a day at a thousand locations around the globe. They meausure temperature, humidity, pressure, and winds at different heights as they ascend. By averaging temperatures throughout the several layers of the atmosphere, we can eliminate local effects that occur near the ground. However, worldwide coverage didn't begin until after 1958.

Weather Satellites—Several satellites have instruments that look down at Earth, measuring the temperature of the lowest several miles of the atmosphere. The measurements almost completely cover the world, thanks to the satellites' orbits; but coverage didn't begin until 1979.

Weather Maps—Using observations of temperature, pressure, and wind at various heights made by a variety of instruments, meteorologists construct weather maps for different levels above the ground. From these, temperatures can be averaged around the globe. A big advantage is that, because of the laws of physics that govern the motion of air, the various measurements—temperature, pressure, and wind—made by very different instruments provide a "check" on each other. But as with balloons and satellites, these maps weren't global until the 1970s.

... since the greenhouse effect is caused by radiation from the ground being intercepted and absorbed—and converted to heat—by gases in the atmosphere, the atmosphere should warm faster than the ground!

Since 1979, all three of these techniques of taking the Earth's temperature have told the same story—that the world's average temperature fluctuates wildly from year to year, but over those 20-plus years there has been no overall trend. Meanwhile, some tabulations of the temperatures recorded by ground-level weather stations suggest the world has warmed by half a degree over the same 20-odd years. Why the discrepancy? Some claim that the ground-level temperature is actually rising faster than the bulk of the atmosphere—but if so, that would be the opposite of what would be expected from the greenhouse effect. If anything, since the greenhouse effect is caused by radiation from the ground being intercepted and absorbed—and converted to heat—by gases in the atmosphere, the atmosphere should warm faster than the ground!

Curiously, when one compares the four different temperature measurements for North America, all four—including weather stations—are in excellent agreement. North America has no shortage of weather stations, and we can pick and choose those from rural locations (to eliminate the urban warming effect) and still have plenty of stations to cover the continent. A reasonable conclusion is that if the rest of the world, including the oceans, had complete coverage by weather stations that weren't subject to urban warming, we would also have an excellent agreement among the techniques. Which means, of course, that the Earth's climate did not warm (or cool, for that matter) by any measurable amount during the last 20 years of the 20th century.

It grieves me to sound so critical of these weather records, since I'm the proud operator of one such weather station—but we must realize that despite the great care and diligence of individual observers, the data we collect has real limitations. However, the original purpose of surface weather stations was not to figure a global average temperature, but rather to provide data for daily weather maps and forecasts, to document local and regional climate patterns (such as variations in rain and snow fall over a watershed) and, later, to aid in aircraft operations—all of which the worldwide network of weather stations does fantastically well.

Western Average Temperatures— The 20th Century

Computing an average temperature for a state, province, or region is a more manageable endeavor than trying to come up with a global average, and the national climate centers of the United States and Canada have done their best. I appreciate their efforts, and have combined their results into average annual temperatures for the entire West—11 states, 3 provinces, and the panhandle of Alaska. No doubt you will draw some of your own conclusions as you look at the graph. Following are some of my interpretations.

〄 During the 107 years of data, there is an overall warming trend of about 0.5 degrees Fahrenheit, similar to the warming trend seen elsewhere around the globe. However, the fat line (consecutive 30-year averages) tells some details of this trend—namely, the temperature rise has not been a steady uphill climb, and may not really be a warming trend at all. The West warmed half a degree between 1900 and 1930, lost that half a degree by 1960, and has since warmed back up to 1930 levels. The warmest years were 1934 and 1987, and the coldest years were 1955 and 1916. Rather than showing a steady upward trend, our climate appears to be alternating every 20 or 30 years between slightly warmer and slightly

Western Climate: the Past 107 Years—Average temperatures across Western North America (11 western states, 5 Canadian provinces and territories, and Alaska) for the past century show little evidence of any long-term climate trends. What this record does show is an enormous year-to-year variability that is, for the most part, still unexplained and unpredictable, superimposed on a longer-term up-and-down cycle that seems to follow some solar and ocean cycles. The Dust Bowl year 1934 was the warmest year on record in the West, with 1987 in second place, while the cool years include 1916, 1955, and 1985.

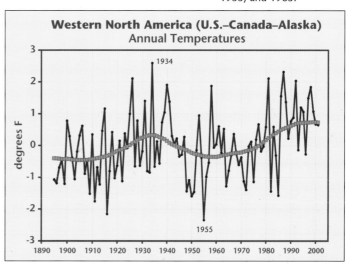

Western North America (U.S.–Canada–Alaska) Annual Temperatures

cooler conditions. Presently we are in a slightly warmer trend; one can only guess what the West's climate may be like in 2030.

A Tale of Three Cities

Another way to assess climate change in the West is to look at the record from places where someone had the foresight to start recording the weather a long time ago and others had the persistence to keep it up over the decades since. Here are temperatures from Santa Fe, New Mexico; San Francisco, California; and Sitka, Alaska. They all have records extending back over 150 years, and all three names begin with S—but that's where the similarity ends. The three cities represent very different climate regimes—Sitka is on an island along the Alaskan coast, subject to frequent Pacific storms and strongly influenced by the nearby ocean but also vulnerable to outbreaks of polar air. Santa Fe is far from any ocean at an elevation of 7,000 feet and has a sunny and dry climate with infrequent storms, and San Francisco, like Sitka, is on the coast but is quite immune to polar outbreaks (but sometimes subject to desert heat).

That's the setting; now the details. None of these cities is very trendy, meteorologically speaking—over 150 years, all three show no warming or cooling trends. More noticeable are the up-and-down wiggles of the 30-year means. Look at the lines and take note of the years that were warm or cold all across the West, as well as the decades when the longer-term wiggles are wiggling in the same direction.

There are also years and decades when the three cities have quite different climate fluctuations. Sitka and Santa Fe had opposite conditions—relatively warm at Santa Fe, cool at Sitka—during the 1860s and in the late 1940s and early 1950s, while both places were relatively warm during the 1930s (as was San Francisco). Meanwhile, all three cities were cool in the 1960s and 1970s. This tells us that over the past 150 years, the biggest climate changes are regional (not global), and that your local climate is affected largely by year-to-year and decade-to-decade shifts in the average positions of weather features such as the Pacific High, the jet stream, and tracks of storms and Arctic High pressure

A Tale of Three Cities— 150 years of temperatures for Sitka, Santa Fe, and San Francisco. DATA FROM NASA GODDARD INSTITUTE FOR SPACE STUDIES

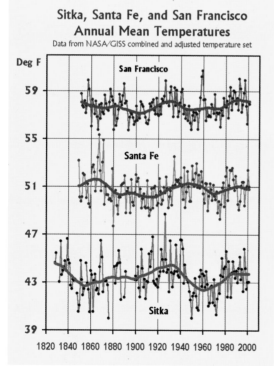

Sitka, Santa Fe, and San Francisco Annual Mean Temperatures
Data from NASA/GISS combined and adjusted temperature set

systems. A glance at the graph shows that anywhere in the West, one year can easily be 2, 3, even 8 degrees warmer or colder than another year, mostly due to random "natural variability" and, perhaps, ocean currents. Compared to that, a half-degree global (or regional) warming or cooling may seem rather insignificant. However, these smaller, slower, and larger-scale climate fluctuations can sometimes become larger, longer-lasting, and global, at which point they may alter the history of humanity (take the Ice Ages, for example—both great and little!).

The "Little Ice Age"

The longest spell of odd weather in the recorded history of North America was a frosty period known as the "Little Ice Age." It could be the reason this book is written in English instead of Norwegian (or Icelandic). Let me explain ...

A thousand years ago the climate was enough warmer than today—perhaps by 2 or more degrees—that Vikings sailed their sturdy little boats from Scandinavia to Iceland, Greenland, Newfoundland, and possibly as far south as Massachusetts (reports that they sailed to Minnesota have been discounted). Greenland was so mild that self-sufficient, crop-raising colonies thrived for more than two centuries. Times got tough in these colonies after A.D. 1200, when a sharp downturn in the climate made agriculture iffy at best. Sailing conditions around Greenland worsened as the ice thickened, and by A.D. 1300, the homeland lost all contact with their colonies (this was during the same time of the severe drought in the Southwest that may have driven the Anasazi to evacuate their land). Explorers returning to Greenland centuries later could find no trace of the Norse colonies, and today the ice-capped island is inhabited by the Inuit, who arrived around the same time as the Vikings but who fished, rather than farmed, and were better able to adjust to the whims of the climate. The Norse settlers in Iceland survived the tough times, and today that island nation is peopled by the descendents of the Vikings. One can speculate about the history of North America had the Greenland colonies also been able to endure and expand southward.

That cold spell—the Little Ice Age—persisted for more than four centuries, with moderations around 1400 and 1600, finally ending around 1720 (some climatologists think the Little Ice Age had a relapse in the early 1800s before expiring completely). When Thomas Jefferson wrote that "snows are less frequent and less deep," he was describing the warm-up that followed the Little Ice Age. There are no temperature records from the time, but evidence ranging from rocks left by glaciers in the Alps and Rockies, to Chinese and European

The longest spell of odd weather in the recorded history of North America was a frosty period known as the "Little Ice Age." It could be the reason this book is written in English instead of Norwegian (or Icelandic).

Bristlecone Pines—
These trees can live for several thousand years, and their growth rings provide an excellent record of climate change.
ARLEN HUGGINS

harvest records, to dates of the Japanese emperor's cherry blossom festivals, as well as the sad history of the Viking settlers, indicate the cooling amounted to 2 degrees or more. In the West, the Little Ice Age is evident in the record of Bristlecone pine tree rings in the White Mountains of California. For trees near timberline, tree growth is limited more by temperature than it is by moisture, and thin rings indicate cold, short summers.

As is the case for all climate fluctuations, we don't know for sure what caused the Northern Hemisphere to cool down for 400 years. However, scientists (notably Jack Eddy, a solar astronomer at the National Center for Atmospheric Research) doing some clever detective work, found that Chinese records of spots on the sun, Scandinavian sightings of the aurora borealis, and variations in the amount of certain kinds of carbon atoms in tree rings all strongly suggest that as Earth cooled, so did the sun.

The same record of solar activity indicates something that looks like a 200-year cycle, with peaks around 1200, in the late 1300s, around 1600, in the late 1700s, and in the late 1900s. Without knowing why such a cycle might occur, we can't be sure it will repeat itself—but if it does, the sun may start cooling down over the coming century, and as the sun chills, so do we.

THE SUN, OUR STAR

Since first grade, we all learn that the sun is a star, but we have always considered it a very special star. So special, in fact, that centuries ago people got into trouble for thinking our star was anything but flawless. We now realize that the sun is indeed not "perfect," but has its blemishes—sunspots. We are also now beginning to realize that like most other stars in the universe, the sun is a variable star—its brightness is not constant, but fluctuates on time scales from seconds to centuries to billions of years.

The best-known of the sun's cycles are the 11- and 22-year-long "Sunspot Cycles." Sunspots are relatively cool (and therefore, dark), Earth-sized patches on the sun, caused by disturbances in the sun's magnetic field (much like storms on Earth are disturbances in atmospheric pressure). For some unknown reason, the number and sizes of these spots varies over an

11-year cycle, with lots of spots around 1989 and 2000, and fewer spots in between. Although the spots themselves are cooler than the rest of the sun, 20 years of satellite measurements show that the entire sun radiates about 0.1 percent more energy with more spots than with less. A quick calculation shows that this might change Earth's temperature by a tenth of a degree—hardly a measurable amount. But not all sunspot cycles are the same. Some have more sunspots than other cycles, and some are quicker (9 years) or slower (15 years) than the average.

Fortunately for our understanding of the sun, our star is really fairly ordinary—a middle-aged Main Sequence G2 star almost halfway through its 12-billion-year lifetime, to be specific. By observing the behavior of dozens of sun-like stars in our neighborhood of the galaxy, astronomers are effectively looking at what variations the sun may exhibit over thousands of years. Also, it's a lot easier to determine the precise brightness (and changes in brightness) of other stars, since there are many other stars to compare their brightnesses with (the sun has no comparison!). What we have found from studies of other stars is that the sun's brightness can vary by a few tenths of a percent, and that during the Little Ice Age, the sun was radiating about 0.3 percent less energy than it is now, cooling the Earth by more than a degree.

Since the Little Ice Age ended around 1720, lesser fluctuations of the sun (as indicated by rather detailed sunspot observations made since Galileo observed the sun in 1610) should have caused the Earth's temperature to fluctuate by about one-half degree Fahrenheit, which is about twice the theoretical change due to the carbon dioxide–induced greenhouse effect. But while increasing concentrations of carbon dioxide should cause a steady rise in temperatures, the erratically varying sun would lead to a more irregular change in Earth's temperature—cool in the 1800s, a warming trend into the 1940s, then cooling through the 1960s, and a warming again to the end of the 20th century. If the timing of these warming and cooling spells sounds familiar, they should—since 1895, the fluctuations of the West's temperatures have closely paralleled the ups and downs of the sun's energy output (as best as scientists can figure).

Western Climate, the Past 1,200 Years—Nature's record of the climate is written in the growth rings of trees. Just as trees in arid climates grow more during a wet year, trees surviving near timberline grow more when their growing season is unusually warm. The widths of the rings in bristlecone pines in the White Mountains of California, averaged over 20-year intervals, tell the story of the past ten centuries. The record reveals a warming from the 9th through the 12th centuries A.D., while the Anasazi were flourishing in the Southwest. With warmth came drought, however, and the Anasazi culture disappeared in the 1200s. We are now in another slow warming trend that began three centuries ago. Longer-term records show that the current century, along with the 1100s, are the warmest centuries since 2700 B.C.
DATA FROM LAMARCHE

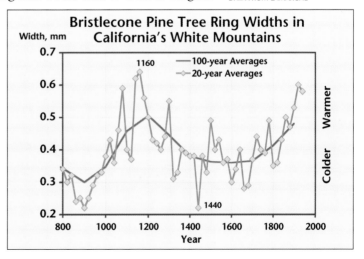

Bristlecone Pine Tree Ring Widths in California's White Mountains

THE GREAT ICE AGE

If there was a Little Ice Age, it figures that there must have been a "Big" Ice Age. And there were—several of them, collectively known as the Great Ice Age. No worries about inaccurate thermometers and half-degree temperature differences here; the evidence is literally carved in stone all across the West. All across the Cascades, Sierras, Rockies, and other mountain ranges throughout the West, glaciers gouged wide valleys and broad, round basins known as cirques, often so close together that only knife-edge ridges separate them. The rocky rubble from this grandest of earth-moving schemes piled up at the sides and ends of the glaciers into pebble- and boulder-filled moraines. Half-mile-deep "rivers of ice" from Colorado's San Juan Mountains invaded the suburbs of Durango, a scene repeated near many other future cities of the West. Farther north, the locations of some of the West's greatest cities—Seattle, Vancouver, Calgary, Edmonton, Wolf Point—were under thousands of feet of solid ice. Medicine Lake, Montana, where the mercury soared to 117° F during the Dust Bowl, was frozen solid year-round. Looking eastward, sheets of glacier ice extended as far south as New York City and Saint Louis; the Ohio and Missouri Rivers form the approximate boundaries of the ice sheet. Other ice sheets covered Antarctica and parts of Europe, from Great Britain to Russia.

The greatest ice sheet of all time, the Laurentide Ice Sheet, initially formed around Hudson's Bay, and spread over the northeastern half of the continent. This mass of ice extended all the way to the foothills of the Canadian Rockies in Alberta, but in the United States it just barely entered northern Montana. Mountain glaciers in the northern Rockies and Cascades, along with the Coast Mountains of British Columbia and the Alaska Range, grew and coalesced into a smaller ice sheet, the Cordilleran Ice Sheet, which filled Puget Sound and other fjords along the northern Pacific Coast, and which later merged with the larger Laurentide Ice Sheet. Meanwhile, the Yukon Valley and Arctic coast of Alaska remained ice-free.

The Northern Hemisphere: Ice Age vs. Today—18,000 years ago, mile-deep ice covered almost all of Canada and a good portion of the northern United States. Today, the Ice Age lingers on in Greenland and on a few small ice caps in northern Canada. NOAA

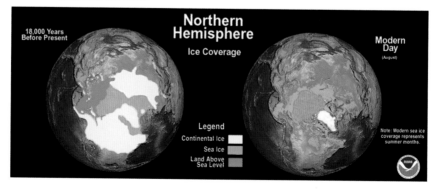

Although most of the western United States escaped the ice sheet, a great deal of evidence shows that the regional climate was vastly different from today's climate. Mountain glaciers in the southern Rockies and Sierras grew for miles beyond their present locations, and what are now alkali flats and salt lakes in the Great Basin were then huge freshwater lakes more than 100 miles across. The largest of these was Lake Bonneville, which extended for 300 miles across Nevada, Utah, and Idaho. At times, glaciers from the Wasatch Mountains may have flowed into this inland sea. All this points to a much cooler and wetter climate than we have now.

The Way It Was—The Gilkey Glacier, near Juneau, Alaska, is what much of the Sierras and Rockies looked like during the Great Ice Age.
RICHARD A. KEEN

Not only was it colder during the Ice Age, it was also windier. Geologic relics from the old days, such as wind-scoured rocks found along the eastern slopes of the Rockies, suggest that the prevailing westerlies blew stronger back then. We might expect this, since the Arctic cooled off much more than did the tropics, increasing the equator-to-pole temperature difference. This, in turn, would strengthen the jet stream. However, the same strong westerlies that brought more moisture to much of the West would have diverted the northward flow of moisture from the Gulf of Mexico, leaving the High Plains area east of the Rockies in perpetual drought. Thus, western weather during the Ice Age may have seen continuous storms blasting the West Coast and dumping snow in the mountains, with incessant chinook winds howling east of the Rockies—even during summer. It's speculative, of course, but plausible.

The climate of the West has warmed and dried considerably since the Ice Age. Lake Bonneville is now gone; in its place are the Great Salt Lake and the seasonally wet Bonneville Salt Flats. At its peak, Lake Bonneville was more than 1,000 feet deeper than present-day Great Salt Lake, and the lines of ancient beaches can now be seen high and dry on the slopes of the mountains ringing the Salt Lake Basin. Compared to the 20-foot fluctuations of the level of the Great Salt Lake, in recent years (see graph on page 32) we can see how incredibly different the climate of the Ice Age truly was.

Apparently there were many ice ages—various counts range from 4 or 5 to 20 or more. The whole mess started about 2 million years ago, and the ice has advanced and retreated every 100,000 years or so ever since. It's hard to tell how exactly how many times the glaciers grew and shrunk, since each advance often erased the geological evidence of the previous glaciers. Between each of these ice ages the climate was much like it is today. The last round began 80,000 or 90,000 years ago, and the glaciers reached their maximum extent 18,000 years ago (or 16,000 B.C.). Around 12,000 B.C., the world's climate suddenly warmed up to near-present temperatures, and the Big Melt began. By 5,000 B.C., most of the West's glaciers had withered away to their present size, leaving only glorified snow patches on many formerly glacier-fringed peaks and ranges, and breaking the Cordilleran Ice Sheet into a group of separate ice fields in Alaska and British Columbia. At this same time, the last patch of the Laurentide Ice Sheet disappeared from northern Quebec. Remnant ice caps dot some islands of northeastern Canada, while the Ice Age still lives in Antarctica and Greenland.

Inside a Glacier—Blue light filters into an ice cave on the Lemon Creek Glacier, near Juneau. The cave was carved by running melt water.
RICHARD A. KEEN

Many theories exist about the cause of the ice ages, and some of them may actually be true. One plausible theory was put forth in 1920 by a Serb named Milutin Milankovitch and concerns the wobbles of the Earth and its orbit. Like a spinning top, the axis of Earth's poles wobbles around and

changes its tilt in cycles of 26,000 and 40,000 years, while the shape of the Earth's orbit around the sun changes over several longer cycles—up to 100,000 years. The actual size of the orbit never changes, and, over an entire year, the total amount of sunlight reaching the Earth never changes. Thanks to these wobbles, however, the solar heating of the different hemispheres during different seasons varies by up to 5 or 10 percent over thousands of years. If the Northern Hemisphere gets less sunlight during the summer, that season is cooler. As it is now, the winter snows that cover the far north barely melt before the summer is over; if the summers were 5 degrees cooler, the snow might not melt at all from some places. That means the snow would build up year after year. Once the snow cover gets thick enough, it can increase the cooling by reflecting sunlight back into space. Keep that up, and in a few thousand years there's an ice sheet.

The Milankovitch theory predicts several cycles that might affect the buildup of snow, and some of them do fit the cycles of the ice ages. The theory also predicts that the past ice age was not the last one, and that we may have already passed the peak of the warming separating the last ice age from the next. In Alaska, there's evidence that some glaciers—such as Taku Glacier near Juneau—now occupy valleys that were melted clear a few thousand years ago.

Other ice age theories put forth that epochs of increased volcanic activity spew global clouds of dust into the upper atmosphere that block the sunlight, cool the planet, and get the glaciers growing, or that in it's enormous orbit around the center of the Milky Way Galaxy, the solar system passes through clouds of interstellar dust and gas that have the same effect as the volcanic dust (not many climatologists subscribe to this theory). Yet another possibility has to do with our old nemesis, the natural variability of the atmosphere that we see from year to year (we expect that no two winters will be alike, and that one will, of course, be snowier than the other). If, by chance, the world has a sequence of several *extremely* cold summers and snowy winters, arctic ice sheets can build up in the winter while not melting in the summer. It's the same setup as the Milankovitch theory postulates, but instead of ice ages being triggered by the well-ordered wobbles of the Earth, they are triggered by a random extreme of weather that could happen next year—or not for another million years. Stay tuned!

In Alaska, there's evidence that some glaciers—such as Taku Glacier near Juneau—now occupy valleys that were melted clear a few thousand years ago.

What's It All Mean?

Yet no matter how large the computer, no matter how many thousands of acres of virgin forest are devastated to provide paper for its maw, the results it produces are no better than the ideas and data that went into their production.

—Craig Bohren, *Clouds in a Glass of Beer*

If nothing else, you have probably realized how amazingly complex climate and climate change are. Sunspots, ocean currents, carbon dioxide, volcanoes, ice ages—all have caused (or maybe are causing) the climate to change over past and future years, centuries, and millennia. Dozens of "climate modelers" around the world spend a great deal of computer time generating forecasts of what the world's climate will be like when they're no longer around to answer for their attempts. It has been said that only fools and charlatans dare predict the climate or the stock market. I generally agree with that assessment. Having spent so many pages discussing the possible causes of climate variations, however, I feel obligated to tie it all together in the form of a prediction, so, here goes. ...

Sunspots, ocean currents, carbon dioxide, volcanoes, ice ages—all have caused (or maybe are causing) the climate to change over past and future years, centuries, and millennia.

First of all, we have no way of knowing what El Niño, the PDO, and volcanoes will do in the future, except that they'll continue doing their thing intermittently when they darn well feel like it. In my opinion, solar activity appears to be the largest factor influencing the temperature of the West (and the world) over the past 150 years (and, indeed, the past 1,000 or more years, as evidenced by tree rings), and I expect that to continue. But what will the sun do in the near future? If the sun is now headed into a downward half of a supposed 200-year cycle, we could see a cooling of a degree or so, back to the levels of the 1800s—unless, of course, our star has other plans.

Then there are the future effects of increasing carbon dioxide, which depends on two things—how much current levels of this greenhouse gas have already affected our climate, and how much more carbon dioxide there will be in, say, the next century. For the first question, the close link between solar variations and temperature doesn't leave much room for a big effect due to carbon dioxide, and it's likely that the *direct* effect of carbon dioxide is all we're getting—that is, one-quarter of a degree over the past century. No positive feedbacks, as climate modelers like to put into their computer programs; just the rather small direct effect of this gas. On the second question, the growth rate of carbon dioxide in the atmosphere has slowed down over the past 20 years. At the current rate of growth, carbon dioxide levels will reach 500 parts per million, or nearly twice the pre-Industrial Age amount of 280 parts per million, around the year 2100. If this is the case, the world will warm by another half a degree Fahrenheit over the coming century, a change smaller than what the climate has already undergone during most of our lifetimes, and which could easily be countered by other "natural" causes (such as a dimming sun). These predictions are nothing fancy—just statistical correlations of what has happened in the past and extrapolations of what might happen in the future.

Not everyone agrees with this assessment, of course. Some scientists, like Dr. William Gray at Colorado State University, think the main thing driving climate change from one decade to the next is not in the sky above, but deep in the oceans below. It's the great "Oceanic Conveyor Belt," a huge, circuitous current that links the surface and deep waters of all the world's oceans and provides a connection between the North Atlantic Oscillation, the Pacific Decadal Oscillation, El Niño, and perhaps a few more of these things we haven't thought of yet. It's an intriguing idea, especially since it's championed by one of the very few people who regularly and successfully predicts the following years' weather (he makes annual forecasts of hurricane activity in the Atlantic Ocean).

Doubtlessly, each and all of these possible causes of climate change— wobbles of the Earth, the varying sun, ocean currents, volcanoes, gases in the

Dry Falls—The melting ice cap at the end of the last ice age sent tremendous amounts of water running to the sea. In eastern Washington, the runoff was blocked for years by a lingering lobe of glacial ice. When the lobe melted, one of the greatest floods in history was unleashed, carving channels and waterfalls that are now dry. RICHARD A. KEEN

atmosphere, and autovariability—have some effect. The big question is: Which ones have the greatest influence, and which ones are relatively unimportant? It will be a long time before climatologists agree on the correct answer.

But Not to Worry …

Astronomers tell us that ever since the sun coalesced out of a swirling cloud of gas and dust, it has been slowly brightening, and that it is now about 30 percent brighter than it was 4.5 billion years ago. At that rate, when the sun brightens another 10 percent in about a billion years, the Earth will heat up by 20 or 30 degrees, giving Seattle an equatorial climate.

Let's say we survive "global warming," or the next ice age (whichever comes first). Then what? Astronomers tell us that ever since the sun coalesced out of a swirling cloud of gas and dust, it has been slowly brightening, and that it is now about 30 percent brighter than it was 4.5 billion years ago. At that rate, when the sun brightens another 10 percent in about a billion years, the Earth will heat up by 20 or 30 degrees, giving Seattle an equatorial climate. Not too bad, you say, until you realize that the Tropics would also warm up by 20 or 30 degrees. At those temperatures, rapid evaporation of the oceans will create a water vapor greenhouse that no amount of cloudiness can counteract. At this point a "runaway greenhouse effect" will begin, and before long the oceans will disappear completely, turning the Earth into a not-quite-so-hot version of Venus. A sad end to our blue-green planet, the loveliest in the solar system? Only if you underestimate the creativity and spirit of our species—there are already discussions about how to deal with this problem by nudging an asteroid out of its orbit so that it swings by the Earth every few centuries. Each time the asteroid swings by the Earth, its weak gravity would tug our planet a little farther from the sun. Widening the Earth's orbit by 1 mile every 200 years would work just fine.

LIGHTS IN THE SKY

Now this science is far more beautiful and useful than others, and therefore more delightful—because we take special delight in vision, because light and color have singular beauty.

—Roger Bacon,
Perspectiva, 1267

Long before flying saucers were first reported in 1947, humans have looked up at lights in the sky with attitudes ranging from amusement to awe. It's a good thing, too, because that's how meteorology began. Even if we choose to ignore that bit of the universe that lies above and beyond the atmosphere and confine ourselves to things within the Earth's sheath of air, there's still a fantastic variety of visual phenomena. Here are a few of my favorites:

METEORS

Meteors seem like a good place to begin, because what would meteorologists study if not meteors? We have all taken high school science and know that meteors are pieces of space dust burning high in the atmosphere that are sometimes called "shooting stars." Of course, meteorologists study other stuff, right? Wrong! The dictionary defines "meteor" as, among other things, "a phenomenon in the atmosphere, such as lightning, a rainbow, or snow." "Shooting stars" also occur in the atmosphere, so we may add them to the list. It just happens that this last definition has become the one most commonly used nowadays.

Most of the confusion comes from the fact that meteorology has changed somewhat since it became a science and received its name some 2,500 years

Meteor Shower—On the morning of November 18, 2001, meteors radiating from the constellation Leo streaked across the sky at the rate of 2,000 per hour. One of the brightest that night slashes across Orion, while a fainter meteor skims nearby.

RICHARD A. KEEN

Meteor Train—As the brilliant meteor disintegrated, it left a trailing cloud of glowing dust and gas called a "meteor train." This train was visible twisting in the wind (yes, there are winds 60 miles up!) for several minutes afterward.

RICHARD A. KEEN

ago. The name is Greek, and comes from *meteoros,* meaning "high in the air," and originally *anything* that appeared in the sky was fair game for meteorologists. We now associate meteorology with things in the lower part of the atmosphere, and the higher stuff—like "shooting stars"—belongs to astronomers.

By the common definition, meteors are indeed pieces of space dust burning up in the atmosphere. The study of these meteors is called "meteoritics." The dust particles range in size from microscopic to basketball-sized, with "typical" shooting stars being about the size of a pinhead. Anything larger than a basketball is likely to reach the ground and become a "meteorite." Most appear to the remains of disintegrated comets. The European "Giotto" space probe to Halley's Comet in 1986 and the U.S. "Deep Space 1" mission flyby of Comet Borrelly in 2001 revealed that comets are mountain-sized masses of ice and dirt, much like that found in urban snowbanks. Comets become visible when the ice evaporates and forms a cloud of sunlit water vapor and other gases. As the ice evaporates over millions of years, leftover dust is strung out along the comet's orbit. The comet disappears when all the ice is gone, leaving an orbiting stream of dust. When our planet plows through the dust, we see meteors.

The combined orbital velocities of the Earth and ex-comet send the meteor particles into our atmosphere at speeds of 10 to 45 miles per *second.* For comparison, space shuttles come back in at 5 miles per second, and even at that speed they glow red hot. Meteors get white hot, briefly reaching temperatures of 5,000° to 10,000° F before they're gone. They first appear at altitudes of 70 miles or so, and most burn up completely in a second or two, by which time they're down to 40 or 50 miles above the ground.

The bright thing we see as the meteor or shooting star is not so much the burning pinhead of dirt as it is a glowing ball of air surrounding the particle. The collision of dust particle and air molecules heats the air, too, causing it to shine—just like the extremely hot air inside a lightning flash. Some of the larger and faster (and therefore hotter) meteors leave long, glowing trails of hot gases and burnt meteor dust in their wake. These trails can last for minutes, sometimes even an hour, after the meteor has gone, by which time they have become contorted into fantastic shapes by the winds in the upper atmosphere. Using observations of meteor trails to measure these winds, scientists have come up with speeds of 100 m.p.h. and faster. This is how the earliest measurements of high-altitude winds were made, which gets us back where we started—meteorologists *do* study meteors!

***Challenger* over the Rockies**—The space shuttle *Challenger* soars above the Continental Divide in this pre-dawn time exposure. The International Space Station, lauched in 1998, is now the largest object ever flown by humans, and is easily seen over most of the planet. Log on to HTTP://SPACEFLIGHT.NASA.GOV and click on the "skywatch" link to find out when the shuttle flies over your house. RICHARD A. KEEN

Columbia Comes Home—Looking like a golden star with a silver trail, the space shuttle Columbia streaks across the sky above southern Colorado on a successful return to Earth in 1995. The sight of people coming home from a trip into space is one of the most beautiful in the heavens. The double trail was caused by the wind shaking the camera tripod during this time exposure. RICHARD A. KEEN

Why Is the Sky Blue?

Probably the first thing we ever notice about the sky is that it is blue. We surely would consider any other color odd, but always at the back of our minds the question nags ever so slightly: "Why is the sky blue?" The answer has to do with sunlight and molecules, and with a process called "scattering."

Spend a day on a fishing pier, and if the fish aren't biting, you might notice what happens when waves strike the pilings. Big waves splash against the pilings, but most of the wave continues on its way. Small waves, or more like ripples, bend around the pilings, with the ripples rounding either side of the post heading off in opposite directions. Since the waves and ripples go off in various directions, their bending is called scattering.

Light is also a wave, but made of electric and magnetic fields instead of water. Waves of visible light are quite small, too, with their ripples being about 1/50,000th of an inch apart (this distance is the wavelength). Like all waves, light scatters, but the bending is caused by things like molecules of air. And again like waves in the ocean, shorter wavelengths of light (ripples) scatter more than longer wavelengths (waves). One way to visualize it is that to shorter waves, molecules look larger and present more of an obstacle to their forward motion.

To us sunlight appears white or pale yellow, but its light is really a mixture of all colors, from blue to green, yellow, orange, and red. Blue light has a shorter wavelength than red light, so when a sunbeam shines through the molecules of air over our heads, blue light is scattered the most, while red light, which is scattered the least, continues in a straight line. When you look at the sky away from the sun, then, blue more than red, yellow, or green is being scattered in your direction. That's why the sky is blue!

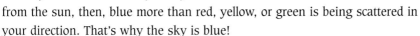

Death Valley Twilight— Rays of sunlight from the distant setting sun passing high overhead are scattered by the thin air, producing the greens and violets of twilight. RICHARD A. KEEN

TWILIGHT

When you look at the sun, your eyes take in a beam of light that has had more blue light than red light scattered out of it. So the sun, which looks white in outer space, appears slightly yellowish. When setting, the sun shines through 20 to 40 times as much air as it does when it's high in the sky, and proportionately more blue light is scattered away. That's why the setting sun appears red. (The same is true for the rising sun, of course.)

Long after the sun has set, its light continues to scatter off the molecules of the upper atmosphere. Twilight can last an hour or two after sunset, by which time the glow you see low in the west is sunlight scattered by molecules 40 to 50 miles high and 600 miles away. Even though the light reaching these molecules from the distant setting sun is red, the molecules still prefer to scatter blue light. The result is a mixture of reds, greens, and blues.

Light waves are small, but molecules are even smaller. A typical air molecule is about one hundred-millionth of an inch across, or less than a thousandth the size of a wavelength of light. Particles that are larger than one or two wavelengths, like dust and cloud droplets, scatter light quite differently—these particles look big to all wavelengths of light, and all wavelengths of visible light are scattered equally well. That's why clouds look white.

Volcanic Twilight—
Several times in the past century, volcanic eruptions around the world have sent more massive clouds of sulfurous gases into the stratosphere. These gases remained for years, causing brilliant lavender sunsets and sunrises (such as this one two years after the 1982 eruption of El Chichon), and possibly affecting the global climate. RICHARD A. KEEN

Most clouds are confined to the lower atmosphere, but on occasion clouds can form in the stratosphere, 15 to 40 miles up. Every now and then, ice-particle clouds form high above the Arctic in the summer, but this is extremely rare south of 50 degrees latitude. At lower latitudes, the most common stratospheric clouds are the layers of sulfuric acid droplets spewed out by exploding volcanoes. These larger particles scatter the setting sun's red light much more effectively than do molecules, and twilights take on a different hue. Instead of greens and blues, we see much brighter yellows, reds, and purples scattered by the globe-circling layers of volcanic acid. Sometimes shadows of distant clouds are casted on the volcanic layer, creating dark rays on the bright twilight sky. These spectacular twilights usually last two or three years after major volcanic eruptions, of which there have been only four in the past century (some on the other side of the world!).

Aurora Borealis

Some say the Northern Lights are the glare of the Arctic ice and snow;
And some that it's electricity, and nobody seems to know. ...
—Robert Service,
The Ballad of the Northern Lights

Of all the lights in the sky, none give the cool shivers like the aurora borealis, or northern lights. They often begin as a pale green arch hugging the northern horizon, but then searchlight beams crisscross the sky and multiply and merge into red and green curtains that march overhead and off to the south. At times, the entire sky shines and shimmers like an incongruous mixture of fire and jello. Watching an outbreak of the northern lights is one of the most memorable ways one can spend a clear night, as Frederick Whymper recalled in *Travel and Adventure in the Territory of Alaska* (1868):

It was not the conventional arch, but a graceful, undulating, every-changing "snake" of electric light; evanescent colours, pale as those of a lunar rainbow, ever and again flitting through it, and long streamers and scintillations moving upward to the bright starts, which distinctly shone through its hazy, ethereal form.

For centuries no one could figure out what was going on. "Aurora" means "dawn" in Latin and "borealis" means "north"; down under in Australia, the southern equivalent is called the aurora australis. The Vikings figured the lights to be the souls of their warriors ascending to Valhalla, while some Eskimo groups felt that the aurora was caused by the souls already in heaven, joyfully playing ball with a walrus skull. Other Eskimos thought they were seeing the dancing spirits of lost children, or of deer, seals, and whales. In more recent centuries, most attempts at scientifically explaining the "northern dawn" involved peculiar kinds of twilight—for example, sunlight reflecting off the polar ice back into the sky. Sometimes the aurora was blamed on distant forest fires lighting the sky, or even spontaneous combustion of the air itself. Of course, none of this is true.

The aurora works on the same principle as fluorescent or neon lights, or outdoor mercury and sodium vapor lamps. The idea is to run energetic, high-speed electrons through a gas. In the case of the aurora, the gases are mostly oxygen and nitrogen. The high-speed electrons strike the gas molecules, shaking the molecules' electrons out of their little orbits. When the molecular

Red Rays—Narrow beams of fluorescent nitrogen atoms line up along the Earth's magnetic field in this exceptionally brilliant auroral display over Colorado. RICHARD A. KEEN

Green Beam—A greenish beam of glowing oxygen pierces the sky above the Knik River, north of Anchorage, Alaska. The aurora was so bright that even the glare of the nearly full moon didn't dim the show. SCOTT McGEE

It's Curtains—Green and violet curtains appear to radiate from the sky above Mount McKinley (Denali), Alaska. The violet fringe on the bottom of the aurora is due to glowing nitrogen atoms at altitudes of 60 to 70 miles. SCOTT McGEE

Purple Rays—An aurora so bright that it outshines the evening twilight shimmers in the sky above the Juneau Ice Field, Alaska. The greenish curtains of glowing oxygen are capped with reddish-purple beams of glowing nitrogen atoms. The color of this high-altitude nitrogen is due to a different atomic process than the violet color of lower-altitude nitrogen.
SCOTT McGEE

electrons drop back to their original orbits, they lose the energy they picked up from the high-speed electrons. This energy radiates away as light.

Fluorescent lights get their electrons from the house current, with an extra kick given by the lamp's ballast mechanism. The aurora is lit by electrons from the sun, which need no boost. Electrons thrown out by hot spots in the solar atmosphere known as solar flares can travel the 93 million miles to Earth in less than a day. The solar electrons never quite make it to the ground, however. Several thousand miles up they get caught in our magnetic field. Earth's magnetic field looks just like the familiar magnetic pattern around a bar magnet, with broad loops connecting the north and south poles. The electrons are deflected north or south along these loops, and as they approach the poles they dip down into the atmosphere. To an electron, the magnetic field looks somewhat like an apple, with electrons on the surface of the apple forced to moved "north" or "south" into one of the dimples. The electrons are finally funneled into the top of the atmosphere

Aurora Borealis—A gigantic solar flare bathed most of North America with brilliant, multicolored auroras on several nights in 1989, a year of exceptional solar activity. Reddish glows were seen as far south as Mexico, Guatemala, and the Caribbean. Exceptionally powerful electrical particles from the sun penetrated deep into the Earth's magnetic field and atmosphere, causing nitrogen atoms to glow red at unusually low latitudes. RICHARD A. KEEN

Surface of Sun—Million-degree electrons race along magnetic field lines above the turbulent surface of the sun. NASA TRACE SATELLITE IMAGE

in a ring (called the "auroral oval") surrounding each of the magnetic poles.

Electrons are always funneling down to the earth, and there's always an aurora—albeit faint most of the time—along the auroral oval. After a solar flare the solar electrons are much more energetic and penetrate much deeper into the magnetic field before getting caught. Their trajectories bring them into the atmosphere farther from the poles, the (northern) auroral oval expands south, and we see the northern lights.

The aurora gives us a chance to glimpse the very highest reaches of our atmosphere. Most auroras shine between 60 and 200 miles up, but occasionally a really big show can reach as high as 600 miles—higher than most satellites! In contrast to these enormous vertical dimensions, the curtains themselves are only a few thousand feet thick. The curtains usually shade from greenish on the bottom to red at the top; both colors come from oxygen atoms. Occasionally, a deep violet glow from nitrogen atoms appears in the higher reaches of the aurora.

The north and south poles of Earth's magnet—the dimples on the apple, so to speak—are not exactly at the geographic north and south poles, but about 1,000 miles away from each. That places the magnetic north pole over Ellesmere Island in the Canadian Arctic. This quirk of our magnetic field is a boon for North American aurora watchers, since it brings the magnetic north pole—and the auroral oval—1,000 miles closer, increasing the frequency of auroras. At the same geographic latitudes in Asia, auroras are much less frequent than they are in North America (especially in the eastern United States and Canada).

Over North America the auroral oval usually runs from northern Alaska, across the Canada's northern Northwest Territories, into northern Quebec and Labrador. These are the places to go if you want to see the aurora almost every clear night. Farther south the frequency drops off—to 30 nights per year at Anchorage, Juneau, and Edmonton, 10 at Victoria and Yellowstone, 5 at Denver, 1 at Phoenix, and once every other year at San Diego. (Remember that about half of these auroras will be clouded out.) The southernmost aurora borealis on record was seen from the Cayman Islands (19 degrees north) in the Caribbean in March 1989. The frequency of auroras closely follows the 11-year cycle of solar activity known as the "sunspot cycle." The last peak was in 2000–2001, when several spectacular shows lit up the southwestern states; the next peak should arrive around 2012.

REFRACTION

Light does not always travel in straight lines, nor does it always travel at the so-called "speed of light," 186,283 miles per second. This number is actually the speed of light in a vacuum; however, light slows down when it goes into something thicker than a vacuum, such as air, water, or glass. In water or glass, light slows to two-thirds its vacuum speed, but in air the deceleration is much less—about 50 miles per second out of the 186,283. Besides slowing down, light also changes its direction when it goes from a vacuum into glass or air. It's very much like the uncomfortable experience of running the right wheels of your car off the edge of a paved road onto a muddy shoulder. The resistance of the mud slows the right side of the automobile, pulling the car off the road. If you didn't steer back to the left, your car would end up in the mud. Light beams don't have anyone on board to steer them back, so they simply change direction when they enter the glass or air—just like your tire tracks.

The bending of light is called "refraction," and the amount of bending depends on several things. Generally, the denser the material (glass is denser than water, and water is denser than air), the more the bending. Refraction is also greater if the light rays strike the surface of the glass or air at more of a glancing angle, like your car just edging off the road. The smaller the angle between the incoming light and the refracting surface (or edge of the road), the greater the bending. If the light strikes the surface head-on, there's no

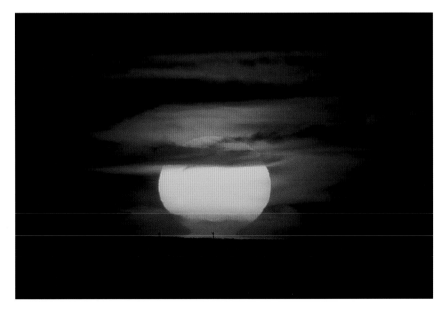

Setting Sun—Refraction by ripples and layers in the atmosphere distorts the sun's lower edge (and highlight fishermen on a jetty). RICHARD A. KEEN

bending—just as if you drove straight off the end of a parking lot into the mud, you would slow down but still be going straight. Finally, shorter wavelengths of light (e.g., blue) bend more than longer wavelengths (e.g., red)—in our automotive analogy, a short wheelbase Volkswagen gets tugged off the road faster than does a Greyhound bus.

Harvest Moon

Of the 12 or 13 full moons every year, there's something special about the first one of autumn—the Harvest Moon. Astronomically, October's (or sometimes late September's) moon is quite ordinary, but after a summer of leaf-filled trees, it's the first full moon we can easily see as soon as it comes over the horizon. In milder climates the leaves don't fall until November, and the spectacle is saved for the Hunter Moon. In either case, the rising Harvest (or Hunter) moon does indeed look huge, like an extra-large pizza. And if you catch the rising moon when it's sitting right on the horizon, it also looks a bit squashed, like a football lying on its side (after all, it is football season!). The squashing effect is caused by the atmosphere, so let's look at that one first.

... if you catch the rising moon when it's sitting right on the horizon, it also looks a bit squashed, like a football lying on its side ...

Light entering the atmosphere from any object in space is refracted toward the ground. The shallower the angle of entry, the greater the refraction. For those of us on the ground looking up, the object appears higher in the sky than it would without refraction—the only exception being an object directly overhead at the zenith, which cannot appear any higher! The lifting effect is greatest for objects on the horizon, where it amounts to half a degree, or just about the apparent diameter of the moon. Refraction actually causes the moon (and sun) to rise earlier (and set later) than they would on an airless Earth.

The angle of refraction decreases for objects progressively higher on the horizon. When the moon is sitting on the horizon, its top edge is refracted less that its lower edge. This compresses the apparent distance between the top and bottom of the moon. Meanwhile, the moon's horizontal width appears its normal size, since atmospheric refraction works only in the up–down direction. The result is a squashed moon.

None of this explains why the moon should appear so big when it rises, however. Refraction actually shrinks the overall size of the rising moon. Even without refraction the moon should appear slightly smaller when it is on the horizon, since it's almost 4,000 miles (half the Earth's diameter) farther away than when it is overhead. However, the moon's average distance from the Earth's center is 239,000 miles, and that 4,000 miles doesn't make a noticeable difference in the moon's size. The "pizza pie" effect is an opti-

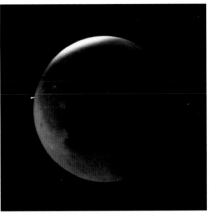

Lunar Eclipses—The bright coppery luster of a normal lunar eclipse (left) comes from sunlight refracted through the earth's atmosphere. The dull grey eclipse of December 30, 1982 (right), darkened by volcanic dust from El Chichon, required such a long time exposure that stars appear as dashes.
RICHARD A. KEEN

cal illusion created by our mind's interpretation of what the eye sees. When the moon is high in the sky, we (consciously or not) compare its size with nearby objects such as branches, roofs, and streetlights. When the moon sits on the horizon, comparison objects, such as houses, hills, and trees, are more distant (and larger). So the moon, instead of appearing as big as a leaf, looks more the size of a house. The effect strikes us in October because, once again, it's the first time we've seen the moon on a clear horizon in a while. Doubters can prove it for themselves by taking photographs of the moon at different elevations above the horizon, or, more cleverly, comparing the moon's apparent size with that of a small (one-third of an inch) object taped to the end of a yardstick.

LUNAR ECLIPSES

There's another special kind of full moon that occurs about once a year, on average, although it's just as likely to happen in March, or any other month, as in September or October. Rather than stunning us with its size or brightness, though, this full moon nearly disappears by passing into the Earth's long, tapered shadow, or "umbra." It is, of course, an eclipse of the moon (or lunar eclipse). Although lunar eclipses are less common than the more dramatic eclipses of the sun, they can be seen from the entire half of the Earth from which the moon is visible at the time. Most of you have probably seen a lunar eclipse at one time or another, while very few have found themselves within a total solar eclipse's narrow path of visibility.

The moon is completely outside Earth's atmosphere, so it may seem that its eclipses belong entirely to the realm of astronomy, rather than meteorology. The Earth's atmosphere, however, along with such phenomena as refraction,

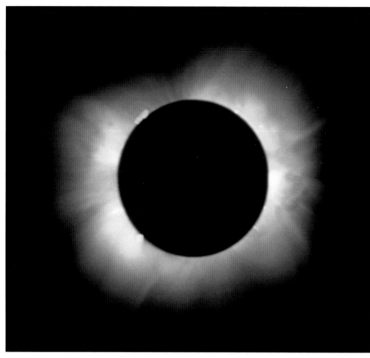

Total Solar Eclipse— Glowing electrons flying into space from the surface of the sun create the corona, which is visible to human eyes only when the moon covers the sun during a total solar eclipse. This eclipse, on February 26, 1979, was visible from Washington to North Dakota and Manitoba. After an eclipse in the Arctic on August 1, 2008, North America's next total solar eclipse on August 21, 2017, will be seen from Oregon to South Carolina. RICHARD A. KEEN

scattering, and even volcanic eruptions, play important roles in the phenomena we see during a lunar eclipse.

Normally the eclipsed moon shines a bright copper orange, or, as one 19th-century observer wrote, "like a glowing iron." Once in a while, the moon turns dark and grayish or even disappears completely. Although the dark eclipses are the unusual ones, it is the bright orange luster of "normal" eclipses that require some explaining. During a total eclipse the moon is completely immersed in the umbra, and, one might expect, totally cut off from sunlight. Why then doesn't the moon always disappear during an eclipse? The answer lies in the Earth's atmosphere: like a thin lens encircling our planet, the atmosphere refracts rays of sunlight as they pass by the edge of the Earth, focusing them into the umbra. As at sunset, scattering reddens the rays as they pass through the atmosphere, except here the red sunlight shines onto the moon.

The degree of refraction depends on the density of the air the sunlight passes through—the denser air in the lower atmosphere refracts sunlight deep into the umbra, while the thin air higher up bends light rays only slightly. At the distance of the moon, most of the light refracted into the umbra passes through the stratosphere, 15 to 40 miles up. Since the stratosphere is normally cloudless, the umbra (and, therefore, the eclipsed moon) is relatively bright.

The robot lunar lander Surveyor III observed a lunar eclipse in 1967 from a completely different perspective, and photographed the passage of the sun behind the Earth. At mid-eclipse the night side of the Earth was surrounded by a thin, but brilliant, ring of sunlight, broken here and there by the tops of the highest clouds. The total brightness of this ring was 10 to 100 times that of the full moon as seen from Earth. When future astronauts and cosmonauts (none of the *Apollo* astronauts were so fortunate) witness this spectacle, they will, in a way, be gazing upon a most memorable sunset, with the setting sun stretched all the way around the horizon that is the edge of the planet Earth.

If the atmospheric lens that illuminates the moon becomes dirty enough, light will be blocked from entering the umbra. Volcanoes are the most common source of stratospheric dirt. The most recent large eruption was that of the Philippine volcano Pinatubo in June 1991. The following year, when there was a total lunar eclipse, Pinatubo's 5-mile-deep cloud of sulfuric acid had spread around the globe. More a haze layer than a cloud, the volcanic cloud was fairly transparent compared to most earthly clouds. However, light rays grazing the Earth's edge on their way into the umbra passed nearly horizontally through the haze layer. After a 500-mile passage through the haze, only 1 percent of the light remained to enter the umbra. When the moon crossed the umbra on December 9, 1992, it appeared dim and gray, and observers in cities had trouble seeing the moon at all!

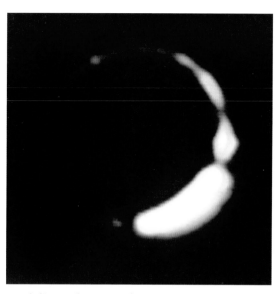

An Eclipse of the Sun—by the Earth!—A sight never seen by human eyes, this eclipse of the sun by the Earth was photographed in 1967 from the surface of the moon by Surveyor III, an unmanned lander that paved the way for the Apollo missions a few years later. From Earth, humans saw this event as an eclipse of the moon. NASA

Pinatubo was by no means the first volcano to tarnish the coppery glow of a lunar eclipse. Dark eclipses followed major eruptions in 1902, 1912, 1963, and 1982. The infamous paroxysms of Krakatoa (1883) and Tambora (1815) preceded dim, almost invisible eclipses. In 1620, the great astronomer Johannes Kepler observed an eclipsed moon so dark that "nothing could be seen of it, though the stars shone brightly all around," and although he was unaware of any volcanic eruptions, he correctly attributed the darkness to "mists and smoke" in the Earth's atmosphere. It may have been another unknown volcanic upheaval around A.D. 753 that ultimately led a reporter for the "Anglo-Saxon Chronicle" to describe the eclipsed moon that year as "covered by a horrid black shield," in contrast to a more normal eclipse appearing "sprinkled with blood" 13 years earlier.

Volcanoes are one of nature's most awesome phenomena. In seconds they can reduce cities and countryside to steaming mounds of dust, and globe-girdling volcanic clouds can change the color of the sky and even influence our planet's climate. Now we see that volcanic eruptions can literally cast shadows on the moon, a quarter of a million miles away.

THE GREEN FLASH

It sounds like the name for a comic book superhero, but the green flash is really just the sun (a superhero in itself!) putting on a rare and spectacular show at setting time. The cause is the same that lifts the squashed moon off

Green Flash—The same atmospheric refraction that distorted the sunset (see page 207) can sometimes create a "green flash," which lingers briefly after the rest of sun has set.
RICHARD A. KEEN

the horizon—refraction—but with an extra twist. Refraction bends blue light more than red, so at sunrise and sunset, the sun's blue (and green) light is lifted a little higher off the horizon than is the red and orange light. The shifting of different colors is not great, but is enough to grace the sun's upper edge with a bluish or greenish fringe. The lower edge of the sun gets a reddish fringe out of the deal, but that's not so obvious, since the whole setting (or rising) sun is tinted red. The separation of colors is exactly the same as you see when sunlight shines through a prism or crystal, except now the atmosphere is doing the job.

It's easy to see that when the sun sets, the last part to go is the blue-green fringe on top. Unfortunately, haze and junk in the atmosphere usually dull the colors, and the sun simply disappears. When the air is exceptionally clear, however, that blue-green fringe can shine alone for a second or two before it too disappears. The brilliant green color can appear quite suddenly, giving it the name "green flash." Since the atmosphere needs to be clear and the horizon should be flat (no mountains or trees), the best places to observe the green flash are over the ocean or from an airplane. Be patient, though. In 40 years I have seen it only about a dozen times—mostly when the sun set over a clear ocean and once from an airplane.

RAINBOWS

Rainbows, and theories attempting to explain them, have been around for a long time. To Noah, the rainbow at the end of the Great Flood was God's message that it would never again rain quite so much. In the 4th century B.C., Aristotle, who didn't know about refraction, blamed rainbows on sunlight reflecting from clouds only at one particular angle. He had little to say about the rainbow's colors, but he did correctly explain the bow being an arc of a certain angular diameter. Two thousand years after Aristotle, Isaac Newton finally—and correctly—explained the colors of rainbows in terms of refraction, much to the dismay of his contemporary poets.

Contrary to popular conception, raindrops are not teardrop-shaped. Most drops are almost perfectly spherical, but drops larger than a sixteenth of an inch actually flatten out as they fall. It's the little spheres that make rainbows. When sunlight shines into a raindrop, refraction bends its path and breaks it up into its component colors. The light may exit the backside of the drop and continue on its way, or it may reflect off the inside of the drop and exit the drop heading back in the general direction of the sun. For a perfect sphere, reflected light can deviate as much as 42 degrees from the line pointing directly back toward the sun, with light being reflected at all angles up to 42 degrees.

Most of the sunlight comes back at angles near zero degrees, or straight back toward the sun. Because these light rays go straight into the drop and straight out again, there's not much refraction (mostly reflection), and the light does not separate into colors. This kind of reflection is quite bright, though—like the glass beads on stop signs reflecting your headlights. At increasing angles, the reflected light becomes relatively dim, until it grows bright again as the angle approaches 42 degrees. Increasing angles also bring greater refraction and color separation. To an observer with his or her back to the sun, refracted light coming back at any angle will form a colored ring of that angular diameter surrounding the point opposite the sun.

We now have rainbows forming at all angles up to 42 degrees; however, at angles less than 42 degrees the rainbows overlap and their colors wash out. Only the last—and brightest—bow, the

Double Rainbow—A rain shower on Mount Thorodin, Colorado, ends with a spectacular double rainbow. Note that the sequence of colors reverses between the inner and outer bows. RICHARD A. KEEN

Fish-eye View of a Rainbow—A fish-eye lens catches the full extent of a double rainbow.

RICHARD A. KEEN

one at 42 degrees, survives to become a rainbow. Occasionally several of the outer bows, called supernumerary arcs, are visible as colored fringes inside the main rainbow.

Sunlight may reflect more than once inside the drop before exiting. With two reflections, the light may leave the drop at angles greater than 50 degrees, creating a secondary rainbow 50 degrees from the point opposite the sun. The extra reflection reverses the color sequence—red is on the inside, blue on the outside. Between the two rainbows the sky is relatively dark, since neither case reflects at angles between 42 and 50 degrees.

A third reflection within the drop sends the light in the same general direction as the original sunbeam. Therefore there's no third rainbow. Since each additional reflection further dims the light, higher order rainbows—fourth, fifth, and so on—have never been observed.

Rainbow over Snow—Although rainbows do not occur when it's snowing (they require round drops of clear water to be seen), they can occur when snow is on the ground. RICHARD A. KEEN

Moon Halo—Ice crystals floating within a thin veil of cirrus clouds produce a ring around the moon, along with two moon dogs, one on either side. The bright horizontal line between the moon and both moon dogs is a "parhelic circle," which appears curved in this wide-angle photo.
PAUL NEIMAN

HALOES AND SUNDOGS

Dazzle mine eyes, or do I see three suns?
—Edward in William Shakespeare's
Henry VI, Act 3

"In this the heaven figures some event," continued Edward's brother Richard, neither apparently aware that the two extra suns were caused by ice crystals miles above the ground. Nor did they suspect that haloes, crosses, and many other omens in the sky were likewise beams of sunlight shining through ice crystals. Had they known, their minds would have been boggled by the vast variety of visual phenomena ice crystals can produce.

Most ice crystals have six sides and two flat ends, but the relative proportions of length versus width can vary greatly. Two common shapes are responsible for most of the phenomena: hexagonal (six-sided) plates and hexagonal columns. Plates look like flat, six-sided wafers, and columns resemble segments of a six-sided pencil. Both shapes have eight surfaces that refract and reflect light. The most common form of refraction through a hexagonal shape bends light at angles of 22 degrees and greater, with the angle being least for red light. It's much like light shining through a three-sided prism. If the sky is full of hexagonal columns, those oriented at right angles to the sun refract sunlight into a 22-degree halo surrounding the sun, with red on the inside and blue on the outside.

As they fall, ice crystals more than a few thousandths of an inch across orient their longest dimensions horizontally. Plates fall flat and columns lay on

Multiple Halo—Although the most common halo around the sun or moon has a radius of 22 degrees, haloes of other sizes occasionally occur when the ice crystals are of the right size and orientation. The smaller, inner halo in this picture is caused by the pyramid-shaped tips of minute pencil-shaped crystals. PAUL NEIMAN

their sides. Horizontal hexagonal plates are capable of the same refraction by which columns create the 22-degree halo, but only if they are at the same elevation above the horizon as the sun. This produces bright, colored spots 22 degrees to the left and right of the sun known as "mock suns" or "sundogs." Along with the real sun in the middle they made Edward's three suns.

Ice crystals also reflect light. Like a myriad of mirrors, horizontal plates may reflect the setting sun into brilliant pillars extending above and below, but no wider than, the sun. Vertically oriented reflecting surfaces, like the end faces of horizontal columns or the edges of plates, can generate a band of light extending horizontally from the sun. Sometimes this band extends all the way around the horizon at the same elevation as the sun, and is called a "parhelic circle." The horizontal band and vertical pillar occasionally combine to form a cross centered on the sun. Unlike refracted sundogs and haloes, these reflection phenomena are mostly colorless—unless, of course, the setting sun is turning red.

These examples are a mere fraction of the possible arcs and haloes that have been observed, and even more are theoretically possible. Exotic crystal shapes, such as pyramids, add even more variety to the picture. And just as there are sun haloes and sundogs, night owls can enjoy moon haloes and moon dogs created by the refracted light of our moon.

TWINKLING

Twinkle, twinkle, little star
How I wonder what you are
—Anonymous

Sorry, kids, but stars' twinkling actually tells us very little about what they are and, as far as astronomers are concerned, it merely confuses the issue and hinders their studies. True, some stars do vary their brightness, but that takes hours or days or, in some cases, years. The rapid flickering many call twinkling, and scientists call scintillation, originates not in the stars, but in the air surrounding our own planet.

Our atmosphere is riddled with temperature contrasts, and the temperature changes from place to place within the atmosphere are not always smooth. Between the ground and the beginning of the stratosphere, 8 or 10 miles up, the temperature may drop from 60° F to –60° F. The vertical rate of cooling comes out to 12 or 15 degrees per mile, but very rarely is that rate a steady one. Somewhere in that 120-degree spread there's bound to be several layers of relatively warm air overlying a layer of cooler air. Winds in the warm layer blowing across the top of the cool layer can create waves, just as winds in the atmosphere create waves on the surface of the ocean. And like their oceanic counterparts, waves in the atmosphere can grow and break, mixing turbulent bubbles of cold and warm air. Jet streams, with their strong winds and temperature contrasts, are just about the best places in the atmosphere for these bubbles to form.

Cold air, being denser, refracts light with more strength than warm air, so cold bubbles act like weak lenses and focus light rays together, while warm bubbles spread light rays apart. The temperature differences between the bubbles are usually quite small, a degree or two, so the bending of the light rays is very slight. If the bubbles are 8 or 10 miles up, however, the light can be deflected several feet. The net effect of the spreading and focusing of starlight by hot and cold bubbles is a blotchy pattern of light and dark moving along the ground with the same speed and direction as the winds aloft that blow the bubbles around. When bright and dark parts of the pattern pass by your eyes, you see the star flash accordingly—this is twinkling.

We don't see starlight patterns on the ground at night because individual stars aren't bright enough, and the combined patterns from the thousand or so naked-eye stars average each other out. If there were a single, extremely bright star overhead, the ground would shimmer like the bottom of a swimming pool on a sunny day. We do have an extremely bright star—the sun—but it does not twinkle, and neither does the moon. There is one exception—during eclipses of the sun, when the visible disk of the sun is reduced to the thinnest of crescents, ripples of sunlight often dance across the ground. It's one of the many rare phenomena you can see during a solar eclipse, and one of the reasons eclipse watchers travel thousands of miles to see an event that lasts a few minutes at best. Nor do any of the planets, like Jupiter or Mars, twinkle

Corona—This pattern of colored rings around the sun (which is hidden by the wind gauge) is called a corona, but it's not caused by hot electrons from the sun. Rather, the effect is due to sunlight passing through cloud droplets, all of which happen to be about the same size.
RICHARD A. KEEN

very much. When they do, it's in a more sedate manner, because all these objects appear as sizeable disks in the sky, although it takes a telescope to see the planets as disks. Stars, even through a telescope, always look like brilliant points of light. Light rays reaching our eyes from a planet arrive from a variety of slightly different directions and pass through slightly different places in the atmosphere. At jet stream levels, the slightly different places are 5 or 10 feet apart. For a planet not to twinkle, then, the twinkling effects for light rays even a few feet apart must cancel each other out, and means that the blobs of hot and cold air are typically no bigger than a medicine ball!

The very slight refraction by the hot and cold bubbles causes noticeable focusing only at very large distances, and most of the twinkling we see comes from the highest bubbles in and near the jet stream. Knowing this, astronomers made some of the first measurements of jet stream wind speeds by simply timing twinkles from a star as they appeared in two telescopes several yards apart. Twinkling may still leave us wondering what stars are, but it tells us a surprising amount about the atmosphere!

... during eclipses of the sun, when the visible disk of the sun is reduced to the thinnest of crescents, ripples of sunlight often dance across the ground. It's one of the many rare phenomena you can see during a solar eclipse, and one of the reasons eclipse watchers travel thousands of miles to see an event that lasts a few minutes at best.

WATCHING THE WEATHER

CHAPTER 13

You can observe a lot by just watching.

—Yogi Berra

On July 1, 1776, as he put the final touches on his draft of the Declaration of Independence, Thomas Jefferson began another endeavor that would occupy him for the next 50 years—he picked up a thermometer from Mr. Sparhawk's store and started recording the daily temperature. Three days later, on July 4, he paid for the instrument, and on July 8 he bought a barometer. Throughout his terms as governor of Virginia, ambassador to France, and president of the United States, and during his travels and his years of retirement at Monticello, Jefferson logged the weather conditions in his *Weather Memorandum Book.* It is no wonder then that Jefferson made sure Lewis and Clark log the weather on their epic journey to the Pacific Ocean and back in 1803–1806.

James Madison, the nation's fourth president, also watched the weather, and for his last 33 years, George Washington kept an "Account of the Weather." Thus, the first, third, and fourth presidents of the United States knew the joys (and importance) of watching the weather. They understood that the best way to learn about something is to participate in it, and to participate in the changing weather means to observe it closely. Humans haven't always known what makes the weather work. That knowledge came over the centuries by paying close attention to the passages of clouds, wind, and rain, and to the vagaries of temperature, humidity, and pressure, and finally fitting all the observations together until they made sense. The knowledge also came from carefully observing the new climates in new lands as they were explored, as Lewis and Clark did. There is no need for you to re-create these early days of discovery, of course, but if you watch the skies carefully enough and long enough you will come to understand the weather in a way no book can teach you.

Halfway Up—A climber tracks an approaching thunderstorm from the summit of Mexico's highest mountain, 18,700-foot-high Pico de Orizaba. At this altitude the air pressure is half of what it is at sea level, and anyone on this peak has ascended through half of the atmosphere! RICHARD A. KEEN

Observing the weather is an activity that can be done at nearly any level of dedication and expense. On one extreme, you can note what kind of weather occurs each day by simply watching the clouds and what falls out of them. You don't need to spend a cent on weather instruments since you already have the most remarkable weather instrument ever devised—a pair of eyes. On the other extreme, you can invest thousands of dollars in automatic recording weather devices, perhaps even hooked up to a home computer. Most of you will fall somewhere in between these two extremes; you may want to watch the weather with the help of a thermometer and a rain gauge. If you would like some guidance from Jefferson, his instructions to Lewis and Clark were to observe the "Climate, as characterized by the thermometer, by the proportion of rainy, cloudy, and clear days; by lightning, hail, snow, ice; by the access and recess of frost; by the winds prevailing at different seasons; the dates at which particular plants put forth or lose their flower and leaf; times of appearance of particular birds, reptiles, or insects." That is a fairly complete list of things to observe, I'd say!

Now that you're convinced you want to set up a small, inexpensive weather station, what instruments should you get? Should you buy them or make them yourself? Where do you put them and how often do you read them? And what do you do with your records? Of course, your choices are individual ones. But perhaps this veteran weather buff can give you some hints and cautions to ease you into a fascinating hobby that only gets more captivating with time.

No matter how large or small your weather station is, or even if you're using no instruments at all, keep in mind that some form of record keeping is essential. Memories change with time, with big storms getting bigger and small storms smaller. Most days disappear entirely. Twenty years from now, you probably won't remember what today's weather was. Write it down, and two decades from now your notebook will be one of your prized possessions. If you only have a dollar to spare, invest in a notebook. Roomy calendars and appointment books work just fine, as do business ledgers and cash books.

Now for the instruments. It pays to be somewhat picky in your choice of instruments and to be careful about how and where you set them up. You want your records to be as accurate as possible. Not only is it a matter of personal pride, accurate records can be of use and interest to others. The following suggestions should help you get the best weather records for your dollar.

TEMPERATURE

The most basic instrument—and one that most people already own—is a thermometer. Most household thermometers, however, don't give very accurate readings. This is not to say the thermometers themselves are inaccurate, but rather they are situated where their readings are not representative of real weather. A window-mounted thermometer picks up some heat from the house and may read 5 or 10 degrees higher than the actual outside air temperature. A thermometer sitting in the sun might read 50 degrees too high. While temperatures "in the sun" may mean *something,* it is difficult to say what. Consider that the reading of a thermometer set in the sun is affected by wind speed, angle of the sun, where the thermometer is mounted, type and brand of thermometer, and actual air temperature. In other words, you don't learn much from thermometer readings taken in the sun. That is why meteorologists around the world have chosen to take readings "in the shade." If your thermometer readings are taken the same way, they can be compared directly with temperatures from Bangkok to Siberia, or even from a spacecraft on the surface of Mars.

To a meteorologist, "in the shade" doesn't necessarily mean under a tree. In fact, it has been found that thick groves of trees generate a local "microclimate" that is substantially cooler than surrounding areas. Good locations for thermometers are on the north sides of buildings or under porch roofs, although even here reflected sunlight can affect the readings by

No matter how large or small your weather station is, or even if you're using no instruments at all, keep in mind that some form of record keeping is essential.

a few degrees. The best location for a thermometer, and the one chosen as an international standard by the World Meteorological Organization, is in a white louvered box at eye level above open ground, as far as possible from trees, walls, buildings, or other obstructions. While setting the thermometer out in the open may seem to contradict the "in the shade" requirement, the louvered box (called an "instrument shelter") actually provides more effective shade than any tree or wall, while still allowing free flow of air around the thermometer. Anybody willing to invest $30 and a day's work can build a suitable box. A design that has served me well for many years is described in Appendix 2, "Building Your Thermometer Shelter." Making one would be an easy project for a novice do-it-yourselfer.

Nearly two centuries ago, weather watchers found that the average of readings taken at sunrise, 2 P.M. and 9 P.M. came reasonably close to the actual average temperature for the day.

Whether or not you make a box, weather watching is a lot easier if your thermometer can tell you what the temperature *has been,* as well as what it is now. The simplest (and cheapest) way to do this is to get a maximum–minimum thermometer, called simply a "max–min" in the trade. This kind of thermometer indicates the highest and lowest temperatures that have occurred since you last checked it. Simply read the high, low, and current temperatures, reset the high and low indicators, and come back the next day. The best max–min thermometers are the liquid-in-glass type. Good ones made by Taylor and Airguide are sold in hardware and department stores for $20 to $30. There are cheaper max–min thermometers of the coiled metallic-spring type, but their metal springs have a tendency to shift and stretch with time, causing the temperature readings to lose accuracy. For $50 or more you can get computerized thermometers that give you the same information and more. Over the past few years some inexpensive electronic thermometers have appeared on the market, such as the "HOBO" temperature data loggers made by Onset Computers (of course, you'll also need a computer to read the data from these units). Temperatures are best recorded on a daily basis. With an ordinary thermometer, readings made at the same time every day, say 7 A.M. or. 6 P.M., give a good account of day-to-day excursions of weather. By taking 24 readings—one every hour on the hour—and averaging them, you get the average temperature for the day. That's a lot of work (unless you're using an electronic data logger). Fortunately there's a better way. Nearly two centuries ago, weather watchers found that the average of readings taken at sunrise, 2 P.M., and 9 P.M. came reasonably close to the actual average temperature for the day. Since the max–min thermometer was invented in the last century, an even easier way to figure average temperature was discovered: simply average the high and low temperatures for the day. All you have to do is read your max–min thermometer once a day and

you've got the day's average. Read it each day for a month and you can figure the average for the month, and so on.

Even with a max–min, there are good times and not-so-good times to read your thermometer. For example, if you read your max–min at 6 A.M., the temperature is near the minimum for the day. If that minimum was 48° F, for example, the temperature when you take the reading may be 50° F. When you reset the thermometer, it remembers that 50-degree temperature. Now imagine that the weather warms up over the next 24 hours (probability says this happens about half the time!), and the next morning's minimum is 60° F. When you take the reading, however, the thermometer will show a low of 50° F, left over from the previous, cooler morning. This happens often enough that your computed averages can be as much as 2 degrees lower than the actual average temperature. The opposite problem occurs if you take your daily readings in the afternoon—your averages will be 1 or 2 degrees too high. The best time to read a max–min thermometer is when the

An Alpine Weather Station—This weather station atop Niwot Ridge, west of Boulder, has been maintained by the University of Colorado's Institute of Arctic and Alpine Research for over 50 years. JOHN MARR, UNIVERSITY OF COLORADO ARCHIVES

The One That Got Away—A storm chaser gazes wistfully at a tornado-producing supercell thunderstorm, which popped up suddenly and too far away to investigate.
RICHARD A. KEEN

temperature is normally midway between the high and low. Studies of this problem have shown that these times are about 9 A.M. or 10 P.M. The National Weather Service has chosen the calendar day–midnight max–min readings for their weather stations. Your choice of a time depends on your lifestyle. One important thing to remember is that the key to good and useful records is consistency. Pick a time that you can stick with over the long run. Many false "climate changes" occur in weather records the world over, which are really changes in weather station locations or observation procedures. Try not to change your horse in midstream, and your records will be all the better for it.

HUMIDITY

Much of what we call "weather"—clouds, rain, snow, frost, fog, and so on—is caused by moisture in the atmosphere. This is why humidity is so important. Humidity is also difficult to measure accurately. Most common humidity indicators, or "hygrometers," rely on the fact that some substances, such as hair and paper, expand when they absorb moisture from the air. Unfortunately, these substances attract dust and bugs and tend to stretch over time. As a result, the humidity readings are not much more accurate than noting how clammy your skin feels when you're outside.

Another problem with hair or paper hygrometers is that they measure *relative* humidity, which is the amount of moisture in the air expressed as a percentage of the amount the air could hold at that temperature. The interesting thing to measure, however, is the *absolute* humidity—the actual amount of moisture in the air. Meteorologists prefer to express absolute humidity in terms of the "dew point." If you take outside air and cool it, the dew point is the temperature at which the water vapor in the air condenses. In other words, when night cooling drops ground temperature to the dew point, then dew forms. Higher dew points mean more moisture in the air.

The most economical way to measure dew point is with a "wet bulb hygrometer," available for $30–$40. If you don't like the price, it's easy to make your own for a few dollars. This little gadget consists of two thermometers mounted side by side. One thermometer has a wet cotton wick attached to its bulb; the other end of the wick is dipped in a small reservoir of water. The dry thermometer reads the ordinary air temperature, or "dry bulb" temperature, while the wet thermometer gives, not surprisingly, the "wet bulb" temperature. Because of evaporative cooling, the wet bulb reading is always lower than the dry bulb reading. Using a small chart supplied with the hygrometer, you can convert wet and dry bulb temperatures into dew points.

Another version of the wet bulb hygrometer is the "sling psychrometer." This also has dry and wet bulb thermometers mounted side by side, with the whole thing attached to a hinge or a chain. Soak the wet bulb wick, twirl the thermometers around (to get better ventilation), and read the dry and wet bulb temperatures. With either version, the situation gets complicated when the wet bulb temperature is below freezing. Ice evaporates or, more properly, sublimates more slowly than liquid water, so when the wet wick freezes, the ice bulb temperature reads higher for the same dew point temperature. There are separate charts for converting ice bulb readings to dew points.

Watch the dew point closely, especially during summer, and you'll see how the air's moisture content changes with different air masses. In desert areas, dew points rise with the onset of the summer monsoon. If it gets above 60° F, thunderstorms may be in the offing. In coastal regions, the dew point changes sharply as winds switch to and from the ocean. Eventually, you'll find that the dew point is a handy number to know when making your own forecasts.

Much of what we call "weather"— clouds, rain, snow, frost, fog, and so on—is caused by moisture in the atmosphere. This is why humidity is so important.

RAINFALL

Measuring rainfall is the epitome of simplicity. "One inch of rain" from a storm simply means that the ground is covered with 1 inch of water (assuming none of the rain runs off or soaks into the ground). Rain is a lot easier to measure than temperature, and in some ways it is more interesting. Rainfall rates can vary dramatically over distances of a few miles or less. Unless you live close to a weather station, you really need your own measurements to know how much rain you have received.

Rain is a lot easier to measure than temperature, and in some ways it is more interesting. Rainfall rates can vary dramatically over distances of a few miles or less.

Official-type rain gauges cost several hundred dollars, but fortunately small gauges that are nearly as accurate can be found for about $10. At the bottom of the price range, my favorite is the plastic "wedge" made by Tru-Chek; for a bit more (about $30) you can purchase a round, clear plastic gauge with a removable funnel that gives excellent results. To set up your rain gauge, mount it on a fence post, clothes pole, or (for you apartment dwellers) up on the roof. About the only rule to remember is not to place the gauge near or under anything that might interfere with the rainfall. The rule of thumb is to keep the gauge as far away from trees, buildings, and the like as the obstructions are high. Read the rainfall at the end of each storm (don't wait too long, or some rain might evaporate). If you prefer, make daily readings when you check your thermometer. Don't forget to empty the gauge each time and, above all, remember to write down the amount before you forget it.

SNOWFALL

Although snowfall is one of the trickiest phenomenon to measure, its measuring instrument is certainly the simplest and most commonplace of all weather instruments. Believe it or not, even the pros at the National Weather Service use an ordinary ruler (or yardstick) to measure snowfall. The difficulties arise because of what happens to snow after it falls. If it's warm, snow melts as it hits the ground; if it's windy, snow drifts; and if snow accumulates over 4–6 inches, it settles under its own weight. Because of the varied fates of grounded snowflakes, snow depth on the ground sometimes decreases even as the snow continues to fall. So really, there are two things to measure. One is snow depth; the other is snowfall.

To measure snow depth, simply go out and stick your ruler into the snow in several places and take an average depth. If there has been a lot of drifting, take more measurements until you feel confident you have a good average. This technique is simple and straightforward. Snowfall, on the other hand, requires an

attempt to measure the amount of snow that would have accumulated had there been no melting, drifting, or settling. To do this, measure snow depth on a surface where relatively little melting has occurred—wooden decks and picnic tables are favorites. Some people prefer to use a special "snow board," a white-painted piece of wood set on the ground. Measure the snow every few hours, or whenever 4–6 inches accumulate, and write down your measurement. Clear off the table or set the snow board back on top of the snow. Let the snow start accumulating again and take another measurement in a few hours. This eliminates the settling problem. Your snowfall total is the sum of the individual measurements. It's not really all that difficult, once you have the procedure down.

Measurements of snow depth and snowfall often differ, particularly in bigger storms. Snowfall is always the larger of the two. The National Weather Service measures both, but uses *snowfall* for the official record of a storm. If you live near an official weather station and wonder why they always have more snow than you, it may be because you're comparing their snowfall with your snow depth.

"Keen Eye" on Weather—The author reads the max-min thermometer in his weather station after a 72-inch Colorado snowstorm in March 2003.
RICHARD A. KEEN

WIND

Wind can be as tricky to measure as snowfall and a lot more expensive. There are an incredible variety of wind gauges—or anemometers—available on the market. Most are of the familiar three-rotating-cup variety. For about $100 you can buy one that tells you wind speed; for twice that they throw in wind direction. For $300 there are anemometers that recall the peak gust since you last reset it, similar to a max–min thermometer. For the same amount of money you can get one that gives a continuous chart recording of wind speed. On the opposite end of the price scale is an elegant little device that measures wind speed by using the pressure of the wind to push a red fluid up a tube. Made by Dwyer, this gauge sells for about $40. Whichever design of anemometer you may decide to buy, remember to place it high enough that trees and buildings don't interfere with its readings. Above all, ground it well to protect it from lightning.

Whichever design of anemometer you may decide to buy, remember to place it high enough that trees and buildings don't interfere with its readings. Above all, ground it well to protect it from lightning.

Anemometers, with their rapidly fluctuating dials, are fun to watch. However, you don't absolutely need to buy one to measure wind speed. You may very well have one or more anemometers growing in your backyard, because trees are fairly accurate indicators of wind speed. The idea of watching the effects of wind to estimate wind speed was first formalized in 1806 by Sir Francis Beaufort of the British Navy. Beaufort tabulated descriptions of sea wave heights, roughness, whitecaps, and the like—corresponding to different wind speeds, for use by mariners. Later, Beaufort devised a similar table for land use. More recently, Theodore Fujita of the University of Chicago expanded the scale to the extremely high wind speeds found in tornadoes and severe hurricanes. These wind scales are described in Appendix 3, "Wind Speed Scales," and you can use them to make surprisingly good estimates of wind speed.

The diehard do-it-yourselfer might want to make his or her own anemometer. It's not impossible, as the basic concept is really rather elementary. The wind pushes on the three round cups and makes them spin about the axis. This in turn rotates a small electric generator, which creates a voltage (proportional to wind speed) that moves the needle on a voltmeter. A small direct-current motor from a hobby shop works as well as a generator, and an inexpensive voltmeter makes a great readout dial. Making the cups and attaching them securely to the motor can be tricky, as can waterproofing the motor from the rain. An effective way of calibrating the device is to drive a car at specific and constant speeds while holding the cup mechanism out the window and comparing the current readout with the speedometer. Enlist a friend to help you with the driving.

The not-so-diehard do-it-yourselfer may prefer to build a wind vane, which simply indicates wind direction. The standard design is essentially a large-tailed arrow balanced on a pivot, so the arrow always points into the wind. This can be as simple as a plywood arrow that pivots on a nail. Let your imagination run free on this project. When you record wind directions, though, remember that meteorologists always talk about the direction the wind blows *from*.

BAROMETRIC PRESSURE

Undoubtedly, the most popular instrument for do-it-yourself weather forecasters is the barometer. Most weather books contain tables describing tomorrow's weather based on today's barometric readings. Unfortunately, these tables don't always work in the West. We all know that falling pressures mean stormy weather and rising barometers mean clearing, right? Not necessarily so! There are places in the western states where the heaviest storms begin as the pressure starts to rise and places where falling pressures bring sunny weather. You're on your own here. Buy a barometer—decent ones are $20 and up—and read it once or twice a day (preferably at the same time each day). Don't forget to write your readings down, along with the rest of your observations.

WHAT TO DO WITH YOUR WEATHER RECORDS

When you first start taking weather records, the satisfaction you gain will be a personal one. Each time you watch, measure, and record some weather phenomenon, you will notice details about the event that would have otherwise escaped you. You may certainly have some fun gathering your own statistics. After a while, you'll have enough statistics to start tinkering with them. Plotting temperatures, pressures, rainfall, and snowfall on graph paper is an engaging way to display your data, and gives you a real feel for how the weather varies from day to day. This job is easier if you have access to a computer with spreadsheet and graphics software, but plotting it by hand lets you appreciate the data more. After all, the computer doesn't care what these numbers mean! When you have several years of records, you'll be able to calculate "normal" temperatures—rainfall and snowfall for, say, April—and have a record of all-time highs and lows.

Don't forget that there are others who also like statistics. They may be interested in yours. Just look at a newspaper. Check the sports page, the business section, or even the weather column, and what do you see—statistics!

We all know that falling pressures mean stormy weather and rising barometers mean clearing, right? Not necessarily so! There are places in the western states where the heaviest storms begin as the pressure starts to rise and places where falling pressures bring sunny weather.

People love statistics, so don't be shy about sharing yours with them. How you go about doing this depends on where you live. If you're in a city, there's probably an official weather station not too far away. The public, media, and meteorologists are interested in how the weather varies across town, especially during storms. Let your newspaper, radio, or television station—even the National Weather Service office—know you're keeping records. You may be pleased to find they're interested in your reports.

If you live in a small town or in the country away from an official weather station, your records may be the only show in town, and your local newspaper may be delighted to get your weather reports on a regular basis. The National Weather Service has organized a nationwide network of volunteer weather observers in a program called the "Cooperative Observer Network." The observer network was originally championed by the likes of Thomas Jefferson and Ben Franklin, who recognized the need to document the climate of the old and new territories of their country. The role of these cooperative observers is to fill in the large gaps between NWS stations, which are usually located at major airports. Ideally, cooperative observers are spaced about 20 miles apart, with 100 or 200 such observers in each state. The greatest need for weather observers is in isolated regions of the West, and I'm proud to be one of these cooperative observers whose weather station (in the foothills northwest of Denver) fills in one of these data voids. If you live more than 20 miles from the nearest cooperative station, the NWS may want *you* as an observer! If you become a cooperative observer, the NWS will set you up with official U.S. government–design weather equipment. Your responsibilities include taking daily observations on a consistent basis and filling out and sending in a monthly weather summary. The satisfaction comes in seeing your data published in the government publication *Climatological Data,* and in knowing that thousands of subscribers across the country are reading and using your data.

Sharing your interest in the weather can be rewarding. Eventually, however, your greatest satisfaction will probably come from your own growing understanding of the way weather works.

If you like kids, this is your big chance to enrich their lives. Schools and scout groups are always looking for projects and field trips. Wouldn't you have liked to visit a weather station when you were a kid?

Sharing your interest in the weather can be rewarding. Eventually, however, your greatest satisfaction will probably come from your own growing understanding of the way weather works. Even though weather can cause personal hardship—from leaking roofs and snow-slick roads to planes missed because of fog—following it over the years will lead to a familiarity that breeds respect rather than contempt.

Weather Maps

One of the biggest leaps in the science of meteorology came in the mid-19th century, when, for the first time in human history, it was possible to draw a daily weather map. Humans have been observing the weather for thousands of years, and in the 18th century, they began recording and publishing these observations. During the 19th century, a network of weather observers (many at army posts) followed the westward expansion of the United States, and with the invention of the telegraph (and the establishment of a national telegraph grid) it was possible for weather reports from all around the United States—a fair chunk of a continent—to be wired to a central location in near real time. That central location was (and still is) Washington, D.C., and shortly after the Civil War, that's where the first daily weather maps covering a large enough area to show highs, lows, and fronts were drawn.

You can look out the window to see what the local weather is doing, but you need a broader perspective before the weather you see makes any real sense. After learning this in the 19th century, meteorologists developed the weather map. Since then they have devised internationally accepted ways of mapping weather. Weather maps used by meteorologists are loaded with information expressed by hundreds of symbols and numbers. There's no need to learn all the fine details of a weather map, but you may wish to pick up some of the basics. The aim of this chapter is to point out the most important features of the weather map and to show an example of a weather map from a notable day.

Unless you're a sailor or a pilot, you may not have many chances to see a real weather map. Weather maps appear every day in newspapers and on television, but these media maps are often simplified to the point that they tell very little about what's really happening. You can, however, subscribe to a booklet of daily maps published weekly by the National Weather Service, and there are plenty of websites that have detailed and frequently updated weather maps (see "Resources" for the address.)

The first thing you notice when looking at a weather map is a lot of lines. Many of these are "isobars," or lines of equal barometric pressure. They're

Weather Map for September 18, 2003: A Tranquil Day in the West—High pressure over Montana brings light winds and chilly temperatures to most of the western U.S. and Canada. The leading edge of the cold air—a cold front (marked with blue triangles)—marches eastward across the Plains states, triggering rain and thundershowers in the green tinted area. The cold front meets a warm front (marked with red half-circles) at the center of a typical low just south of Hudson's Bay. Another cold front (which becomes an occluded front, shown in purple) is coming ashore over British Columbia. The brown contour lines are isobars, or equal pressure lines; the red numbers (1008, 1012, etc.) are the pressure values in millibars. The big weather story that day, though, is the approach of Hurricane Isabel, marked by a red swirly symbol off the North Carolina coast. NWS

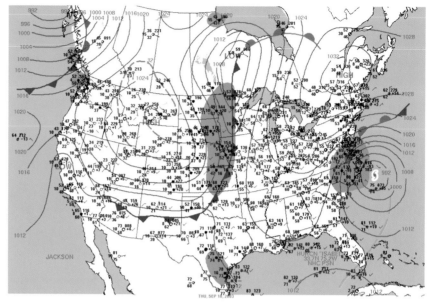

Surface Weather Map and Station Weather at 7:00 A.M. E.S.T.

similar to the contour lines on topographic maps. Winds tend to blow along the isobars, clockwise around highs and counterclockwise around lows, with a further tendency to angle in toward low pressure. The closer the isobars are to each other, the stronger the pressure gradient and the faster the winds. The many isobars around an intense cyclone sometimes look like a bull's eye.

On weather maps, isobars are labeled in "millibars" of pressure. While your barometer probably reads pressure in inches of mercury, meteorologists generally use millibars to measure pressure. The average atmospheric pressure around the world is 1,013 millibars, or 29.92 inches. A typical high pressure may be 1,030 millibars (30.42 inches) or more, while an average low has pressures below 1,000 millibars, or 29.53 inches.

Fronts appear on a weather map as heavy lines with little round or pointed bumps. Round bumps mean a warm front, and pointed bumps a cold front. The bumps point in the direction the front is headed. A line with both round and pointed bumps pointing in the same direction is called an "occluded" front. This is where a cold front has caught up to a slower warm front. The passage of an occluded front usually brings rain or snow and a shift of wind direction, but not much of a temperature change. If the line has round bumps on one side and pointed ones on the other, it's a stationary front. Warm or cold fronts may stall and become stationary fronts, while stationary fronts can start moving. Sometimes part of a front is moving as a warm or cold front while another section is stationary. If you follow maps over several days, you'll see fronts form and disinte- grate, and the temperature contrasts across them strengthen and weaken.

Between all the lines on weather maps, little groupings of numbers and symbols represent plots of data from differ- ent weather stations, called "station plots." At the center of each station

Satellite Image, September 18, 2003— This visible light satellite image is, in effect, a black- and-white television image of North America, taken a few hours after the time of the weather map. A wide band of clouds from Texas to Minnesota marks the cold front, and more clouds are massed around the low near Hudson Bay. More clouds are coming ashore with the cold front along the British Columbia coast, and Hurricane Isabel is coming ashore along the North Carolina coast. NOAA

plot is a small circle; the amount of shading in the circle shows the amount of cloudiness. An empty circle means clear skies, while a completely blackened circle means overcast. A line extending from the circle gives the direction the wind is blowing from, while the number of branches on the line indicates the wind speed. One branch means 10 knots, or 12 m.p.h., two branches mean 20 knots, and so on. The current temperature appears to the upper left of the circle, and the dew point temperature to the lower left. Symbols between the

temperature and dew point mark the current weather. One dot means light rain, two dots mean heavier rain; a six- pointed star means light snow, and so on. Green shaded areas on the map show where precipitation is falling at the time the map was made. Other numbers and symbols

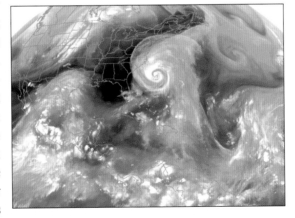

Water Vapor Image, September 18, 2003— This image shows a different perspective on the weather, taken from the same satellite (GOES 12) on the same day. Instead of looking in visible light (the wavelength range that our eyes see in), this picture shows the weather as it appears in a wavelength of light given off by water vapor in the upper atmosphere. Along with high-level clouds, this image reveals the swirls that occur at jet stream level, and also shows where air is rising (white) and sinking (dark). NOAA

give pressures, cloud types, rainfall amounts, and so on. They are all explained in a little pamphlet available from the same folks who publish the weekly booklet of weather maps.

STANDARD WEATHER SYMBOLS

A, B
Direction and Windspeed

Symbol	Speed, knots	Speed, m/sec
◎	Calm	Calm
—	1 - 2	0.5 - 1
—	3 - 7	1.5 - 3.6
—	8 - 12	4.1 - 6.2
—	13 - 17	6.7 - 8.7
—	18 - 22	9.3 - 11.3
—	23 - 27	11.8 - 13.9
—	28 - 32	14.4 - 16.5
—	33 - 37	17 - 19
—	38 - 42	19.5 - 21.6
—	43 - 47	22.1 - 24.2
—	48 - 52	24.7 - 26.7
—	53 - 57	27.3 - 29.3
—	58 - 62	29.8 - 31.9
—	63 - 67	32.4 - 34.5
—	68 - 72	35 - 37
—	73 - 77	37.6 - 39.6
—	103 - 107	53 - 55

→ (wind direction)

A Direction from which wind is blowing (see symbols at left)
B Windspeed (see symbols at left)
C Extent of cloud cover (see symbols at left)
D Barometric pressure reduced to sea level, kilopascals (millibars)
E Air temperature at time of reporting, fahrenheit
F Weather conditions at time of reporting (see symbols below)
G Visibility, miles
H Dewpoint temperature, fahrenheit
I Pressure change during the 3 hr period preceeding observation, kilopascals (millibars)
J Height of base of lowest cloud, miles

Missing or unavailable data are indicated by "M" in the proper location.
(Note: Only those codes which appear on maps in this report are listed).

C
Cloud Cover

Symbol	Percent covered
○	Clear
◔	Up to 10
◔	20 to 30
◑	40
◑	50
◕	60
◕	70 to 80
◕	90 or overcast with openings
●	Completely overcast
⊗	Sky obscured

F
Present Weather Conditions

Symbol	Explanation
∿	Visibility reduced by smoke
∞	Haze
❜	Intermittent drizzle (not freezing), slight
••	Continuous rain (not freezing), slight
••	Continuous rain (not freezing), moderate
✳	Intermittent snow, slight
▽	Slight rain showers
✳▽	Slight snow showers

RESOURCES

I hope that by reading this book, you have had the satisfaction of gaining an understanding and appreciation of the special kinds of weather that occurs in the West. Weather is a fantastically complex subject and, at best, this book just skims the surface. Perhaps it has whetted your appetite for more information. There are many ways to expand your knowledge about weather, ranging from reading books and periodicals to following the daily weather maps and even taking your own weather records. Here are some suggestions for these pursuits.

BOOKS

There are many books about the weather, ranging from kids' books and photo albums to textbooks and technical reports. I suggest going to a library and skimming through their selection, or browsing through www.amazon.com and find one that appeals to you. Here are a few of my favorites:

Weather, by Paul Lehr, Will Burnett, and Herbert Zim (Golden Press, New York). This pocket-sized volume came out in 1957 and has been updated several times since. It's a compact but comprehensive overview of the weather, easy to read with nice illustrations. I have recommended it to audiences from Cub Scouts to mountaineers.

Those of you who won't believe anything until you've done an experiment to prove it will like Craig Bohren's *Clouds in a Glass of Beer: Simple Experiments in Atmospheric Physics,* and the sequel, *What Light through Yonder Window Breaks* (Wiley and Sons, New York, 1987 and 1990).

If you like weather facts, figures, and historical anecdotes, David M. Ludlum has written a series of four books about *Early American Winters (volumes I and II), Hurricanes,* and *Tornadoes,* as well as *The American Weather Book,* available from the American Meteorological Society, 45 Beacon Street, Boston, MA 02108.

The American Meteorological Society also sells the *International Cloud Atlas, Volume II,* a must for cloud watchers. Published in 1987 by the World Meteorological Organization, this lavish (and expensive) volume contains more than 200 photographs of clouds and other weather phenomena and is the international standard for identifying cloud types. Some of the photographs in *Skywatch West* are in this atlas. If you want something quite a bit less expensive, try the cloud charts (and assorted teaching aids) from How the Weatherworks, 1522 Baylor Avenue, Rockville, MD 20850 (www.weatherworks.com), For Spacious Skies, 54 Webb Street, Lexington, MA 02173, and from www.cloudman.com. Between these extremes, you can get *The Audubon Society Field Guide to North American Weather* (Alfred Knopf, New York, 1991), the *Audubon Society Pocket Guide to Clouds and Storms* (also by Knopf), or *The Book of Clouds* (Silver Lining Books, New York, 2002), all of which have a beautiful selection of photographs. If you'd like to know more about rainbows, haloes, and other lights in the sky, I recommend Robert Greenler's book, *Rainbows, Haloes, and Glories* (Cambridge University Press, New York, 1980). And if snow is your passion, you'll want to read *The Snow Booklet,* by Nolan Doesken and Arthur Judson, available from the Colorado Climate Center, Department of Atmospheric Science, Colorado State University, Fort Collins, CO 80523-1371, or at http://ccc.atmos.colostate.edu.

Aurora Photographs

You can decorate your home with large prints of the aurora pictures in Chapter 12, available from Alaska Photographics, P.O. Box 232644, Anchorage, AK 99523-2644 (www.alaskaphotos.biz).

U.S. Government Publications

Those who relish detailed weather information will find a gold mine in some of the publications offered by the U.S. government. Many reasonably priced publications are available from the Superintendent of Documents, U.S. Government Printing Office, P.O. Box 371954, Pittsburgh, PA 15250-7954; 866-512-1800; or go to bookstore.gpo.gov for their general catalog, a special catalog of weather-related publications, and their monthly listing of new books.

The National Climate Center, Federal Building, Asheville, NC 28801 (www.ncdc.noaa.gov), publishes tons of climate data for all sorts of locations. Write for their list.

Storm Data describes hundreds of storms, from hurricanes to dust devils that strike the United States each month. There are maps, photos, and statistics—a real bonanza for storm lovers!

Local Climatological Data (your city)—Monthly summaries of the daily weather for dozens of western cities (mostly cities with airports). All the numbers you ever need to know.

Climatological Data (your state)—Monthly summaries of weather at dozens of cities, towns, and remote locations in each state. Includes temperature, rainfall, snow, and other data.

Climates of the States (your state)—Published for each state of the Union, these booklets provide a narrative description of the climate, several pages of tabulated statistics about temperature, wind, snow, and the like for selected cities, and maps of average temperatures and precipitation. Very informative.

Weekly Weather and Crop Bulletin gives a weekly report on weather conditions state-by-state and around the world, with emphasis on effects on agriculture.

CANADIAN GOVERNMENT PUBLICATIONS

The Canadian Climate Center (4905 Dufferin Street, Downsview, Ontario M3H 5T4) publishes a variety of periodicals, atlases, and data reports. Among these are the weekly "Climate Perspectives and the Monthly Record of Meteorological Observations in Canada," which are somewhat equivalent to the "U.S. Weekly Weather and Crop Bulletin and Climatological Data." Write for their catalog, "Selected Publications in Climate and Applied Meteorology."

PERIODICALS

For more than 50 years, *Weatherwise,* published six times a year by Heldref Publications(4000 Albemarle Street, N.W., Washington, D.C. 20016) has been the only magazine in America devoted solely to weather. Articles cover weather research, history, and recent weather events.

The *Bulletin of the American Meteorological Society* is directed more to the professional meteorologist, but amateurs will enjoy many of the articles and news notes. It's free to AMS members and quite expensive otherwise. Write to the AMS (45 Beacon Street, Boston, MA 02108) or check your library.

The National Weather Association (1697 Capri Way, Charlottesville, VA 22911-3534) publishes the *National Weather Digest* along with slide sets and a manual for interpreting weather satellite pictures. The *Digest* features articles written by forecasters about specific weather events, and gives you a real feel for what these people do for a living.

Science News, by Science Service (31 West Center Street, Marion, OH 43305), is a weekly magazine that reports on the latest discoveries in all the sciences, including meteorology.

WEATHER WEBSITES ON THE INTERNET

Everyone has a website these days, and weather watchers have their fair share. While the Internet is a volatile and ever-changing place (kind of like the weather), and websites can come and go, at least some of the following sites should still be around for a while. Here's a list of some sites that I find useful and go to fairly frequently. Most of these sites have links to other websites— so this list will just get you started.

REAL-TIME WEATHER AND FORECASTS
Canadian Weather Office: **www.weatheroffice.ec.gc.ca**
Lightningstorm.com (U.S. map of lightning strikes over the previous hour): **www.lightningstorm.com**
Meteorological Service of Canada: **www.msc.ec.gc.ca**
Mexican Weather Service: **smn.cna.gob.mx**
National Center for Atmospheric Research (radar, satellite, upper-air, forecast maps, etc.): **www.rap.ucar.edu/weather**
National Hurricane Center (warnings, images, storm names and histories, hurricane flight logs): **www.nhc.noaa.gov**
National Severe Storms Lab (severe storm and tornado forecasts and histories): **www.nssl.noaa.gov**
National Weather Service, U.S. ("Interactive Weather Information System" has current weather data, storm warnings, etc.): **www.nws.noaa.gov**
Storm Prediction Center (tornadoes, etc.): **www.spc.noaa.gov** (or **www.weather.gov**)
Unisys Weather Site (forecast maps, balloon soundings, hurricane information, etc.): **www.weather.unisys.com**
The Weather Channel (national maps, forecasts, etc.): **www.weather. com**
Weather Services, Inc. (weather maps, radar, excellent articles about El Niño, climate change, etc.): **www.intellicast.com**

CLIMATE INFORMATION (PAST WEATHER)
Climate Data Center (El Niño and other climate information): **www.cdc.noaa.gov**
Colorado Climate Center: **http://ccc.atmos.colostate.edu**

CO2 Science (articles and data about climate change): www.co2science.org
Daily U.S. Weather Maps for the past few months:
    www.hpc.ncep.noaa. gov/dwm/dwm.html
Department of Engergy (data about greenhouse gases, etc.): www.doe.gov
National Climate Data Center: www.ncdc.noaa.gov
National Geophysical Data Center (tree rings, sunspots, ice cores, etc.):
    www.ngdc.noaa.gov
National Snow and Ice Data Center (glaciers, polar ice caps):
    www.nsidc.colorado.edu
University of Alaska climate center: climate.gi.alaska.edu
Western Regional Climate Center (one-stop source for climate and snow data
    for western states): www.wrcc.dri.edu

Meteorological Organizations
American Meteorological Society: www.ametsoc.org
National Center for Atmospheric Research: www.ucar.edu
National Weather Association: www.nwas.org
NOAA: www.noaa.gov

More Stuff
Cloudman (nice pictures of the basic cloud types): www.cloudman.com
Colorado Avalanche Center: http://geosurvey.state.co.us/avalanche
Crevasse Zone (information and photos about the Juneau Ice Field and about
    glaciers): www.crevassezone.org (follow the link to "Alaska Photographics,"
    www.alaskaphotos.biz, to see some neat aurora pictures).
Global Volcanism Network: www.volcano.si.edu
National Interagency Fire Center (daily updated wildfire information):
    www.nifc.gov
Science News magazine: www.sciencenews.org
Sky and Telescope magazine (astronomy): www.skyandtelescope.com
Space Environment Center (solar flares, auroras, etc.): www.sel.noaa.gov
Space Flight Now (satellites, earth observation): www.spaceflightnow.com
Space Weather (more about auroras, etc.) www.spaceweather.com
Storm Track (articles by and for storm chasers): www.stormtrack.org
Tornado Project: www.tornadoproject.com
University of Illinois Weather Education Site: ww2010.atmos.uiuc.edu
Weatherwise magazine: www.weather-wise.org

DAILY WEATHER INFORMATION

Ever-changing weather is best appreciated by following it on a daily basis. You don't have to take your own records; there are plenty of data available in the media and elsewhere. Many newspapers carry weather maps and satellite photos, and most have daily high and low temperatures. Most newspaper maps aren't very detailed, and some are just about worthless.

If you want a good weather map, the National Weather Service publishes a weekly booklet with daily maps and upper-air charts. Contact: NNDC/NCDC, P.O. Box 70169, Chicago, IL 60673-0169 or call 866-742-3322, or go to their website: www.hpc.ncep.noaa.gov/dwm/dwm.html.

Television weather broadcasts vary in quality; if the weatherman knows something about the subject, you may learn something by watching. Most show satellite photos of the nation's weather, and some put together time-lapse satellite and radar images of moving storms and clouds. These space views of the weather give a perspective on the workings of weather that was unavailable 30 years ago. Watch them for a while and you'll get a real feel for how storms grow, move, and die.

On cable television, "The Weather Channel" gives comprehensive non-stop weather reports that will satisfy the hungriest appetite for real-time information.

WEATHER ON THE RADIO

The weather is a subject of passing fancy to some and passionate interest to others. However, for many people—notably mariners and aviators—the whims of the winds are matters of economic welfare and personal safety. To fill the needs of these people, an amazing variety of weather information is broadcast over a variety of radio frequencies. The airwaves are free, and all are welcome to listen to these broadcasts—you only need the proper radio for the frequency band of the broadcast. Here's a sampler of what's available:

WEATHER RADIO

Your best bet by far for local weather information are the "weather radio" stations operated by the Weather Services in the United States and Canada. The continuous broadcasts give forecasts, warnings, and observations for the area covered by the 25- to 50-mile range of the stations. Hundreds of these stations exist in the United States, and dozens in Canada, and most of the populace can pick up at least one of them. The National Weather Service (Attn: W/OM15x2, NOAA, Silver Spring, MD 20910) has a free brochure and station list; write to the Windsor Weather Office, Environment Canada, Air Terminal, Windsor Airport, R.R. #1, Windsor, Ontario N9A 6J3, for the Canadian list. The 162 MHz weather band can be picked up on multiband radios, so-called "police band" radios and scanners available at department and electronics stores. Some special Weather Radios are designed solely for these broadcasts and have a neat feature that automatically switches on whenever the local station broadcasts a severe weather warning. Several models in the $20–$50 range are available from Maxon (8610 NW 107th Terrace, Kansas City, MO 64153), and also sold in electronics, hardware, and department stores. By the way, these weather stations are the official U.S. government broadcast outlet for warnings of nuclear attack, replacing the CONELRAD system of the 1950s— just in case you want to be the first on your block to know... .

AVIATION AND MARINE RADIO

Those who live near airports or seaports will find more sources of weather information in the "Very High Frequency" (VHF) marine (156–162 MHz) and aviation (108–136 MHz) bands. Some broadcast continuous weather reports, while others send out warnings and answer requests for specific information. One particularly interesting aviation frequency is 122 MHz, where pilots report their perspective on the weather to the ground. You can buy special marine and aviation radios to receive these transmissions or listen on the VHF bands of multi-band radios and scanners.

The National Weather Service publishes "Marine Weather Services Charts" that show, in map format, weather broadcast stations for 15 U.S. coastal regions, including the Great Lakes and Alaska, Hawaii, and Puerto Rico.

They're available from: NWS (WOS21), 1325 East–West Highway, Room 13100, Silver Spring, MD 20910 (www.nws.noaa.gov/om/marine), or from marine supply shops. Canadian broadcast schedules appear in "Radio Aids to Marine Navigation," available from the Canadian Government Publishing Center, Ottawa K1A 0S9.

SHORTWAVE RADIO

If you yearn to hear some truly exotic weather reports, get a shortwave radio. The so-called shortwave band, 2–30 MHz (2000–30000 kHz), is unique in the radio spectrum in that its signals can travel literally around the world reflecting off ionospheric layers. I've been able to pick up weather reports from Africa, Australia, and Siberia! There's something refreshing about listening to hurricane advisories from Fiji, when the temperature is near zero outside.

Some specific frequencies to check out are:

2670 kHz—Frequent (but not continuous) Coast Guard weather broadcasts from stations up and down the Pacific Coast. The Canadian Coast Guard broadcasts on 2598 kHz.

6753 and 15035 kHz—Canadian and Arctic weather reports broadcast from Edmonton, Alberta; Trenton, Ontario; and St John's, Newfoundland, at 20, 30 and 40 minutes (respectively) past each hour.

6673, 8893, 10015, 11246, 13244, and 13354 kHz—Several of the frequencies used by Air Force and NOAA "Hurricane Hunter" flights. You might even hear a report from the eye of a hurricane!

14325 kHz—A frequency used by amateur radio operators ("hams") to relay weather and relief information to and from hurricane-struck areas.

2500, 5000, 10000, 15000, and 20000 kHz—This is WWV in Fort Collins, CO, the nation's official time station, with beeps every second (exactly!). Along with the beeps, storm positions for the Atlantic, Caribbean, Gulf of Mexico, and North Pacific are broadcast beginning at 8 minutes past each hour. If conditions are right, you might be able to pick up storm warnings for the South Pacific from WWVH (Hawaii), on the same frequencies, at 48 minutes past the hour. Also, check out the solar reports on WWV at 18 minutes past the hour. If they say there's a "Major" or "Severe" geomagnetic storm about to happen, go out and look for the northern lights. If you don't have a shortwave radio, you can listen to the same message by calling 303-497-3235.

You'll have to shop around a bit to get a good shortwave radio. Check out the selection at Radio Shack or a specialty electronic shop like Grove Enterprises

(7540 Highway 64 West, Brasstown, NC 28902; www.grove-ent.com). Pick up one of the monthly radio magazines, such as *Monitoring Times* or *Popular Communications* and scan their ads. Except for the time signal station WWV, all of these weather broadcasts are in Single Side Band (SSB) mode, so make sure your radio has a SSB switch or a Beat Frequency Oscillator (BFO) dial. Also make sure the radio can tune in the frequency bands you want. Finally, don't forget the antenna—for less than $10, you can string up a 50-foot wire that will work wonders.

The broadcast frequencies listed above are in kilohertz (KHz) and megahertz (MHz), which, to you old-timers, are better known as kilocycles and megacycles. One megahertz equals 1000 kilohertz, so, for example, the standard AM broadcast band extends from 530 to 1600 KHz, or 0.53 to 1.6 MHz. Generally, frequencies less than 10000 KHz (10 MHz) are received better at night, and higher frequencies are better during the day.

HAM RADIO

When severe weather threatens, the National Weather Service relies on volunteer spotters to call in sightings of hail, funnel clouds, and such. Many of these spotters are amateur radio operators (or "hams") out in their cars with their mobile radio rigs. If you want to listen to these live reports, tune your radio or scanner to the 144–148 MHz band; if you would rather be out there yourself watching and reporting the weather, ask your local weather service office or the American Radio Relay League (225 Main Street, Newington, CT 06111) about joining the "Skywarn" program.

Many locations have amateur weather networks, in which hams call in weather reports from their home weather stations. The moderator of the network forwards the data to the local weather service office. These "weather nets" call in every day at the same time and on the same frequency. You can obtain a complete directory of U.S. and Canadian nets from the Amateur Radio Relay League.

WEATHER EQUIPMENT

Some department and hardware stores carry a fair selection of thermometers, rain gauges, and other weather gizmos. If you would like to see some of the more esoteric equipment, try the catalogs available from:

Edmund Scientific, 60 Pearce Avenue, Tonawanda, NY 14150-6711; 800-728-6999; www.scientificsonline.com.

Wind & Weather, 1200 North Main Street, Fort Bragg, CA 95437-8473; 800-922-9463; www.windandweather.com.

Onset Computers, P.O. Box 3450, Pocasset, MA 02559-3450; 800-564-4377; www.onsetcomp.com.

Forestry Suppliers, 205 West Rankin Street, Jackson, MS 39201; 800-360-7788; www.forestry-suppliers.com.

Also check the ads in *Weatherwise* magazine.

Ask the Experts

You can also obtain literature about weather from the various organizations that deal with the subject. Among these are your local weather service and the agriculture or meteorology departments at colleges and universities. The National Center for Atmospheric Research (P.O. Box 3000, Boulder, CO 80303; www.ucar.edu) is in the forefront of weather research, and their Information Office has some interesting public relations blurbs.

Many places have local chapters of the American Meteorological Society. Check for locations with the American Meteorological Society (45 Beacon Street, Boston, MA 02108). This is a good way to meet some meteorologists and enjoy interesting presentations. Likewise, the National Weather Association (1697 Capri Way, Charlottesville, VA 22911-3534) has local chapters that meet periodically.

A Final Note

Now that you have read *Skywatch West* forward and backward, subscribed to all the magazines and climate reports, and pored over the daily weather map as you listen to Weather Radio and can't walk by your barometer without tapping it, you are a true weather nut. But don't forget to look out your window once in a while. That's where the weather is, and it's putting on a show just for you.

APPENDIX 1
CLIMATIC DATA

One way to appreciate the fantastic variety of climates found in the West is to scan this table of climate data for some representative locations. In this listing you will find places 20 miles apart whose climates are as different as Brazil's is from Britain's. It wasn't easy deciding which weather stations, out of the thousands in the West, to include in this table, but the 119 stations listed here should be a representative cross-section of the West's varied climates. Some of the locations are major urban centers, in or near which many readers might live. Others are popular vacation destinations, ranging from national parks to ski areas. A few are simply places with extreme climates that are exceptionally hot or cold, snowy or rainy. And one very special place is my backyard weather station in Coal Creek, Colorado. I'll admit to showing off a bit of pride about the climate I live in, but there is another reason for including the Coal Creek station in this table. That is to show that with your own weather station, you can come up with your own climate data. After just a few years, you'll be able to compare your home's climate with that of Death Valley, Pikes Peak, or Tombstone, Arizona.

Modern weather stations can produce a bewildering variety of data. The few statistics presented here should give you a fairly complete picture of the local climate. The data included in this listing are:

Elevation—Along with latitude and distance from the ocean, elevation is one of the most important factors in determining a place's climate.

Years Records Cover—The longer weather records have been taken, the more reliable the averages will be. It takes about 10 or 20 years to come up with a truly representative average.

Average Temperature—I've found annual average temperatures to be fairly worthless at describing a place's climate—San Francisco and Albuquerque have the same annual average. The average daily high and low temperatures for July and January give a much better picture of the daily and seasonal ranges of temperature. July is the warmest month of the year in most western cities, but along the Pacific coast, summer may peak in August or

245

September. For these locations, averages for the warmest month—August, and in a few cases, September, are given instead in the July columns.

Temperature Extremes—These are the highest and lowest temperatures since records began. The longer the period of record, the greater the extremes are likely to be.

Average Annual Precipitation and Snowfall—Precipitation includes the water that falls as rain or snow.

Wettest Month—This gives an idea of when the rainy (or snowy) season is.

Average Annual Thunderstorms (Tstm)—This is actually the average number of days with thunderstorms. Some days may have two or more thunderstorms, but this doesn't affect the average. Not all weather stations keep thunderstorm records; for those that don't, the numbers (in italics) were estimated from maps published by the U.S. and Canadian weather services.

Sunshine (Sun)—The number here is the percentage of possible sunshine—the annual number of hours that the sun shines, given as a percentage of the annual number of hours there would be if the sky were always clear. Seattlites will be pleased to find that the sun shines on their city nearly half of all daylight hours! It should be noted that the Canadian and U.S. sunshine statistics are not directly comparable, since Canadians measure only hours of bright sunshine, while Americans include the hours of hazy or dim sunshine. As a rule of thumb, add 5 or 10 points to the Canadian percentages before comparing them to stateside sunshine.

Fog—Number of days per year with fog that reduces the visibility to one-quarter mile or less (one-half mile in Canada).

CLIMATIC DATA TABLE

Station	Elevation	Years Records Cover	Average Temperature				Temperature Extremes		Average Annual		Wettest Month	Avg. Annual Tstm	Sun
			July max	July min	January max	January min	high	low	precip	snow			
ALASKA													
Amchitka	220	1949–1993	51	44	35	28	60	16	35.7	48	Aug.		
Anchorage	110	1914–2003	65	47	22	9	92	-38	16.1	71	Aug.	1	41
Attu	70	1938–1993	55	46	34	26	72	-15	52.6	76	Oct.		
Barrow	30	1920–2003	47	34	-10	-22	79	-56	4.2	30	Aug.	0	
Denali Park	2,070	1922–2003	68	44	11	-7	91	-54	15.3	82	July		
*Denali summit	20,320		-3	-13	-33	-43	30	-77					
Fairbanks	360	1919–2003	73	52	0	-19	99	-66	10.3	68	Aug.	7	
Fort Yukon	440	1938–1990	73	51	-11	-28	100	-78	6.6	42	Aug.		
Juneau	12	1916–2003	64	49	31	21	90	-22	58.3	97	Oct.	0	30
Juneau Ice Field	3,950	1991–2003	49	40	21	14	81	-17	100.0	600	Oct.		
Kodiak	14	1931–2003	61	49	35	25	86	-16	75.4	78	Oct.	0	
Little Port Walter	10	1949–2003	62	49	38	29	88	0	223.7	115	Oct.		
Nome	13	1906–2003	59	47	13	-2	86	-54	16.6	63	Aug.	1	42
Sitka	10	1899–2003	62	52	39	31	88	-8	86.1	39	Oct.		
Thompson Pass	2,500	1952–1974	58	41	10	-1	75	-39	77.3	552	Oct.		
ARIZONA													
Flagstaff	7,006	1898–2003	82	50	43	17	97	-30	22.9	100	Aug.	49	78
Grand Canyon													
North Rim	8,400	1931–2003	77	47	38	17	92	-25	25.4	140	Jan.	50	
South Rim	6,950	1916–2003	84	50	41	17	101	-22	17.3	47	March	50	
Phantom Ranch	2,570	1935–2003	106	77	56	37	120	-9	9.5	0	Aug.	50	
Page	4,270	1957–2003	96	69	44	27	109	-11	6.8	5	Oct.	30	
Phoenix	1,112	1876–2003	104	81	65	43	122	16	8.3	0	March	24	85
Tombstone	4,610	1894–2003	93	66	60	36	112	3	13.9	3	July	65	
Tucson	2,584	1891–2003	100	73	65	39	117	6	12.2	1	Aug.	41	85
Yuma	194	1873–2003	107	81	70	46	124	22	3.0	0	Aug.	7	90
CALIFORNIA													
Avalon/ Santa Catalina	20	1948–1988	74	61	62	47	104	29	13.1	0	Feb.	5	

* (Temperatures estimated from weather balloon data)

Climatic Data Table

Station	Elevation	Years Records Cover	Average Temperature July max	min	January max	min	Temperature Extremes high	low	Average Annual precip	snow	Wettest Month	Avg. Annual Tstm	Sun
CALIFORNIA (*CONTINUED*)													
Bakersfield	475	1889–2003	97	69	56	39	118	13	6.5	0	March	3	
Death Valley	-178	1912–2003	115	86	66	39	134	15	2.3	0	Feb.	5	
Eureka	43	1887–2003	64	55	56	41	87	20	38.1	0	Dec.	4	51
Los Angeles	270	1878–2003	85	66	68	49	112	28	15.1	0	Feb.	6	73
Red Bluff	342	1878–2003	98	66	56	38	121	17	24.1	2	Jan.	10	77
Sacramento	20	1877–2003	92	58	54	39	115	17	17.9	0	Jan.	5	78
San Diego	13	1875–2003	78	67	66	50	111	25	10.8	0	Jan	3	68
San Francisco	52	1849–2003	69	56	58	46	103	27	22.3	0	Jan.	2	66
Mt. Shasta City	3,535	1888–2003	83	49	44	26	105	-13	39.1	104	Jan.	13	
Tahoe	6,230	1914–2003	78	45	41	20	94	-16	32.7	188	Jan.	20	
Yosemite	3,970	1905–2003	91	55	48	28	110	-6	37.5	58	Jan.	15	
COLORADO													
Alamosa	7,540	1932–2003	82	46	33	-4	96	-50	7.3	33	Aug.	42	
Aspen	7,928	1925–2003	77	46	34	7	94	-33	24.8	178	March	50	
Berthoud Pass	11,310	1950–1987	62	39	21	1	76	-34	37.5	391	April	70	
Coal Creek Can.	8,950	1982–2003	73	46	33	14	89	-36	24.9	200	April	84	
Denver	5,283	1871–2003	88	59	43	15	105	-30	15.8	60	May	42	69
Durango	6,600	1894–2003	85	51	40	12	102	-30	19.3	69	Aug	50	
Estes Park	7,497	1916–2003	79	47	39	18	98	-39	14.0	33	May	60	
Grand Junction	4,855	1892–2003	92	61	37	16	105	-23	9.0	24	Oct.	36	71
Lamar	3,617	1903–2003	92	62	44	14	111	-30	15.8	27	May	40	
Leadville	9,940	1948–2003	71	39	31	3	86	-38	11.6	145	Aug.	60	
Mesa Verde	7,070	1922–2003	84	56	38	17	100	-20	18.0	82	Aug.	35	
Pikes Peak	14,134	1874–1888	48	34	9	-4	64	-39	29.7	553	July	70	
Pueblo	4,684	1888–2003	91	59	45	14	109	-31	12.4	33	Aug.	40	76
IDAHO													
Boise	2,838	1864–2003	89	60	37	24	111	-23	12.2	21	Jan.	15	64
Lewiston/ Moscow	1,413	1879–2003	88	59	39	28	117	-23	12.7	16	May	15	
Pocatello	4,454	1899–2003	88	51	33	16	105	-31	13.6	42	March	24	64
Sandpoint	2,126	1910–2003	82	48	32	20	104	-37	32.0	71	Dec.	10	

CLIMATIC DATA TABLE

Station	Elevation	Years Records Cover	Average Temperature July max	July min	January max	January min	Temperature Extremes high	low	Average Annual precip	snow	Wettest Month	Avg. Annual Tstm	Sun
IDAHO (CONTINUED)													
Sun Valley	5,980	1937–2003	80	43	31	5	96	-46	18.7	114	Dec.	40	
MONTANA													
Billings	3,567	1896–2003	86	58	33	15	112	-49	14.8	57	May	28	60
Glasgow	2,284	1893–2003	84	57	20	2	113	-59	11.6	29	June	28	
Helena	3,828	1881–2003	83	52	31	10	105	-42	11.4	47	June	32	59
Kalispell	2,965	1897–2003	82	47	29	14	105	-38	17.2	65	June	22	
Medicine Lake	1,950	1911–2003	83	54	18	-2	117	-58	13.0	26	June	25	
NEVADA													
Elko	5,050	1888–2003	90	49	37	14	108	-43	9.6	39	Jan.	21	
Ely	6,253	1897–2003	87	47	40	10	101	-30	10.0	50	May	33	73
Las Vegas	2,162	1914–2003	104	78	57	37	118	8	4.5	1	Feb.	13	85
Reno	4,404	1888–2003	91	51	46	22	108	-19	7.5	24	Jan.	14	79
Winnemucca	4,301	1878–2003	92	52	42	19	109	-37	8.3	23	May	15	68
NEW MEXICO													
Albuquerque	5,311	1893–2003	92	65	48	24	107	-17	9.5	11	Aug.	41	76
Carlsbad	3,120	1895–1968	96	68	58	28	114	-17	14.2	3	Sept.	39	
Chaco Canyon	6,175	1922–2001	90	55	43	13	104	-38	9.5	15	Aug.	48	
Cimarron	6,540	1903–1974	84	52	47	16	101	-35	17.9	36	Aug.	80	
Cloudcroft	8,669	1914–2003	71	46	41	17	89	-21	28.2	72	Aug.	50	
Roswell	3,650	1893–2003	95	67	56	24	114	-29	13.3	12	Aug.	38	74
Sandia Crest	10,690	1953–1979	66	47	27	13	82	-20	23.0	116	Aug.	60	
Santa Fe	7,200	1876–2003	86	54	43	16	99	-18	14.2	17	July	54	74
OREGON													
Astoria	8	1884–2003	68	53	48	37	101	6	67.1	4	Nov.	7	
Burns	4,151	1939–2003	85	46	35	14	107	-28	10.6	41	Dec.	14	
Crater Lake	6,475	1919–2003	69	41	34	18	90	-21	67.1	526	Dec.	12	
Eugene	359	1890–2003	82	51	47	33	108	-12	50.9	6	Nov.	5	
Pendleton	1482	1898–2003	88	58	40	27	119	-28	12.8	17	Nov.	10	
Portland	21	1874–2003	80	57	46	34	107	-3	37.1	7	Dec.	7	48

CLIMATIC DATA TABLE

| Station | Elevation | Years Records Cover | Average Temperature | | | | Temperature Extremes | | Average Annual | | Wettest Month | Avg. Annual Tstm | Sun |
			July max	min	January max	min	high	low	precip	snow			
SOUTH DAKOTA													
Rapid City	3,162	1888–2002	86	58	34	11	110	-33	16.6	40	May	42	63
TEXAS													
El Paso	3,916	1888–2002	95	72	57	33	114	-8	9.4	5	Aug.	36	84
UTAH													
Alta	8,730	1948–2003	71	49	29	14	86	-26	52.3	511	Dec.	50	
Bryce Canyon	7,910	1948–2003	78	47	34	9	98	-29	16.4	87	Aug.	36	
Moab	4,020	1890–2003	101	64	44	20	114	-24	9.4	10	Oct.	30	
Salt Lake City	4,221	1874–2003	91	63	37	21	107	-30	16.5	59	May	37	66
WASHINGTON													
Moses Lake	1,210	1943–1987	87	55	34	18	113	-33	8.0	13	Dec.	10	
Mt. Rainier	5,427	1917–2003	62	43	32	20	92	-20	116.3	679	Dec.	15	
Quillayute	179	1942–2003	69	50	45	33	99	5	101.7	13	Dec.	7	32
Seattle	19	1892–2003	75	57	47	36	100	3	38.3	7	Dec.	6	43
Spokane	2,356	1882–2003	83	55	33	22	108	-30	16.7	49	Dec.	11	54
Stampede Pass	3958	1944–2003	66	51	30	22	91	-21	84.2	439	Dec.	7	
Yakima	1,060	1909–2003	87	51	38	21	111	-25	8.3	25	Dec.	7	
WYOMING													
Cheyenne	6,126	1871–2003	82	53	37	15	100	-38	15.5	56	May	51	66
Jackson	6,230	1917–2003	82	40	27	5	101	-52	16.0	74	May	40	
Laramie	7,266	1891–2003	79	47	32	9	95	-50	10.4	49	May	47	
Sundance	4,750	1908–2003	85	54	31	7	105	-42	18.9	74	June	45	
Yellowstone (Mammoth Spgs.)	6,241	1887–2003	80	47	29	10	99	-41	15.2	71	June	40	56
(Old Faithful)	7,360	1978–2003	75	39	27	-2	93	-49	24.4	221	Dec.	40	
CANADA													
ALBERTA													
Banff	4,540	1887–2002	71	45	24	7	94	-60	18.6	92	June	6	40
Calgary	3,557	1881–2002	73	49	27	5	97	-49	16.2	50	June	25	50
Edmonton	2,373	1880–2002	72	49	18	-2	99	-57	19.0	48	July	21	51
Lethbridge	3,047	1908–2002	72	51	29	7	103	-45	15.2	107	June		

CLIMATIC DATA TABLE

Station	Elevation	Years Records Cover	Average Temperature July max	July min	January max	January min	Temperature Extremes high	low	Average Annual precip	snow	Wettest Month	Avg. Annual Tstm	Sun
BRITISH COLUMBIA													
Atlin	2,210	1899–2002	65	46	11	-3	87	-58	13.7	61	July		
Boat Bluff	35	1974–2002	66	51	42	33	91	-4	198.0	9	Nov.	1	
Fort Nelson	1,253	1937–2002	73	51	2	-14	98	-61	17.8	70	July		
Kamloops	1,133	1951–2002	83	57	31	18	105	-35	11.0	30	June	13	
Penticton	1,129	1907–2002	83	55	34	24	105	-17	13.1	26	June	14	45
Prince George	2,268	1942–2002	72	48	22	8	102	-58	23.7	85	June	22	
Prince Rupert	116	1962–2002	62	51	40	28	90	-12	102.1	50	Oct.	3	
Vancouver	14	1899–2002	71	56	43	33	92	0	47.2	19	Nov.	6	44
Victoria	63	1898–2002	67	49	44	33	97	4	34.8	17	Dec.	3	50
Yoho Nat Park	5,400	1974–1993	65	40	17	3	88	-45	34.8	188	Dec.		
NORTHWEST TERRITORIES													
Fort Smith	673	1943–2002	73	50	-3	-20	103	-71	14.3	60	Aug.		
Tuktoyaktuk	15	1957–2002	59	44	-10	-23	86	-58	6.6	38	Aug.		
Yellowknife	675	1942–2002	70	54	-9	-24	91	-60	11.1	60	Aug.	6	
SASKAT- CHEWAN													
Saskatoon	1,652	1892–2002	77	53	11	-8	105	-58	13.8	38	June	18	55
Yellow Grass	1,902	1911–2002	79	53	14	-6	113	-50	17.1	42	June		
YUKON													
Dawson	1,214	1976–2002	74	47	-9	-24	94	-68	12.8	63	July		
Mayo	1,653	1924–2002	73	49	-5	-24	97	-80	12.3	58	July		
Whitehorse	2,317	1942–2002	69	46	8	-8	94	-62	10.5	57	July	6	42

APPENDIX 2
BUILDING YOUR THERMOMETER SHELTER

When we think of weather, the first thing we think of measuring is temperature. For temperature readings to be of real use, they must be read from a thermometer that is properly protected from sunlight, rain, and snow. There are a variety of ways to provide this protection, the most common being to place the thermometer in a louvered wooden box. The following design has served me well for many years.

PARTS NEEDED
The following items are sold in most hardware or lumberstores:

- 1—2-foot x 4-foot x $3/4$-inch outdoor grade plywood
- 2—36-inch-high x 15-inch-wide louvered pine shutters
- 1—3-foot pine 2x4
- 1—7-foot cedar or redwood 4x4
- 2—2.5-inch hinges with screws
- 1—latch with screws
- 2—5-inch x $1/4$-inch lag bolts with washers
- 50—2.5-inch nails
- 1 pint can exterior-grade white paint

The louvered shutters should have a solid wood crosspiece in the middle of the louvered area. The metal hinges, latch, and nails should be zinc-plated to resist rust. The paint pigment should be titanium dioxide, which is very effective in reflecting sunlight. Check the label on the side of the paint can for the listing of ingredients.

TOOLS NEEDED
A hammer, saw, drill, screwdriver, adjustable wrench, paintbrush, and shovel.

Putting It Together

Cut the louvered shutters in half along the solid wood crosspiece. This results in four 15-inch x 18-inch louvered panels, each with solid cross pieces at the top and bottom. Cut the plywood into one 18-inch x 21-inch and two 15-inch x 18-inch pieces. Cut the 2x4 into one 18-inch length, two 3-inch lengths, and two 2-inch lengths.

Now, center one of the 15x18 plywood pieces on the end of the 4x4 beam. Drill two holes through the plywood and into the end of the beam for attaching the two together with the lag bolts (don't attach them yet).

You now make a box, with the drilled 15 x 18 plywood piece forming the bottom, the other 15x18 plywood forming the top, and the louvered panels forming the sides. Nail the back and side louvered panels to each other and to the bottom pieces, with the back panel fitting "inside" the side panels. The side panels should be about three-eighths of an inch farther apart at the front than at the back. This will allow room for the hinged front panel.

Next, attach the front louvered panel using the hinges and screws. Put the latch on the door. Nail down the top 15x18 plywood piece. Place the 18-inch 2x4 vertically inside the box. Locate it near the center of the box, just behind the two drilled holes in the bottom piece, and nail each end with two nails. This vertical 2x4 will soon be holding your thermometer, so make sure it's firmly in place.

The 18x21 plywood piece forms the roof and shades the box from direct sunlight. Nail the two 3-inch 2x4s on top of the box, near the front, and the two 2-inch 2x4s near the back. Nail the roof to the 2x4 pieces; the roof should slope down toward the back. If you live in a windy location, you may want to beef up the construction with steel angle brackets and screws.

Paint your box, inside and out, with two coats. Dig a two-foot-deep post hole and set the 4x4 beam into it (make sure the end with the drilled holes is up!). Bolt the box to the post, place the thermometer on the 2x4 mounting board, and start reading the temperature.

APPENDIX 3
WIND SPEED SCALES

BEAUFORT

Wind Scale	Wind Speed (m.p.h.)		Wind Type	Descriptive Effects
0	0–1	m.p.h.	Calm	Smoke rises vertically.
1	1–3	m.p.h.	Light wind	Smoke drifts slowly.
2	4–7	m.p.h.	Slight breeze	Leaves rustle; wind vanes move.
3	8–12	m.p.h.	Gentle breeze	Leaves and twigs in motion.
4	13–18	m.p.h.	Moderate breeze	Small branches move; raises dust and loose paper.
5	19–24	m.p.h.	Fresh breeze	Small trees sway.
6	25–31	m.p.h.	Strong breeze	Large branches sway; telephone wires whistle.
7	32–38	m.p.h.	Moderate gale	Whole trees in motion; wind affects walking.
8	39–46	m.p.h.	Fresh gale	Twigs break off trees.
9	47–54	m.p.h.	Strong gale	Branches break; shingles blow from roofs.
10	55–63	m.p.h.	Whole gale	Trees snap and uproot; some damage to buildings.
11	64–72	m.p.h.	Storm	Some damage to chimneys and TV antennas.
12–22	73–201	m.p.h.	Hurricane	Hurricane damage; see Saffir-Simpson scale on page 256.

FUJITA (TORNADOES)

Wind Scale	Wind Speed (m.p.h.)	Wind Type	Descriptive Effects
F0	40–72 m.p.h.	Minimal tornado	Twigs and branches break off trees; signs damaged; windows broken.
F1	73–112 m.p.h.	Weak tornado	Cars pushed off road; mobile homes pushed or overturned; sheds destroyed.
F2	113–157 m.p.h.	Strong tornado	Roofs torn from frame houses; trailer homes destroyed; cars blown from highways
F3	158–206 m.p.h.	Severe tornado	Walls torn from frame houses; cars lifted off ground; trains derailed.
F4	207–260 m.p.h.	Devastating	Frame houses reduced to rubble; bark removed from trees; cars and trains thrown or rolled considerable distances.
F5	261–318 m.p.h.	Incredible	Whole frame houses tossed from foundations; cars fly through air; asphalt torn from roads.

Saffir-Simpson (Hurricanes)

(Note: This "Hurricane Damage Potential Scale," developed by Florida engineer Herbert Saffir and Dr. Robert Simpson, former director of the National Hurricane Center, rates hurricanes on a scale from 1 to 5, based on the combined effects of wind and high seas on coastal and low-lying areas in the path of the storm.)

Wind Scale	Wind Speed (m.p.h.)	Wind Type	Descriptive Effects
1	74–95 m.p.h.	Minimal damage	Damage primarily to shrubbery, trees, and mobile homes; low-lying coastal roads flooded by storm surge of 4–5 feet above normal tides.
2	96–110 m.p.h.	Moderate damage	Some trees blown down; damage to roofs, windows and mobile homes, but no major structural damage. Six- to eight-foot-storm surge floods coastal escape routes and marinas, and tears small craft from moorings.
3	111–130 m.p.h.	Extensive damage	Large trees down; structural damage to small buildings; mobile homes destroyed. Coastal buildings damaged or destroyed by waves and floating debris on 9- to 12-foot storm tide.
4	131–155 m.p.h.	Extreme damage	Complete roof failures on many small residences; 13- to 18-foot storm surge floods areas up to 6 miles inland and erodes beaches.
5	156 m.p.h. or more	Catastrophic	Some residences and other damage completely destroyed; small buildings overturned or blown away. Storm surge in excess of 18 feet may flood areas 10 miles inland.

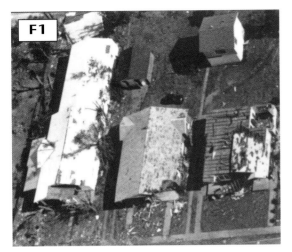

EXAMPLES OF THE FUJITA SCALE FOR DAMAGING WINDS

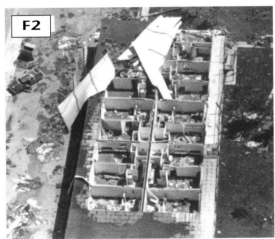

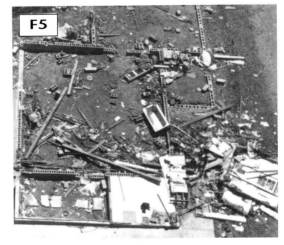

INDEX

Experience Nature at Its Best
with Fulcrum Publishing

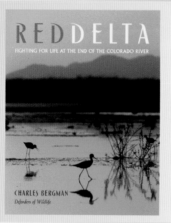

Red Delta
Fighting for Life at the End of the Colorado River

Charles Bergman
with Defenders of Wildlife

From a rare and endangered bird to a village of impoverished Cucapá people, see the variety and abundance of life on the Mexican delta.

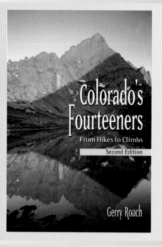

Colorado's Fourteeners
From Hikes to Climbs
SECOND EDITION

Gerry Roach

Climb Colorado's highest mountains with this up-to-date, full-color edition of the best-selling guidebook to the state's 14,000-foot peaks.

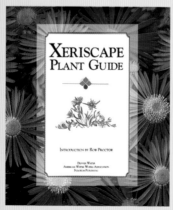

Xeriscape Plant Guide
100 Water-Wise Plants for Gardens and Landscapes

Denver Water
Introduction by Rob Proctor

A plant-by-plant full-color guide.